Mary B. Duffield, Isabella G. D. Stewart, Sally B. Sill

Home Messenger Book of Tested Receipts

Mary B. Duffield, Isabella G. D. Stewart, Sally B. Sill

Home Messenger Book of Tested Receipts

ISBN/EAN: 9783337306861

Printed in Europe, USA, Canada, Australia, Japan

Cover: Foto ©Lupo / pixelio.de

More available books at **www.hansebooks.com**

REVISED EDITION.

HOME MESSENGER

BOOK

OF

TESTED RECEIPTS

TOTAL ABSTINENCE.

Respectfully Dedicated to the Patrons and Friends of the
DETROIT HOME OF THE FRIENDLESS,

BY THE COMPILERS,

MESDAMES

ISABELLA G. D. STEWART,   FANNIE L. CARTER,
SALLY B. SILL,   MARY B. DUFFIELD.

PRICE, $1.00.

The Profits of this Volume are Devoted to the Detroit Home of the Friendless.

THIRD EDITION

PRINTED BY
THE POST AND TRIBUNE JOB PRINTING CO.
1886.

Entered according to Act of Congress by the officers of the Home of the Friendless, Detroit, in the office of Librarian of Congress, Washington, D.C., in the Year, A. D. 1886.

PREFACE

TO THE

REVISED EDITION OF THE HOME MESSENGER RECEIPT BOOK.

The Home Messenger Book of Tested Receipts was published somewhat hastily in October, 1873, and several thousand found a ready sale. It contained 137 pages, or 380 receipts, sold without an agent for $1.25.

In December, 1878, a second edition was brought out, 288 pages, 801 receipts, price, $1.00, Total Abstinence principles. Five thousand were sold promptly, and for the past two years not a copy could be bought. The demand for a third edition has been so great that we now issued the present book, which is, by far, the best of all.

The effort has been to give exact measures in cups and tablespoons rather than weighing the articles. It is a significant fact that the cooks, either amateur or professional, are the ones who demand the book. This third edition contains 288 pages, 810 Receipts; price, $1.00, Total Abstinence. The very best of the old receipts have been retained, and new ones from such practical cooks as Miss Parloa, Margery Daw, Mrs. Welch, Warne's Great English Book, The National Training School of Cookery in England, Mrs. Henderson, The Virginia Cook Book, translations of tested French receipts, etc. It will find its way into thousands of homes in Michigan and in the United States generally. We bespeak for it your confidence, because it is indeed an advance in gastronomic art and science; for these receipts have been tried, tested, criticised and reformed, until in a plain and practical way we consider them faultless.

By the exercise of forethought much better meals can be had with far greater economy. Decide as far as possible *the night before* what are to be your meals for the following day; by this means you can use yeast instead of baking powder, have cold tapioca puddings or well-set creams and your soup stocks on hand, etc. Nothing is wiser policy than to face the inevitable *in time*, for like seed time and harvest (only far more frequently), come Breakfast, Dinner and Supper.

No cookery book alone will make a good cook. Judgment in baking, boiling, stewing, frying and compounding is only to be attained by experience; but the acquisition of that experience may be greatly expedited by such instructions as are to be found herein. Here are receipts that will enable any lady to get up for her own family, or ceremonious guests, a delightful breakfast, lunch, dinner or tea, a tea-company, or large evening entertainment. We have endeavored to make them so explicit that a lady can follow them herself, or *stand by* her cook, and see that she follows them.

THE COMPILER.

INDEX.

* The Asterisks designate favorite receipts of the compilers.

COFFEE, TEA AND CHOCOLATE.

	PAGE		PAGE
*Good New England Coffee	1	*Tea	3
*Vienna Coffee	1	English Breakfast or Oolong	3
Soyer's Cafe au Lait	1	Iced Tea	4
Coffee for two persons	2	*German Chocolate	4
Cream and Milk for Coffee	2	*Chocolate	4
Tea and Coffee for Children	3		

SOUPS.

Several Hints	5	Tomato Soup	14
Why Soup is Wholesome	6	*Veal Soup	14
*Perfect Mock Turtle	6	*Black Bean Soup	15
*Bouillon	9	Pea Soup	15
*Corn Soup	10	*Croutons	15
*Summer or Winter Corn Soup	10	Browning for Soup	15
Corn Soup	11	*Oyster Soup	16
Potato Soup	11	Oyster Soup	16
*Parker House Tomato Soup	11	Miss Parloa's Green Pea Soup	16
*Very Rich Beef Soup	12	Soup Dumplings	17
Turkey Soup	12	*Green Pea Soup	18
*Sorrel Soup	13	*White Almond Soup	19
Calves' Head Soup	13	Clam Soup	19
*Okra Soup	14		

OYSTERS.

To Stew Oysters	20	*Oyster Pie	24
*Panned or Griddled Oysters	20	Oyster Pattie	24
*Devilled Oysters	20	Scalloped Oysters	25
*Roasted Oysters	21	Oyster Omelette	25
*How to Broil Oysters	21	*Croustade of Oysters	25
*Fried Oysters	22	*Chicken and Oyster Croquettes	26
Fried Oysters	22	Pickled Oysters	26
Fried Oysters	22	Pickled Oysters, No. 2	27
*Oyster Fritters	28	Lobster Croquettes	27
Oysters Broiled in the Shell	22	Oyster and Clam Fritters	27
Teal's Cream Oysters	23	Batter for Oyster Fritters	28
*Unsurpassed Fricasseed Oysters	23	Raw Oysters	28
Fricasseed Oysters	24		

FISH AND FROGS.

	PAGE		PAGE
*Boiled Fish	29	*Codfish Balls	31
*Boiled Fish, Vegetable Flavor	29	Baked Lobster or Lobster Turbot	31
To Broil a Whitefish	29	Pickled Fish	31
Fish Chowder	30	*Picked Codfish (delicious)	32
*Turbot, No. 1	30	Codfish for Friday Dinner	32
Turbot, No. 2	30	Frogs	33

SAVORY SAUCES.

	PAGE		PAGE
*Drawn Butter Sauce	34	Mushroom Sauce	37
Drawn Butter Sauce	34	Horseradish Sauce	37
Egg Sauce	35	Mint Vinegar	38
*Oyster Sauce	35	Pepper Vinegar, Tarragon Vinegar	38
Celery Sauce	35	*Fish Sauce	38
*Tomato Sauce	25	*Dutch Sauce, for Fish (Hollandaise)	38
Tomato Sauce	36	*Sauce Tartare (a cold sauce)	39
Pepper Vinegar	36	Mushroom Sauce	39
Mint Sauce	36	Fish Sauce (Grand Hotel, Paris)	39
*Sauce Hollandaise	36	Sauce Hollandaise	39
Chilli Sauce	37		
White Sauce for Fowls	37		

BEEF.

	PAGE		PAGE
Roast Beef	40	To Cook a Steak	43
*Fillet of Beef	41	Miss Parloa's Method for Beef Steak	44
*Beef a la Mode	42		
A la Mode Beef	43	Maitre d'Hotel Butter	44

TO BOIL FRESH AND SALT BEEF AND HAM.

	PAGE		PAGE
To Boil Pickled or Corned Beef	45	*Kate's Monday Stew	47
Boiling Meat	45	To Bake a Ham	48
Beef Stew	46	Glazed Ham	48
Remains of Roast Beef	47	*To Boil a Ham	48

SWEET-BREADS.

	PAGE		PAGE
*To Roast a Leg of Veal	49	*Veal Cutlets	49
Veal Sweet-breads	50	*Broiled Sweet-breads	51
Sweet-breads Stewed	50	*Stewed Sweet-breads	280
*Sweet-breads Roasted	50	*Fried Sweet-breads	280
Sweet-breads, an English Method	51		

MUTTON AND LAMB.

	PAGE		PAGE
Mutton and Lamb	52	*Saddle of Mutton	52
To Boil a Leg of Mutton	52	*Fore Quarter of Lamb Broiled	53
Fore Quarter of Lamb Roasted	52	Mutton Cutlets Breaded	52

PORK.

	PAGE		PAGE
*Leg of Fresh Pork Roasted	54	*To Fry Salt Pork	55
Pork Spare Ribs	54	To Bake Salt Pork	55
Pork Tender Loins	54	*Pork and Beans	5
To Broil Salt Pork	54		

POULTRY AND GAME.

	PAGE		PAGE
*Turkey and Chicken Stuffing	56	Fricassee Chicken, No. 2 (French)	58
*To Roast a Turkey or Chicken	56	Dumpling for Fricasseed Chicken	60
*To Boil a Chicken or Turkey	57	Escalloped Chicken	60
Broiled Chicken	58	*Chicken Pie, No. 1	61
Escalloped Turkey	58	Rice and Chicken Pie, No. 3	61
Prairie Chicken, Partridges and Quail	58	*Chicken Jelly	61
A Nice Way to Cook Pigeons	58	*Chicken Gumbo	62
To Pot Birds	59	*Chicken Pie	62
*Fricassee Chicken	59	Brunswick Stew	64

POTATOES.

	PAGE		PAGE
Potatoes a la Maitre d'Hotel	63	*Potato Puff	64
*Boiled Potatoes, Miss Parloa	63	Potato Fritters	65
*Mashed Potatoes	64	*Creaming Potatoes	65
Fried Potatoes	64		

VEGETABLES.

	PAGE		PAGE
Salsify	65	*Stuffed Tomatoes	68
Oyster Plant	66	*Succotash	69
Fried Salsify or Mock Oysters	66	Green Corn	69
Cooking Carrots	66	Corn Oysters, No. 1	69
Asparagus	67	Corn Oysters, No. 2	69
*A Dainty Way of Serving Asparagus	67	*Corn Oysters, No. 3	70
Radishes	67	*To Boil Turnips	70
Spinach	67	*Egg Plant	70
Tomatoes	68	Boiled Cauliflower	71
Escalloped Tomatoes	68	To Stew Cabbage	71
		Cabbage Jelly	71

YEAST, BREAD AND BISCUIT.

	PAGE		PAGE
*Old School Presbyterian Yeast	72	*Sticks	77
Joanna's Yeast	72	Swedish Bread	77
Mrs. Isham's Potato Yeast	73	*Parker House Rolls	78
*Esther's Bread	73	Miss Parloa's Parker House Rolls	78
To Sponge Bread	73	*French Rolls	79
Brown Bread	74	Steamed Loaf	79
Corn Bread	74	Ways of Baking Graham Flour	79
Mrs. A.'s Corn Bread	74	Graham Gems	80
Phillis' Corn Bread	74	Graham Bread (Miss Parloa)	80
French Bread	74	Graham Bread, No. 2	80
*Miss Parloa's Yeast Bread	76		

CORN-BREAD AND CAKES.

	PAGE		PAGE
*St. Michael's Corn Cakes	81	*Pone	82
Crissie's Corn Bread	81	*Miss Parloa's Spider Corn Cake	82
*Steamed Corn Bread	81	Rye and Indian Bread	83
Corn Bread (most excellent)	81	Old Receipt for Bannocks	83
Corn Bread	82	Brown Bread	83

TEA AND BREAKFAST CAKES.

	PAGE		PAGE
*French Breakfast Rolls	84	*Baking Powder Biscuit	86
*Galettes	84	*Sally Lunn (yeast)	86
Rusks	85	Sally Lunn (soda and cream tartar)	87
*Rusks	85		

MUFFINS, Etc.

	PAGE		PAGE
*Hints on Muffins	87	*Potato Short Cake	89
*Water or English Muffins	87	Potato Cakes	89
Muffins	88	Stirred Bread	90
Indian Muffins	88	English Crumpets	90
Sweet Muffins	88	Puffets	90
Burlington Muffins	88	Breakfast Puffs	91
Rice Muffins	89	Pop-overs	91

WAFFLES.

*Good Ann's Receipt	91	*Rice Waffles	92
Yeast Waffles	91		

GRIDDLE CAKES.

Rice Griddle Cakes	92	Pancakes of Rice	94
*Three Buckwheat Cakes	92	Pancakes	94
*Dessert Pancakes	93	*Pancakes with Bread Crumbs	94
*Pennsylvania Flannel Cakes	93	Wheaten Scones	94
*Corn Batter Cakes	93		

MUSH, OAT-MEAL AND RICE.

How to make Corn-meal Mush	95	*Cooking Oat-meal	95
Cracked Wheat	95	*Mrs. DeLand's Oat-meal Porridge	96
Boiled Rice	95		

MACARONI.

*Macaroni	96	Macaroni a la Solferino	97

EGGS.

Boiled Eggs	98	*Omelet	99
Poached Eggs	98	Baked Eggs	99
*Scrambled Eggs	98	*Eggs sur le Plat	100
Egg Omelet	99	*Egg Vermicelli	100
Ham Omelet	99		

SALADS AND SALAD DRESSINGS.

*Chicken Salad	101	*German Salad Dressing	105
Lobster Salad	102	*Dressing for Mayonnaise	105
Shrimp Salad	102	Salad Dressing made at Table	105
Egg Salad	102	*Salad Dressing, No. 2	106
*Mrs Henry S.'s Chicken Salad Dressing	102	*Salad Dressing, to Keep	106
		Potato Salad	106
Salad Dressing	103	*French Dressing for Salad	107
*Miss Smith's Cream Dressing	103	Simple Potato Salad	107
*Mayonnaise Sauce	104	*Fresh Tomato	107
Dressing for Salad	104	*Tomato Mayonnaise	107

INDEX.

PIES.

	PAGE		PAGE
*Pastry	108	Lemon Pie	113
*Plain, Good Family Pie Crust	108	*Cocoanut Pie	113
Prof. Blot's Pie Crust	108	Cocoanut Pie	113
*Plain Pie Crust for Two Pies	108	Orange Pie	113
*A Celebrated Puff Paste	109	*Orange Pie	113
Tart Crust	109	*Pie Plant or Rhubarb Pie	114
*Rich Mince Pie	109	*Strawberry Pie	114
*Mince Pie	110	*Pumpkin Pie	114
Plain Mince Meat	110	Pumpkin or Squash Pie	115
Summer Mince Pies	110	*Cream Pie (unsurpassed)	115
Mock Mince Meat	111	Peach Pie	115
*Lemon Pie, No. 1, very fine	111	*Apple Custard Pie	115
*Lemon Pie, No. 2	111	Sweet Potato Pudding	116
Lemon Pie, that will keep a long time	112	Irish Potato Pudding	116
*A Substitute for Corn-Starch	112	*Whortleberry Pie	116
*Lemon Pie, No. 3	112	Apple Pie	116
Apple Lemon Pie	112	Custard Pie	117
		Washington Pie	117

PUDDINGS.

	PAGE		PAGE
*Mace Compound	118	Sponge Pudding	128
*Genuine English Pudding	119	Brown Bread Pudding	128
English Plum Pudding, without Eggs	119	*Steamed Graham Pudding	128
English Plum Pudding, with Eggs	120	*Baked Indian Pudding	129
Phillis' Christmas Plum Pudding	120	*Mrs. Ward's Corn-meal Pudding	129
*Black Pudding	120	*Boiled Indian Pudding	129
*Farina Pudding	120	Sweet Corn Pudding	129
*Tapioca Pudding	121	*Chocolate Pudding	129
Sago Pudding	121	Chocolate Pudding	130
Very Nice Rice Pudding	121	*Chocolate Pudding	130
Rice Pudding	121	*Queen of Puddings	130
Rice Pudding	122	*Mountain Dew Pudding	131
*A Delicate Pudding, Cocoanut and Rice	122	*Delmonico Pudding	131
*Poor Man's Rice Pudding	123	California Bread Pudding	131
Lemon Rice Pudding	123	*Bread and Butter Pudding	131
*Mrs. S.'s Boiled Lemon Pudding	123	*Poor Man's Pudding, No. 1	132
Lemon Pudding	124	Poor Man's Pudding, No. 2	132
Apple Souffle	124	*Almond Pudding	132
Apple and Tapioca Pudding	124	Marrow Pudding	133
A Cheap Apple Pudding (Eng.)	125	Vanity Fair	133
Apple Pudding	125	Gipsy Pudding	133
Margie's Brown Betties	126	Whortleberry Pudding	133
*Apple, Snow Pudding	126	*Fried Bread Pudding	134
*Fig Pudding	126	Marlboro Pudding	134
Ginger Pudding	127	*Delicious Hasty Pudding	135
*Cottage Pudding	127	*Old-fashioned Suet Pudding	135
Eve's Pudding	127	Boiled Suet Pudding	135
Plum Duff	128	Quick Puff Pudding	135
		*Pudding in Haste	136
		*Yorkshire Pudding	41

SAUCES.

	PAGE		PAGE
*Foaming Sauce	136	*Fairy or Nuns Butter	138
*Katie's Cream Sauce	136	Strawberry Sauce	138
*Pudding Sauce	137	Sauce for Sponge Pudding	138
Pudding Sauce	137	Raisin Sauce	139
The Eyre Sauce	137	Molasses Sauce	139
Virginia Cold Sauce	138	*Virginia Molasses Sauce	139
Bath Lemon Sauce	138	Maple Sugar Sauce	139
Rappahannock Cold Sauce	138	*Cream Pudding Sauce	139

FRIED CREAM, BATTER PUDDINGS, FRITTERS.

	PAGE		PAGE
*Fried Cream (Creme Frite)	140	Fritters made with Yeast	142
*White Puffs	141	American Fritters	143
*Cream Batter Pudding	141	*Orange Fritters	143
*Batter Pudding	141	Apple Fritters	143
Boiled Batter Pudding	142	Arrow Root Pudding	143
*French Fritters	142	*Kissingen Phanne Kuchen	143

HOME-MADE EXTRACTS.

Almond Flavor	144	Essence of Ginger, Vanilla	144
*Mace Compound	144	Pickled Peach Vinegar	144
*Bitter Almond Flavoring	144		

MERINGUES.

*French Meringues	145	*Italian Meringues	145

CUSTARDS.

Delicate Baked Custard	146	Custard, to turn out	148
*Boiled Custard, No. 1	147	Chocolate Custard	149
*Cream Custard	147	Cocoanut Custard	149
*Boiled Custard, No. 2	147	*Almond Custard	149
Caromel Custard Pudding	148	*Snow Custard (winter)	150
Coffee Custard	148	*Snow Custard (summer)	150
Lemon Custards that will Keep	148		

CREAMS.

*Charlotte Russe, No. 1	152	*Bavaroise	159
*Charlotte Russe, No. 2	153	Genoese Cream	159
*Charlotte Russe, No. 3	153	Italian Cream	159
*Charlotte Russe	154	*Her Majesty's Pudding	160
Chocolate Charlotte Russe	154	Russian Cream	160
A Charlotte a la Parisienne	155	*Blanc-mange	160
*Bavarian Cream (our own)	156	*Cream a la Mode	161
*Mrs. Henderson's Bavarian Cream	156	*Tapioca Cream	161
Chocolate Bavarian Cream	157	Peach Meringue	161
*Spanish Cream	157	Orange Souffle	162
*Almond Bavarian Cream	158	Fruit Charlotte	162
*Riz de l'Imperatrice	158		

ICE CREAMS.

*Ice Cream	163	Norvell House Caramel Ice Cream	165
Ice Cream	163	Caramel Custard Ice Cream	165
*Ice Cream, No. 2	164	*Biscuit Glace	165
White Ice Cream	164	Chocolate Ice	166
*Vanilla Ice Cream (Miss Parloa)	164	*Chocolate Ice Cream	166
Caramel Ice Cream	165	Bisque	166

WATER ICES.

*Water Ices	167	*Iced Coffee	168
*Lemon Ice	167	Tutti Frutti	169
*Lemon Ice (Margery Daw)	168	*Currant Ice	169
Pine Apple Ice	168	*Frozen Strawberries	169
Pine Apple Ice, No 2	168	Orange Ice	169

INDEX.

FROSTING.

	PAGE		PAGE
Frosting	170	*Boiled Icing	170
Confectioners' Icing	170	*Old-fashioned Frosting	171

CAKES.

	PAGE		PAGE
*General Directions for Mixing	171	*Election Cake	175
*Black Wedding Cake	172	*Good Pound Cake	176
Excellent Fruit Cake	172	*Delicate Cake	176
*Mrs. H. M. D.'s Reliable Fruit Cake	173	*Delicate Cake	176
		*Mrs. Henderson's Delicate Cake	176
*Imperial Cake	173	*Angel's Food	178
*White Fruit Cake	174	*Angel's Food	178
*Loaf or Bread Cake	174	*Angel's Food	179
Rich Bread Cake	174	Sunshine Cake	179
*Aunt Fanny's Loaf Cake	175	*Queen Cake (a Delicious Cake)	180
*Short Bread, the True Scotch Receipt	175	*Miss Eliza Horner's Queen Cake	180

LAYER CAKES.

	PAGE		PAGE
*Cakes Nos. 1 and 2	180	Fillings—	
*Cake No. 3	181	*Charlotte Russe Filling, No. 10	184
*Cake No. 4	181	Cake No. 5	185
*Cake No. 5	181	*Orange Filling, No. 11	185
*Chocolate Cake, No. 1	181	Marmalade Filling, No. 12	185
*Icing, No 1	181	*Ambrosia Cake	185
Layer Cake, No. 2	182	Pine Apple Cake	185
Fillings—		Hickory Nut Cake	186
Chocolate Icing, No. 2	182	Minnehaha Cake	186
Jelly, No. 3	182	*Ice Cream Cake	186
Cream Filling, No. 4	182	*Delicate Fruit Cake (very nice)	186
Orange Filling, No. 5	183	*Iowa Chocolate Cake (Delicious)	187
Cake No. 3	183	*Mrs. Millard's Almond Cake	187
*Almond Filling, No. 6	183	Winnie's Caramel Cake	188
*Fig Filling, No. 7	183	Maria's Jelly Cake (Good.)	188
*Cocoanut Filling, No. 8	184	*Custard Cake (Good)	188
Cake No. 4	184	Jelly Roll	188
Almond Custard Filling, No. 9	184		

CAKE.

	PAGE		PAGE
Chocolate Eclairs	189	*Burwick Sponge Cake	196
*New York Cream Cakes	189	*Jumbles	196
Calico Cake	190	*Dora's Cake	197
*Honour K. Cake (Good)	190	*French Cake	197
Marble Cake	190	*Water Sponge Cake	197
Watermelon Cake	191	*Spice Cake	197
*Choice Fig Cake	191	Clove	198
*Aunt Eliza's White Cake	191	*Golden Pound	198
Coffee Cake	191	*Hickory Nut Macaroons	198
*Coffee Cake (Excellent)	192	Grove Cake	198
Leopard Cake	192	Zucker Kuchen	199
*Almond Cake (Very Fine)	192	Berlin Kaffee Kuchen	199
Hickory Nut Cake	192	Coffee Cake	199
*Cream Cake	193	*Gold and Silver Cake	200
Cream Cake	193	Currant Short Cake	200
Cold Water Sponge Cake	193	*Lemon Hasty Cake	201
*Sponge Cake (Good)	193	Quick Loaf Cake	201
*Delicious Sponge Cake	194	*White Mountain Cake	201
Hot Sponge Cake	194	*Lemon Cocoanut Cake	201
Hot Water Sponge Cake	195	*Cocoanut Drops	202
Boston Cream Cake	195	Shrewsbury Cake	202
*Jamaica Plains Lemon Cake	195	Jumbles	202
*Mrs. B.'s Washington Cake	196	*Cinnamon Wafers	202
Composition Cake	196	*Ice Cream Cakes	232
*Mother's Rich Cup Cake	196		

COOKIES.

	PAGE		PAGE
*Cookies, No. 1	203	Brown Sugar Cookies	204
*Cookies, No. 2	203	New Year's Cookies	204
*Cookies, No. 3	203	*Chocolate Cookies	204
Drop Cookies	203		

GINGER CAKE.

*Drop Ginger Cakes	204	Gingerbread	205
Ginger Snaps	205	Molasses Sponge Cake	206
*Lulu's Ginger Snaps	205	*Molasses Pound Cake	206
Soft Ginger Bread	205	*Hard Gingerbread	206
Ginger Cookies	205	*Gingerbread	206

FRIED CAKES.

Yeast for Doughnuts	207	*Queen of Doughnuts	208
*Cup Measure Doughnuts	207	*Fried Cakes	209
*Raised Doughnuts	207	Mrs. May's Doughnuts	209
Delightful Raised Doughnuts	208	Crullers	209

SANDWICHES.

Sandwiches	210	*Oyster Sandwiches	211
*Egg Sandwiches	210	*Tongue or Ham Sandwiches	211
Sardine Sandwiches	210	To Carry Sandwiches	212
*Croquette Sandwiches	210	*Small Roll with Salad Filling	212
*Children's School Lunches	211	Fried Cream	212
Potted Ham and Tongue Sandwiches	211		

BREAKFAST AND TEA RELISHES.

*Bichamelle or Minced Veal	212	Liver	215
Chopped Beef	213	Spanish Toast	215
Beef Collops and Hash	213	To Make Milk Toast	215
*Hash	213	Pressed Beef	216
Hashed Mutton	214	*Beef Loaf	216
Corn Beef to Serve Cold	214	Ham Toast	216
Dried Beef	214	*Veal Loaf	216
Persilade	214	*Breakfast Bacon	217
Stewed Kidney	215	Stewed Kidney	282

ENTREES, CROQUETTES, Etc.

*Chicken Croquettes (619)	217	Chicken or Beef Rissoles	228
Chicken Croquettes (620)	217	Pickled Fowl	219
*Delmonico's Croquettes	281	Canned Salmon and Lobster	219
Fricatelles	218	*Salmon in a Mold	219
*Friteurs	218		

SAVORY JELLIES.

*Savory Chicken Jelly	220	Jellied Tongue	220

INDEX.

CHEESE.

	PAGE		PAGE
Cheese Fondu	221	*Cheese Balls for Dessert	222
*English Welch Rarebit	221		

PICKLES AND CATSUP.

	PAGE		PAGE
*The Best Brine for Cucumber Pickles	222	Yellow Pickle	229
*Cucumber Pickles (633)	222	Peach Pickle	229
*Cucumber Pickles (634)	223	*Sweet Pickle Peaches	230
Sliced Cucumber Pickles	224	Pickled Apples	230
*Tomato Catsup (636)	224	*Chili Sauce	230
Cucumber Catsup	224	Spiced Crab Apples	230
Plum Catsup	225	Watermelon Pickles	231
*White Pickles	525	Pickled Onions	231
*Mustard Pickles	225	*Red Cabbage	231
Sweet Pickles	226	*Tomato Relish	231
Pickled Mangos	226	To Make French Mustard	232
Mustard Pickles	227	*Tomato Mustard	232
*Mustard Chow Chow	227	*Spiced Currants	232
Chow Chow	228	Currant Catsup	232
*Filled Peppers	228	*Spiced Fruit	232
Pickled Cabbage	229	To Make Good Table Vinegar	233

PRESERVING AND CANNING FRUIT.

	PAGE		PAGE
Canning Fruit	233	*Raspberry Vinegar, No. 2	239
Worth Knowing	234	Preserved Citron Melon	238
To Prevent Mildew on Preserves	234	*To Preserve Citron	239
*Currant Jelly (Perfect)	234	Lemon Marmalade	240
*Currant Jelly	236	*Lemon Conserves	240
*Crab Apple Jelly	236	*Lemon and Orange Syrup	240
Cranberry Jelly	236	Ripe Tomato Preserves	240
*Grape Jelly	237	*Preserved Currants	241
Apple Jelly	237	*Preserved Quinces	241
*Pie Plant Jelly	237	Apples for Tea	241
*Orange Marmalade	238	*Grape Jam	242
Raspberry Jam	238	Ripe Peach Marmalade	242
Raspberry Vinegar, No. 1	238	*Preserving Peaches	242

PICKLING BRINE.

	PAGE		PAGE
To Cure Meat	243	Curing Beef and Tongue	244
*Spiced Beef	243	Curing Hams	244

WASHING AND CLEANING.

	PAGE		PAGE
The Use of Borax	245	To Wash Summer Suits	248
To Wash Flannel	245	*To Clean Silk Dresses	248
To Wash Colored Flannels	246	To Restore Old Velvet	249
To Remove Grass Stains	246	Removing Grease from Woolen Goods	249
Glossy Starch	246	*To Clean Boys' Clothing	249
To Remove Iron Rust Stains	246	*Japanese Cream	250
To Remove Mildew	247	Paint Spots	250
To Remove Scorches	247	Stains from Linen, etc	250
To Prevent Blue from Fading	247	To Wash Matting	250
Bluing	247	To Clean Carpets	250
To Wash Black Prints	247	*To Sweep a Carpet	251
*Washing Compound	248		
*Washing Compound	248		

TO BANISH VERMIN.

	PAGE		PAGE
*Bed Bugs	251	To Drive Away Mice	253
Moths	252	*To Banish Rats	253
To Drive Away Red Ants	252	Black Ants	253
Water-bugs and Cockroaches	253		

DAIRY AND COWS.

*To Purify Dairy Utensils..... 254 To Make Cows Give Milk....... 254

GENERAL INFORMATION.

*Useful Notes............ 255   Lamp Chimneys........... 256

THE COMPLEXION.

Removing Sunburn	257	*Glycerine Lotion	258
Another Necessary to the Toilet,	257	Red Lip Salve	259
Care of the Hair	257	*Carrot Salve	259

SPECIFICS AND REMEDIES.

A Remedy for Diphtheria	259	For Neuralgia and Headache	263
Sulphur in Scarlet Fever	260	*Senna Figs	264
To Cure Croup	260	*To Take Senna	264
Remedy for Croup	261	*For Burns	264
To Stop the Bleeding of Wounds,	261	*Relief for Scalds	264
To Cure Corns	262	Toothache	264
Soda Mint	262	Antidote for Poison	265
Wash for Inflamed Eyes	262	For an Overdose of Chloroform	265
For Chilblains	262	*For Piles or Sore Nipples	265
Ugly Remedy for Chilblains	262	*Nipple Salve	266
Flaxseed Syrup	263	*To Remove Milk Crust	266
*Lemon for Colds	263	*Remedy for Piles	266
*Chronic Diarrhœa	263		

MISCELLANEOUS.

To Hasten Cooking	267	*To Preserve Eggs	267
*To Keep Meat Fresh	267		

CANDY.

Pop Corn Balls	268	Vinegar Candy	269
*Mamie's Molasses Candy	268	*Caramels	269
Molasses Candy	268	Lemon Drops	270
*Bell's Candy	268	Raspberry Drops	270
Overton Taffy	269	*Cazenovia Caramels	270
*Butter Scotch	269		

COOKERY FOR THE SICK.

*Beef Tea, Nos. 1, 2 and 3	271	*Ice Cream for the Sick	273
Chicken and Mutton Tea	272	*Scrambling Eggs for One	273
*Beef Juice	272	*Cream Toast for One	274
Gruel	272	The Use of the Lemon	274
*Milk Porridge	272	Milk as a Diet	274
Cracker Gruel	272	To Make Lime Water	275
Oat-meal Gruel	273	*To Make a Mustard Poultice	275
Indian-meal Gruel	273	*Cure for a Felon	276
Arrow Root Gruel	273	Cure for a Run Round	276

INDEX.

INDELIBLE INK, PASTE, CEMENT, Etc.

	PAGE		PAGE
To Mend China	276	Mucilage Which Always Keeps	278
A Cheap Fumigater	276	To Repair Walls	278
To Purify A Sink	277	To Extinguish Kerosene Flames,	278
Indelible Ink	277	For Indoor Whitewashing	279

ODDS AND ENDS.

*Burnt Almonds for Desert	279	*Delmonico's Croquettes	281
*Ice Cream Cake	279	*Veal Pasty	281
*Sweet-breads, Fried	280	*Vanilla Ice Cream	281
*Sweet-breads, Stewed	280	*Coffee Ice Cream	282
*Stewed Kidneys	280		

LUNCHES AND DINNERS.

Courses for Dinners	283	Suggestions for Lunches	283

BILLS OF FARE.

Breakfasts, Nos. 1, 2 and 3	283	Dinners, Nos. 1 and 2	286
Lunches, Nos. 1, 2 and 3	285	Dinner, No. 3	287

ALLOWANCE OF SUPPLIES.

For a Private Entertainment	288	For a Public Entertainment	288
Donation Day at Home for the Friendless	289	Founders' Day at the Thompson Home	289

COFFEE, TEA and CHOCOLATE.

1 Good New England Coffee.

For a family of six take six large tablespoonfuls of best Java coffee, well browned and ground (not too fine), beat into it half an egg and one cup of cold water. After it is thoroughly beaten, let it stand half an hour, well covered. Then put into coffee pot, pour on two-and-a-half quarts of boiling water and put on the stove, stir once or twice at first, to prevent burning. Let it scald fifteen or twenty minutes. If desired to be *very* nice, beat up eight instead of six tablespoonfuls coffee; put six in the pot to boil twenty minutes, and about five minutes before it is done, throw in the rest and cover quickly.

2 Vienna Coffee.

With very little extra trouble morning coffee can be greatly improved. Beat the white of an egg to a stiff froth, mix with an equal quantity of whipped cream, and use in coffee instead of cream; put in cream first, then coffee, and lastly this mixture.

3 Soyer's Cafe au Lait.

One cup of best coffee, freshly roasted, but unground, two cups of boiling water, one quart of boiling milk. Put the coffee in a clean, dry kettle, or tin pail; fit on a close top, and set in a sauce-pan of boiling water. Shake it every few minutes, without opening it, until you judge that the coffee grains must be heated through. If, on lifting the cover, you find that the contents of the inner vessel are very hot and smoking, pour over them the boiling water directly from the tea-kettle. Cover the inner vessel closely, and set on the side of the range, where it will keep very hot, without boiling, for twenty minutes. Then add the boiling milk; let all stand together for five minutes more, and strain through thin muslin into the coffee urn. Use loaf sugar for sweetening.

4 Coffee for Two Persons.

Four rounding teaspoonfuls of coffee tied up in a piece of Swiss muslin (leave plenty of room for expansion), pour on two cups of bubbling, boiling water, cover close and set back on the range about ten minutes. Break one egg in a large coffee cup, give it a good whip with a dover egg-beater, divide it half in each cup, add the usual quantity of sugar, pour on the hot coffee, add warm milk and one spoonful of cream, and with the golden foam standing one inch above the rim of the cup you will think it too pretty to drink, and when you taste it will say you never knew how good coffee was before.

5 Cream and Milk for Coffee.

Sweet rich cream, well beaten to free from lumps is best for coffee, but boiling fresh milk is a good substitute. The white of an egg thoroughly beaten and added to thin cream or rich milk is also very nice.

6 Tea and Coffee for Children.

Tea and coffee dietary for children is as bad in its effects as its use is universal. Dr. Ferguson found that children so fed only grew four pounds per annum between the ages of thirteen and sixteen; while those who got milk night and morning grew fifteen pounds each year. This needs no commentary. The deteriorated physique of tea-and-coffee-fed children, as seen in their lessened power to resist disease, is notorious among the medical men of factory districts.

7 Tea.

Tea is made variously as the taste of people require. Black, green, Japan, and English breakfast, all require different methods. For green or Japan tea, scald the teapot and allow from one-half to one teaspoonful for each person, as the strength of the herb may indicate. Pour over this one-half a cup of boiling water, steep in a hot place, (but do not let it boil) from two to ten minutes, then turn in water at a keen boil, in the proportion of one quart to every three persons, and let stand five minutes.

8 English Breakfast or Oolong.

Take two teaspoonfuls for three persons, and proceed as above, only letting the tea *boil* for ten minutes.

An English gentleman, whose tea was quite famous, put it to steep in cold water, as soon as the one o'clock dinner was over, and left it steeping until supper time, when it was brought to a boil.

Others put it on to steep when the fire is made for supper, and let it stand until the meal is announced, served boiling hot.

9 Iced Tea.

To each glass of tea add the juice of half a lemon; fill up the glass with pounded ice, and sweeten.

10 German Chocolate.

For six persons take four heaping tablespoonfuls of plain chocolate; when grated, put with it the yolks of two eggs, and water enough to mix well together. Place it in the chocolate boiler with one half pint of hot water, and four tablespoonfuls of sugar, taking care to stir well. After scalding five minutes, add one quart of boiling milk, and then the whites of the two eggs beaten to a stiff froth with two heaping tablespoonfuls of sugar, stirring all the while. It must be sent to the table as soon as possible after the whites of the eggs are put in.

Mrs. C. S. I.

11 Chocolate.

Webbs', Bakers, and Mailard's plain chocolates are the best—take four or six heaping tablespoonfuls of grated chocolate, four of sugar, and wet with four of boiling water; rub this smooth. Then stir this mixture into one pint of boiling water; let boil five minutes then add one pint of *boiling* milk. Let all boil three minutes. It is greatly improved by milling, while boiling, with a dover egg-beater. If not desired sweet, omit the sugar.

A dainty addition is two tablespoonfuls of whipped cream, that has been sweetened and flavored with vanilla, laid on the top of each cup.

GENERAL HINTS FOR MAKING SOUPS.

It is not easy to see why soups are held in so little favor by Americans generally, while with almost all other people they form an important article of food.

The French, from the richest to the poorest, have their "*pot au feu*," which literally would be "pot to the fire," but it is the name used to designate the universal soup. The directions for this vary. We give one of the most economical. Put in a pot, which is kept for this purpose alone, four-and-a-half quarts of cold water, and three pounds of rump beef, with what remains of poultry or cooked meat that may be at hand. Put upon the fire until it boils, and then place where it will simmer gently, removing the scum as it rises; add carrots, two turnips, two leeks or small onions, a head of celery, and three or four cloves.

The whole story is meat and vegetables simmered slowly together, and it may be varied in many ways by using different vegetables. The meat and vegetables are removed and the clear soup served, after which the meat and vegetables are served plain, or the meat is dressed with tomato or other sauce. Sometimes a tough fowl is put into the soup pot and cooked until tender, and then put into the oven and browned; the broth thus made serves for a variety of soups; with vermicelli, macaroni, rice, or barley, and soups take those names. By using a variety of vegetables cut fine it makes vegetable soup. Roast an onion until it is thoroughly brown and boil in the broth and you have brown soup.

A soup may be varied in many ways, sometimes by slicing hard boiled eggs into it, after dishing; again, small squares of bread, fried to a brown crisp, as in receipt for croutons, and dropped into the soup when it is ready for the table, imparts a savory relish.

12 Why Soup is Wholesome.

The London *Food Journal* says: Physiologically, soup has great value to those who hurry to and from their meals, as it allows an interval of comparative rest to the fainting stomach before the more substantial beef and mutton is attacked, rest before solid food being as important as rest after it. Let a hungry and weary merchant rush *in medias res*—plunge boldly into roast beef, and what is the result? The defeat is often as precipitate as was the attack. When the body is weary the stomach must be identified with it, and cannot therefore stand the shock of some ill-masticated, half-pound weight of beef. But if a small plateful of light soup be gently insinuated into the system, nourishment will soon be introduced, and strength will follow to receive more substantial material.

13 Perfect Mock Turtle Soup.

Endeavor to have the head and the stock-meat ready for the soup, the day before it is to be eaten. It will take eight hours to prepare it properly.

	Hours.
Cleaning and soaking the head	1
To parboil it to cut up	1
Cooling, nearly	1
Making the broth and finishing the soup	5
	8

Get a calf's head with the skin on (the fresher the better); take out the brains, wash the head several times in cold water, let it soak for about an hour in spring water, then lay it in a stewpan, and cover it with cold water, and half a gallon over; as it becomes warm, a great deal of scum will rise, which must be immediately removed; let it boil gently for one hour, take it up, and, when almost cold, cut the head into pieces about an inch and a half by an inch and a quarter, and the tongue into mouthfuls, or rather make a side dish of the tongue and brains.

When the head is taken out, put in the stock meat (about five pounds of knuckle of veal), and as much beef; add to the stock all the trimmings and bones of the head, skim it well, and then cover it close and let it scald five hours (reserve a couple of quarts of this to make gravy sauces); then strain it off and let it stand till the next morning; then take off the fat, set a large stewpan on the fire with half a pound of good fresh butter, two ounces of onions sliced, and one-fourth ounce of green sage; chop it a little; let these fry one hour; then rub in half a pound of browned flour, and by degrees add your broth till it is the thickness of cream; season it with a quarter of an ounce of ground allspice and half an ounce of black pepper ground very fine, salt to your taste, and the rind of one lemon peeled very thin; let it simmer very gently for one hour and-a-half, then strain it through a hair sieve; do not rub your soup to get it through the sieve, or it will make it grouty; if it does not run through easily, knock your wooden spoon against the side of your sieve; put it in a clean stewpan with the head, and season it by adding to each gallon of soup two tablespoonfuls of Tarragon vinegar and two tablespoonfuls of lemon juice; let it simmer gently till the meat is tender; this may take from half an hour to an hour; take care it is not overdone; stir it frequently to prevent the meat sticking to the bottom of the stewpan, and when the meat is quite tender the soup is ready.

A head weighing twenty pounds, and ten pounds of stock meat, will make ten quarts of excellent soup, besides the two quarts of stock you will have put by for made dishes.

Obs.—If there is more meat on the head than you wish to put in the soup, prepare it for a pie, and, with the addition of a calf's foot boiled tender, it will make an excellent ragout pie; season it with zest and a little minced onion; put in half a teacupful of stock, cover it with puff-paste and bake it one hour; when the soup comes from table, if there is a great deal of meat and no soup, put it into a pie dish, season it a little, and add some little stock to it; then cover it with paste, bake it one hour, and you have a good mock-turtle pie.

To Season the Soup.—To each gallon put four tablespoonfuls of lemon juice, two of mushroom catsup, and one teaspoonful of mace, a tablespoonful of curry powder, or a quarter of a drachm of cayenne, and the peel of a lemon pared as thin as possible, let it simmer for five minutes more, take out the lemon peel, add the yolks of four hard boiled eggs, and the soup is ready for the tureen.

While the soup is doing, prepare for each tureen a dozen and a half of mock turtle forcemeat balls, and put them into the tureen. Brain balls, or cakes, are a very elegant addition, and are made by boiling the brains for ten minutes, then putting them in cold water and cutting them into pieces about as big as a large nutmeg; take savory or lemon thyme dried and finely powdered, nutmeg grated, pepper and salt, and pound them all together; beat up an egg, dip the brains in it, and then roll them in this mixture, and make as much of it as possible stick to them; dip them in the eggs again, and then in finely-grated and sifted bread-crumbs; fry them in hot fat, and send them up as a side dish.

A well blanched veal sweet-bread, not too much done or it will break, cut into pieces the same size as you cut the calf's head, and put in the soup, just to get warm before it goes to table, is a superb "*bonne bouche;*" and pickled tongue, stewed till very tender, and cut into mouthfuls, is a favorite addition. We order the meat to be cut into mouthfuls, that it may be eaten with a spoon; the knife and fork have no business in a soup-plate.

N. B.—In helping this soup, the distributer of it should serve out the meat, force-meat and gravy, in equal parts; however trifling or needless this remark may appear, the writer has often suffered from the want of such a hint being given to the soup-server, who has sometimes sent a plate of mere gravy without meat, to others, of meat without gravy, and sometimes scarcely anything but force-meat balls.

Obs.—This is a delicious soup, within the reach of those who "eat to live;" but if it had been composed expressly for those who only "live to eat," I do not know how it could have been made more agreeable; as it is, the lover of good eating will "wish his throat a mile long, and every inch of it a palate."

14 Bouillon.

To five pounds beef cut in small pieces add five quarts cold water; simmer slowly six hours. A shank of beef, broken twice across and once lengthwise is equally good. After boiling three hours slowly, add salt, black pepper, one tablespoonful allspice, two onions cut small, one grated carrot, one head celery, two tomatoes, one dozen whole cloves, boil slowly three hours longer, strain and set away. Next day remove the fat, and boil; just before serving, adding a little nutmeg and mace. In summer, if one dozen ochras are boiled in the soup, it will require but little spice. Made entirely of lean meat, it can be used the same day. Serve in bouillon cups.

15 Corn Soup.

Cut the grains from twelve ears of sweet corn and scrape the milk, add one quart of water; let it boil until quite done, thirty or forty minutes, then add two quarts of new milk, and when it boils stir in one quarter of a pound of butter rubbed into two tablespoonfuls of flour; pepper and salt to taste. Beat the yolks of two eggs with two tablespoonfuls of cream, place in the bottom of the tureen and pour the soup into it boiling; stir all the time for a minute and a half.

16 Summer or Winter Corn Soup.

Boil a leg of mutton or shank of beef in six quarts of water for four hours, (or less, if the mutton is to be eaten for dinner). After the meat and fat have been removed (it is better to stand over one day to cool, so that the grease may all be taken off), add a quart or more of sweet corn nicely cut from the cob, and boil twenty or thirty minutes. In cutting the corn (with a sharp knife) take off only *the point* of the kernels, and *scrape* the milk and pulp, thus avoiding the hull or skin, which is indigestible and unpalatable. Just before serving, add to the soup a coffee-cup of cream, with two tablespoonfuls of flour stirred smoothly in and boil for a minute. This can be made in winter by using the Yarmouth canned corn or the dried corn soaked over night, and boiled till tender. The corn flavors mutton better than beef stock.

17 Corn Soup.

One pint grated corn, one quart milk, two tablespoons butter, one slice of onion, salt and pepper to taste. Cook the corn in two quarts of water thirty minutes. Let the milk and onion come to a boil. Have the flour and butter mixed, and a little boiling milk, and cook eight minutes, then take out the onion and add the corn.

FISHER'S ISLAND, 1882.

18 Potato Soup.

Ten large potatoes boiled soft; pour off the water and mash. Add one quarter of a pound of butter and pour on three pints of cold milk; let it come to a boil, stirring to prevent burning. Season with pepper and salt; put some toasted crackers or bread fried in butter into the tureen, and strain the soup on them through a colander, serve hot.

19 Parker House Tomato Soup.

For one gallon of soup take three quarts of good beef stock (a shank of beef will make six quarts); one medium sized carrot, one turnip, one beet and two small onions; peel and cut them in pieces; add to this three quarts of red tomatoes; boil all for one hour and strain through a colander. Put five ounces of butter in a pan, heat it until it becomes a light brown; take it off the fire and add three tablespoonfuls of flour while hot; mix well and pour a pint or more of the soup into the frying pan, then return all to the soup kettle; season with salt, pepper, and a dessert spoonful of sugar. Set it over the fire and stir it till it boils; boil and skim five minutes. For winter soup of this kind strain the soup before adding the tomatoes, and use in place of the raw tomatoes, two quart cans of sealed tomatoes.

20 Very Rich Beef Soup.

Fry an onion in the bottom of your soup digester, then place four pounds of meat upon it and let it heat until the juices of the meat start well. Then add one onion, one turnip, one carrot, sliced quite thin, two or three stalks of celery, some parsley, a blade of mace; four whole cloves, salt and pepper, a tomato, if in season, a tablespoon of caramel or burnt sugar. Boil slowly and gently, keeping it covered until the vegetables are tender, then strain, and it is ready for use.

21 Turkey Soup.

Place the rack of a cold turkey and what remains of dressing or gravy in a pot, and cover it with cold water. Simmer gently three or four hours, and let it stand until the next day. Take off what fat may have arisen, and take out with a skimmer all the bits of bones. Put the soup on to heat till boiling, then thicken slightly with flour stirred into a cup of cream, and season to the taste. Pick off all the turkey from the bones, put them in the soup, boil up and serve.

22 Sorrel Soup (Soup a la Bonne Femme).

This is a most wholesome soup, which would be popular in America if it were better known. It is much used in France. Sorrel can be obtained in season, at all the French markets in America.

For four quarts of soup, put into a saucepan a piece of butter the size of an egg, two or three sprigs of parsley, two or three leaves of lettuce, one onion and a pint of sorrel (all finely chopped), a little nutmeg, pepper and salt. Cover, and let them cook or sweat ten minutes, then add two tablespoonfuls of flour; mix well, and gradually add three quarts of boiling water (stock would be better). Make a liaison, *i. e.*, beat the yolks of four eggs (one egg to a quart of soup), and mix with them a cupful of cream, or rich milk; add a little chevril (if you have it) to the soup; let it boil ten minutes; then stir in the eggs or liaison, when the soup is quite ready.

23 Calf's Head Soup (Simple Process).

Take the head, pluck and feet. Put them into a pot with cold water. Be careful to skim well when it boils. Chop a dozen small onions and let them all boil together until the meat cleaves from the bones. Then strain it. After putting the liquor into the pot again, add thyme, cloves, salt, pepper and cayenne to your taste. Cut all the meat from the head and feet, half the liver and lights, the whole of the heart and tongue; put all into the pot and boil about three-quarters of an hour. Before it is done take half a pound of butter with as much flour as will make into balls; stir until dissolved. Then add two tablespoonfuls of tarragon vinegar, four hard boiled eggs cut in slices, and a lemon to improve the flavor. This will make two gallons, and may be kept several weeks, to be used as occasion requires.

24 Ockra Soup.

Take two quarts of good strong stock; chop a carrot, two onions, and a very small turnip; let these fry well in two tablespoonfuls of butter; take out the vegetables and in the butter left in the pan, slightly brown two tablespoonfuls of flour, add to this a little stock to get it very smooth, then pour the vegetables and browned flour into the stock. Wash and cut one dozen ockras in wafers an eighth of an inch thick and let them simmer with the stock and vegetables from one and-a-half to two hours. Add pepper and salt and serve with sippets of toast.

25 Tomato Soup.

One quart of water, eight good sized ripe tomatoes cut up; boil twenty minutes and add one half teaspoonful of soda; then boil and add one pint or more of milk, and season as you do oysters. We have three friends who think this soup is delicious, and six who pronounce it abominable.

26 Veal Soup.

Take a veal shank and boil it eight hours in three quarts of water; set the liquor in a cool place until an hour before dinner; skim it well and dry off the top with tissue or blotting paper. It should be a jelly. Let it scald for half an hour with an onion unbroken or cut at the bottom of the pot; then add a pint of cream into which two tablespoonfuls of flour have been well stirred; season with salt and pepper, and a little chopped parsley, or as in sorrel soup.

27 Black Bean Soup.

One quart of black beans, soaked over night, and boiled until perfectly soft; mash them through a colander; have ready three quarts of strong beef stock; add to it the beans and one small onion; boil one hour. Have in the soup tureen three hard-boiled eggs, minced fine ; slice in one lemon; one teaspoonful of brown sugar, a pinch of cloves, two of cinnamon, black pepper and salt; also two tablespoonfuls of the mace compound. Pour the soup into the tureen and serve at once.

Mrs. A. S.'s "Lizzie."

28 Pea Soup.

One quart of soaked split peas, two pounds of salt pork, five quarts of water. Boil five hours, and strain through a sieve while hot.

29 Croutons.

These are small pieces of bread, cut the size of a dice, and fried crisp and brown, to be used in soup.

30 Browning for Soups.

Many of the nicest soups owe their attractive appearance to burnt sugar, which is prepared as follows: Put three tablespoonfuls of brown sugar and an ounce of butter in a small frying pan or iron skillet and set over the fire; stir continually until it is of a bright brown color and sends forth a burning smell, add half a pint of water, boil and skim, and when cold, bottle for use. Add to soups at discretion.

31 Oyster Soup.

This is one of the finest soups we have ever tasted. To one quart of oysters add a teacup of water, shake well and strain off; putting the oysters in a double boiler to heat, then take the strained liquor set it over the fire and as soon as it becomes scalding hot pour it over a piece of butter the size of an egg, into which you have braided, while the liquor is boiling, a tablespoonful of flour; let butter, flour and liquor cook a few minutes, stirring well, then add half a pint of sweet milk or cream and then the oysters, seasoning with salt and a little cayanne pepper. Do not let the soup boil, but keep it quite hot for a moment or two after adding the oysters. Have both soup and oysters cooking so equally that neither waits for the other. This is the secret of success.

32 Oyster Soup.

For four cans of oysters have twelve crackers rolled fine, two quarts of boiling water, one pint of good rich milk. Let the milk and water come to a boil, add the crackers, salt and pepper, boil one minute briskly; pour in the oysters, which have been heating in the double boiler, and let all come to a scald; add about a quarter of a pound of butter as they are poured into a tureen.

33 Miss Parloa's Green Pea Soup.

One pint of the peas having already been thoroughly cooked, are put in a pot on the stove with a slice of onion added. When they have been brought to a boil they are removed and mashed, and a pint of stock is added. Then two tablespoonfuls of butter are melted, and a tablespoonful of flour is mixed in the stewpan. This is poured into the mixture of peas and stock and a pint of cream added last.

34 Soup Dumplings—Mrs. Ewing.

Three tablespoonfuls of flour, white of one egg, and one tablespoonful of marrow out of the beef bone minced with a fork. In seasoning, salt, pepper, a little lemon peel, and a little minced parsley were used. This dumpling was said to look lovely in amber soup. The materials have to be pounded together with the white of egg until well blended, then form into little balls the size of marbles.

"Does the suet moisten the dumpling?" inquired a pupil in the body of the hall.

"The white of egg moistens," replied Mrs. Ewing.

A soup bone should be at least half meat if rich broth was desired. Place in a stock pot or digester, differing from the ordinary kettle in that it had a close fitting lid. Cover with cold water, add a teaspoonful of salt. The meat and bone takes about two quarts of water. The water to be put on cold and salt added at the time, in order to draw out the slime and blood, and assist in its rising in the scum so that it might be carefully skimmed off. When the water comes to the boil it must be carefully skimmed. If allowed to boil in, the soup would not be so clear nor half so finely flavored. The most important point in regard to flavor is that the soup made shall be fresh and not salt. When the soup has been properly skimmed the cover should be put on and screwed down close and the soup be allowed to simmer, not to boil rapidly, for four hours. Longer cooking simply extracts more of the gelatine that is in the bone, while affecting the clearness of the soup. All the juices of the meat could be perfectly extracted in four hours. A fine strainer or fine hair sieve was the best for straining, but a napkin would answer the purpose.

The draining process completed, the soup should be set to cool in the coldest obtainable place—not a refrigerator—but in a draught of cold air, for the sooner the soup stock cools the more perfect the flavor and the longer it keeps. A knife run along the bowl removes every particle of grease.

Amber colored stock can be made with a pound of the lean beef that comes from the round, such as is used for beef tea, cooked in a skillet, or cast-iron spider. Round lean beef gives the soup stock its beautiful amber color and fine flavor. Another way is to take the soup bones and spread a little butter over the lean meat; then place in a bake pan and put in the oven and brown nicely before being put in the stock pot. To every quart of simple stock apply a pound of beefsteak browned on a hot pan, clarifying with shell and white of egg. One vegetable added to a plain soup or clear soup changes it immediately to a vegetable soup, and no multiplication of vegetables would make it anything other than this. In vegetable soup the main thing is to get the vegetables mixed in proper proportion to combine things that harmonize or taste well together. The maximum of success was attained when no one of the various ingredients could be tasted distinctly.

35 Green Pea Soup.

Take a small slice of salt pork, a quart of fresh shelled green peas, or, if in winter, a can of French or Marrowfat peas, pour over them a quart of boiling water and let them boil until they can be washed and strained through a seive or fine colander. Then pour in three pints of boiling milk; salt and pepper to taste. Let all scald together for ten minutes; have the yolks of two eggs beaten with two tablespoonfuls of milk in your soup tureen, pour the scalding soup upon them, and add a spoonful of fresh butter. Serve with croutons, or toasted bread, or crackers.

36 White Almond Soup.

A shank of veal put into five quarts of cold water and boiled down to four; put one carrot, one bunch of celery, one good sized onion, and two cloves into a bag, and put them into the soup kettle with the veal and boil half an hour, or until the flavor is extracted. Then take them out. When the liquor is boiled down to four quarts set it aside until the next day. When you wish to serve, put the jelly in the soup kettle and add two ounces of blanched almonds chopped fine, and half a pint of sweet cream, cook a few moments, and send to the table.

37 Clam Soup.

Put thirty clams in a pot, add four quarts of water. Let them scald two hours and then take them out and chop fine, return to the pot and add a little mace and a few pepper corns. Boil one hour longer. Rub smoothly together a piece of butter, the size of an egg, with two tablespoonfuls of flour, and stir this with a pint of boiling milk. Into the clam soup, which has now boiled three hours, stir in the thickened milk and pour into tureen.

Canned clams make a nice soup after the above recipe.

OYSTERS.

(*For Oyster Soups, see Soups.*)

---

38 To Stew Oysters.

Put the oysters with the broth to boil, and when they begin to curl, skim them out of the kettle into a pan of cold water; let them lie in the water until the broth has been skimmed and seasoned with butter, salt and pepper; add mace if you like; then drain off the water and return the oysters to the broth. When they begin to boil up again they are ready to serve, and will be found to be more plump and hard by the process.

39 Panned or Griddled Oysters.

Wash large oysters free from the liquor. Heat a griddle very hot, butter it and lay large oysters all over it; when brown on one side, turn as you do griddle cakes. In the meantime have the liquor boiled and skimmed, and turned over the oysters when served, first seasoning it with butter, salt and pepper; serve on toasted bread.

40 Devilled Oysters.

To one quart of chopped oysters, add six tablespoonfuls of rolled cracker, four tablespoonfuls of melted butter, half a teaspoonful of salt, one-fourth of a teaspoonful of pepper; bake in hot oyster shells fifteen or twenty minutes.

41 Roasted Oysters.

One quart of oysters, rounds of thin toast delicately browned, butter, pepper and salt. Have ready silver or scalop shells, or several pans of block tin, the ordinary "patty pan" will do if you cannot get anything better. Cut stale bread in thin slices of a size that will just fit in the bottom of your pans, toast these quickly to a light brown, and lay within your tins. Wet with a great spoonful of oyster liquor, then with a silver fork arrange upon the toast as many oysters as each patty will hold without heaping them up. Dust with pepper and salt, put a bit of butter on top, and set the pans, when they are full, upon the floor of a quick oven. Cover with an inverted baking pan to keep in steam and flavor, and cook until the oysters "ruffle." Eight minutes in a brisk oven should be enough; send very hot to the table in the tins in which they were roasted. Next to roasting in the shell this mode of cooking oysters best preserves the native flavor of the bivalves.

42 How to Broil Oysters.

Now let me tell you how we broil oysters here. Given a double gridiron that folds together, and a sufficient number of the bivalves in their natural state, to roll them in anything is to spoil them; grease the bars of the gridiron, which prevents their sticking; then dip each individual—as Audubon always said in reference to birds—into melted butter; place them on the utensil. A brisk fire of charcoal is of course necessary, over which they are to be broiled. Meantime they should be constantly turned and basted with butter. When done, serve on very hot toast and dishes, and you have a dish that Brillat-Savarin, with all his gastronomic ideas, never thought of, and which would have driven him mad with envy.

43 Fried Oysters.

Select the largest, drain them on a cloth or hair sieve, dip them in rolled cracker crumbs that have been sifted and seasoned with pepper and salt; fry in equal parts of butter and lard until they are browned. Grated bread crumbs are even more delicate than cracker crumbs, and do not require sifting.

44 Fried Oysters.

Dry large oysters on a soft towel, dip them into well beaten egg and roll in sifted cracker crumbs; then fry in equal parts of butter and lard, which should be very hot.

45 Fried Oysters.

Beat an egg and a tablespoonful of milk together, add to this enough finely sifted cracker crumbs to make a thin batter, dry the oysters, dip them into this batter and draw them out well covered with it, plunge them into boiling batter and lard and fry.

46 Oyster Fritters.—Madame Pierson.

Take the liquor from the oysters, boil and skim it, add to every teacupful an equal quantity of milk, three eggs and six tablespoonfuls of flour, into which has been stirred a teaspoonful of baking powder; pour a tablespoonful of butter in a small cake on the griddle, lay an oyster in the middle and let it cook through.

47 Oysters Broiled in the Shell.

The oysters should be of the largest size. Clean the shells with a stiff brush, then open, and save the juice;

turn boiling water over the oysters for only a minute or two; drain it off, and lay the oysters on one-half of the shell, putting it on a well-heated gridiron over a very hot fire. Boil the liquor that came from the oysters when opened, add it to the shells with a sprinkle of salt, pepper, and a bit of butter; serve hot on the shells, laid on large platters.

48   Teal's Cream Oysters.

Fifty large oysters, one quart sweet cream, butter, pepper, and salt to taste; put the cream and oysters in separate kettles to heat, the oysters in their own liquor and let them come to a boil; when sufficiently cooked skim them, take out the oysters and put in a bowl to keep warm, put the cream and oyster liquor together, season to taste and thicken with powdered crackers, when thick as cream add the oysters.

49   Unsurpassed Fricasseed Oysters.

For one can of oysters use one pint of thin cream; clean all the liquor from the oysters and put them in the double boiler until hot; at the same time thicken the cream with two even tablespoonfuls flour and season with salt, pepper and a small pinch of mace, and the same of cinnamon and a very little butter; cook this well, and when done thoroughly, add to it the liquor of the oysters which has been scalded and well skimmed until clear; then add the oysters, letting them remain just long enough to get plump (if left too long they shrivel and grow tough). Have ready some toast cut in two inch squares on a platter and pour the whole over it, or have leaves and triangles of rich paste around the dish and partially moistened by the fricassee. Your platter must be very hot, as fricasseed oysters chill like a new-born baby.

50 Fricasseed Oysters.

Drain the liquor from a quart of oysters, which should be placed to heat in the double boiler, strain half a pint of the liquor and put in a porcelain kettle and when it boils put in the oysters, have ready two tablespoonfuls of flour rubbed into a tablespoonfuls of butter. When the oysters begin to swell, stir this into the sauce, cook until the oysters are white and plump; then add a gill of cream, and pepper and salt.

51 Oyster Pie.—Mrs. S. P. B.

Two cans of oysters, or three pints of solid oysters, one quart of sweet cream, one dozen rolled butter crackers, pepper, salt, etc. Stir all together and pour into a dish lined with thick puff paste, cover with another paste and bake three-quarters of an hour. This is a delicious mode of cooking oysters.

52 Oyster Patties.

Put the oysters in a saucepan with enough of the liquor to cover them; let them come to a scald, skim well, add two tablespoonfuls of butter for one quart of oysters, season with pepper and a little salt. Two or three spoonfuls of cream will add to the richness. Have ready small tins lined with puff-paste; put three or four oysters in each, according to the size of the patty; cover with paste and bake in a quick oven twenty minutes; when done wash over the top with beaten egg and set in the oven for two minutes to glaze.

53 Scalloped Oysters.

Have a pint of grated bread crumbs or fine crushed cracker crumbs, seasoned with salt and pepper, either soda or butter crackers; put a thin layer in the bottom of a buttered two-quart pudding dish; wet slightly with oyster liquor and milk, mixed; next a thick layer of oysters; season with salt and pepper and small bits of butter; then more crumbs and oysters, alternately, until the dish is full. Let the top layer be of crumbs. Beat an egg and mix it with a little milk to pour over the top; place little lumps of butter all over the top, cover the dish and bake half an hour; remove the cover a few minutes before taking from the oven to let it brown. The oysters must be done through but not overdone.

54 Oyster Omelette.

Beat six eggs separately; add, by degrees, one gill of cream to the beaten yolks; season with salt and pepper, add the whites, well beaten. Have ready one dozen large oysters cut in half; put into a saucepan to heat, one tablespoonful of butter; pour the eggs into it, drop the oysters on evenly. Fry a light brown, then set in the oven to brown the top, or turn like an ordinary omelette.

55 Croustade of Oysters.

Have a loaf of bread baked in a round two-quart basin. When two or three days old, with a sharp knife cut out the heart of the bread, being careful not to break the crust, and plunge it into a deep pot of boiling lard for one moment, or butter the entire surface of the bread, and bake in a hot oven, being careful not to burn. Break up the crumbs very fine, and dry them slowly in an oven; then quickly fry three cupfuls of them in two tablespoonfuls of butter. As soon as they begin to look golden and are crisp, they are done. It takes about two minutes over a hot fire, stirring all the time. Put one quart of cream to boil, and when it boils, stir in three tablespoonfuls of flour which has been mixed with half a cupful of cold milk. Cook eight minutes. Season well with salt and pepper. Put a layer of the sauce into the croustade, then a layer of oysters, which dredge well with salt and pepper; then another layer of sauce and one of fried crumbs. Continue this until the croustade is nearly full, having the last layer a thick one of crumbs. It takes three pints of oysters for this dish, and about three teaspoonfuls of salt, and half a teaspoonful of pepper. Bake slowly half an hour. Serve with a garnish of parsley around the dish.

56 Chicken and Oyster Croquettes.

Take equal quantities of chicken and oysters; over the latter pour scalding water; parboil for a moment, and then plump in cold water; chop both chicken and oysters fine; add a cup of sifted bread crumbs, a tablespoonful of butter, stirred well together, then moisten with one well beaten egg and enough thick sweet cream to make just thick enough to handle; season with salt and pepper, and if liked, a little mace; form into long, slender rolls; dip into beaten egg, roll in sifted cracked crumbs, and fry in lard to a light brown; serve in a napkin, and garnish with celery tops or parsley and slices of lemon.

57 Pickled Oysters.

Strain the liquor from the oysters; boil and skim until clear; drop in the oysters and let them come to a boil;

skim them out and put them in a jar. Take about half the liquor remaining, add vinegar until it tastes sharp, a few whole cloves and allspice; boil and pour over the oysters, hot; cover them and let them stand two or three days before using. If you wish to use them any sooner take a little more vinegar.

58 Pickled Oysters, No. 2.

Take the oysters from the liquor, boil and skim it. Rinse the oysters if there are any bits of shell attached to them; put them in the liquor while boiling; boil them one minute, then take them out of it, and to the liquor put a few pepper corns and a blade or two of mace, and a little salt, and the same quantity of vinegar as oyster juice. Let the whole scald fifteen minutes, then turn it on to the oysters. If you wish to keep the oysters a couple of weeks, bottle and cork them tight as soon as cold.

59 Lobster Croquettes.

Chop the meat of a well-boiled lobster fine, add pepper, salt and mace, if liked; mix with this one-fourth as much bread crumbs as you have meat; with two tablespoonfuls of melted butter and yolks of two eggs, form into balls, roll these in beaten egg, then in cracker crumbs and fry in hot lard.

60 Oyster and Clam Fritters.

Twelve clams, minced fine, one pint milk, three eggs; add the liquor from the clams to the milk; beat up the eggs and put to this, with salt and pepper, and flour enough for a thin batter; lastly add the chopped clams.

Fry in hot lard, trying a little first to see if fat and batter are right. A tablespoonful makes a fritter of moderate size. Fry quickly and serve hot.

61 Batter for Oyster Fritters.

One egg, one tablespoonful of flour and half a cup of milk; pour scalding water over the oysters in a quart can; then chop them and add to the batter.

62 Raw Oysters.

Should be served at a party or small entertainment on a handsome block of ice, that has been hollowed out on the top. Set the ice on a platter and garnish the edges with quarters of lemons. Be careful that in its melting the water does not overflow. For a second course at dinners or lunches lay three or four oysters on an individual oyster dish, garnished with lemon; lay a sprig of the yellow heart of celery across. Have pepper, salt and vinegar at hand.

FISH AND FROGS.

63 Boiled Fish.

Rub the fish with a fresh lemon, inside and out. To four quarts of boiling water add half a teacupful of salt, a bouquet of sweet herbs, and half a teacupful of vinegar; boil gently, or scald, as the size of the fish may require, allowing from six to ten minutes for each pound of fish. Serve on a napkin, with egg sauce or drawn butter, and gravy-boat garnished with cut lemons and hard boiled eggs grated over.

64 Boiled Fish with Vegetable Flavor.

Mince a carrot, an onion, and a small piece of celery; fry them in a stewpan with a little butter; add some parsley, some pepper-corn, and three or four cloves. Now pour on two quarts of water and a pint of vinegar; let it boil a quarter of an hour, skim it, salt it, and use for boiling the fish. Rub the fish with lemon juice and salt, put it in a kettle and cover with the above liquor. Let it only simmer—not boil hard—until thoroughly done.

65 To Broil a Whitefish.

Lay the fish wide open upon a double gridiron, and broil it as you would a steak; salt and pepper.

66 Fish Chowder.

Quarter pound of pork, cut in pieces; put in the bottom of the pot and fry out. Put slices of potatoes on this, then layer of fish, cut up, two onions, sliced, and layer of soda crackers; repeat these layers. Then pour boiling water over till well covered. Stew twenty-five minutes, but do not stir it. This is excellent, made of whitefish as well as cod.

67 Turbot, No. 1.

Take a fine large white fish, steam until tender; take out the bones and sprinkle with pepper and salt. For the dressing heat one quart of milk and thicken with one-quarter pound of flour stirred smooth in a cup of milk. When cool add two eggs and one-quarter pound of butter. Put in the baking-dish a layer of fish, then a layer of sauce, until full. Season with onions, parsley and thyme. Cover the top with bread crumbs and bake three-quarters of an hour.

68 Turbot, No. 2.

Five pounds of white fish, boil and cool. For dressing take one quart of milk, one quarter-pound of flour, wet with a little milk, one-quarter pound of butter, two eggs, two small onions, one-half bunch of thyme, one-half bunch of green parsley, pepper and salt. Boil together until it thickens. Put in the baking dish a layer of fish, then a layer of dressing, a layer of bread crumbs. Grate cheese over the top, and bake half an hour.

69 Cod Fish Balls.

Pick carefully and take out all bones, and skin enough to fill level full a pint bowl. Lay this in the bottom of your kettle, and place on top two heaping bowls of raw potatoes freshly peeled; pour over boiling water enough to cover both fish and potatoes; boil thirty minutes, then mash both together until very fine and smooth; break into this mixture two raw eggs, stir with a wooden spoon or pot-stick until all are light and well blended; add a bit of butter the size of an egg, then flour your hands and make up into croquets or flat cakes, as you prefer, and boil in a frying-pan. We prefer croquets but old time folks like genuine fish balls. The secret of success is mixing fish and potatoes while both are hot.

70 Baked Lobster; or Lobster Turbot.

Two tablespoonfuls of flour (even), mixed well with one tablespoonful of butter. Put over the fire one teacupful of milk. When it comes to the boiling point, stir in the flour and butter; add yolks of three hard-boiled eggs, salt and one teaspoonful of curry powder or anchovy sauce, and red pepper. This makes the sauce. Put in a baking dish a layer of lobster, and then one of sauce; bake thirty or forty minutes and serve piping hot.

M. ROMEYNE, PER MRS. LOTHROP.

71 Pickled Fish.

Skin the fish and pack in a deep dish; cover with olive oil or butter; spice vinegar with pepper, cloves, cinnamon, allspice and salt; scald and pour over the fish; cover closely and bake until done.

72 Picked Codfish (Delicious).

Pick, very fine indeed, of the thick part of the codfish one pound, put it into the spider, pour over sufficient boiling water to cover it well, then scald it well for a minute; pour off all this water, and if the fish is still too salty drain it off and repeat the process. Get ready a cup and a half of sweet (fresh) milk. Take from this amount of milk four tablespoonfuls and mix into it two tablespoons of sifted flour and stir till it becomes a smooth batter. Pour on to the fish the fresh milk and set on the stove. Add to it two ounces of butter. Allow it to cook till the butter melts, then stir in the prepared batter very slowly and let all boil ten minutes, stirring all the time. If too thick add a little milk; if too thin, add a little flour. After dishing, sprinkle a little pepper over it. Cream can be used without the flour.

73 Codfish for Friday Dinner.

One quart picked codfish, one pint bread crumbs, one-half pint cream, four ounces butter, one teaspoon pepper; wash the fish thoroughly and soak over night in cold water. When ready to use pick it fine; put it in a baking-dish, in layers, with the crumbs and pepper (adding a little mustard if you like); over the top layer, which must be crumbs, spread the softened butter; pour the cream over the whole and bake half an hour. Milk may be used instead of cream.

74 Frogs.

Scald them in salted boiling water, rub them with lemon juice and boil for three minutes; wipe them; dip them first in cracker dust, then in eggs (half a cupful of milk mixed in two eggs and seasoned with pepper and salt), then again in cracker crumbs. When they are well covered with crumbs, clean off the bone at the end with a dry cloth. Put a tablespoonful of lard and a tablespoonful of butter in a spider, over a bright fire, and when hot enough put in the frogs and fry.

SAVORY SAUCES.

75 Drawn Butter Sauce.

Ingredients: Three ounces of butter, one ounce of flour, half a pint of water (or, what is better, veal stock), a pinch of salt and pepper. Put two ounces of the butter into a stew pan, and when it bubbles and boils up, sprinkle in the flour. Stir it well with a wire egg whisk, until the flour is thoroughly cooked and smooth, but without taking any color, and then mix in well the water or stock; take it off the fire and pour through the gravy strainer; then add the one ounce of butter cut in small bits. This sauce may be greatly varied and called by a dozen names. 1st. By the addition of two tablespoonfuls of nasturtions, or pickled cucumber, or cauliflowers, these latter cut fine, or by two tablespoonfuls of capers. 2d. For fish, anchovy paste or anchovy sauce may be added as desired, from one teaspoonful to one tablespoonful, or the inside of a lemon chopped fine, being careful to remove the seeds.

76 Drawn Butter Sauce.

Two heaping tablespoonfuls of flour, a generous half cup of butter and one pint of boiling water, work the flour and butter together until creamy and light, gradually add the boiling water, stir gradually until it comes to a boil, but do not let it boil, take from the fire and serve. A speck of Cayenne pepper may be added if you choose.

77 Egg Sauce.

Cut up three hard-boiled eggs in small dice, salt, pepper, minced onions (one teaspoonful), parsley and thyme; add all these to the drawn butter recipe. It is very nice for boiled chickens, fish or leg of mutton.

78 Oyster Sauce.

Scald one pint of large fresh oysters just enough to plump them, adding one tablespoonful of pepper, vinegar, a little black pepper and salt; pour this into a recipe of well made drawn butter (as above) at boiling point; stir thoroughly, and serve.

79 Celery Sauce.

Cut enough celery into pieces half an inch long to fill a pint bowl, and stew in a small quantity of water (say a cupful) till tender; add one teaspoonful of pepper vinegar, a little salt and pepper; pour in one teacup of cream or milk, and add a teacup of very thick drawn butter.

80 Tomato Sauce.

One quart of canned tomatoes, two tablespoonfuls of butter, two of flour, six cloves, a small slice of onion, cook the tomatoes ten minutes, heat the butter in a small frying pan, add the flour, cloves and onion, stir over the fire until smooth and brown, then stir into the tomatoes, cook five minutes, season to taste with salt and pepper, rub through a strainer fine enough to keep back the seeds; this sauce is nice for meat or macaroni.   Mrs. A. S.'s "Lizzie."

81 Tomato Sauce.

Scald and peel six large, ripe tomatoes; cut them up and stew slowly; cream together one tablespoonful of butter, one tablespoonful of sugar, one tablespoonful of flour; when the tomatoes are thoroughly done and reduced to a fine pulp, add pepper and salt; stir the butter, sugar and flour in; let boil up, and serve. In winter this sauce may be made from nice canned tomatoes.

82 Pepper Vinegar.

Fill a quart bottle or jar with small peppers, either green or ripe; put in two tablespoonfuls of sugar and fill with good cider vinegar. Invaluable in seasoning sauces, and good to eat with fish or meat.

83 Mint Sauce.

Of fresh garden mint take enough to make half a teacupful when chopped fine, two tablespoonfuls of sugar, half a teacupful of cold vinegar; let them stand from one to three hours; when your lamb is ready to serve, add half a teacup of boiling water and let scald.

84 Sauce Hollandaise.

To make one pint of sauce use one tablespoon of butter and one of flour. Mix in a saucepan on the fire until the butter melts. Put in gradually, one-half cup at a time, stirring smooth each time, one pint of water, hot or cold. Season with one salt-spoon of salt, one-fourth as much pepper and a little nutmeg. Let the sauce boil a minute to take away the taste of the flour, then take it off the fire and add yolks of two eggs, stirring quickly. One tablespoon lemon juice, two of salad oil. Put this around, not over, the fish. Garnish with parsley and slices of lemon.

85 Chili Sauce.

Twelve ripe tomatoes, four ripe peppers, two onions, two tablespoonfuls of salt, two of sugar, three teacups of vinegar, a little cinnamon, chopped tomatoes, peppers and onions, very fine; boil one hour; pour into wide-mouthed bottles and seal.

86 White Sauce for Fowls.

Take the neck, gizzard and liver of fowls, with a piece of veal or calf's foot; boil in one quart of water with a few whole peppers, and salt, till reduced to one pint; then thicken with two even tablespoonfuls of flour mixed with two tablespoonfuls of butter; boil five or six minutes; have ready the yolks of two eggs beaten with one teacup of cream from the morning's milk; pour into the saucepan and shake a moment until done.

87 Mushroom Sauce.

Wash and pick one pint of fresh mushrooms (or one can of French mushrooms), put in a saucepan with a little salt, nutmeg (three grates), one blade of mace, one pint of very sweet cream, a lump of butter (size of a pullet's egg) rubbed in one tablespoon of flour; boil up, stir until cooked, and serve with chicken.

88 Horse-radish Sauce.

One teacupful of grated horse radish, one tablespoonful of ground mustard, one tablespoonful of sugar, four tablespoonfuls vinegar and one of olive oil, pepper and salt.

89 Mint Vinegar.

Take a glass can and put loosely into it enough nice, clean mint leaves to fill it; then pour over enough good vinegar to fill the bottle full. Cork tight and let stand for three weeks; then pour off into another bottle and keep to flavor mint sauce, etc.

90 Pepper Vinegar—Tarragon Vinegar.

Fill a quart bottle with small peppers, either green or ripe; put in two tablespoonfuls sugar and fill with good cider vinegar.

Tarragon vinegar can be made after the above recipe, only substituting three ounces of tarragon leaves (to be bought of first-class grocers) for the peppers. The article recommended is *Vinagre Estragone*, prepared in Bordeaux.

91 Fish Sauce.

One heaping tablespoon of flour, three-fourths of a cup of butter, yolks of three eggs. Stir these until smooth, then stir in a little cold water and add boiling water until as thick as you want it. Add the juice of one lemon and slice in the lemon, salt, pepper, nutmeg, a little mustard and parsley. Vinegar if not tart enough. Boil until well cooked and smooth. Strain if necessary.

Mrs. Adams.

92 Dutch Sauce—For Fish (Sauce Hollandaise).

One-half teaspoonful of flour, two ounces of butter, four tablespoonfuls of vinegar—tarragon vinegar is best—yolk of two eggs, juice of half a lemon, salt to the taste. Put all the ingredients except the lemon juice into a stewpan. Set it over the fire and stir constantly until it heats (but not boils). Add the lemon.

93 Sauce Tartare (A Cold Sauce).

We take from Mrs. Henderson this recipe : To a scant half pint of Mayonnaise sauce, made with the mustard added, mix in two tablespoonfuls of capers, one small shallot (a quarter of an onion is a poor substitute), two gherkins or two ounces of cucumber, and one tablespoonful of parsley, all chopped very fine. This sauce will keep a long time bottled and corked, and is delicious for fried fish, fried oysters, boiled cod-fish, cold tongue or salads.

94 Mushroom Sauce.

Take a ladleful of stock, free from grease, from the stock-pot, add to it part of the juice from the can of mushrooms; thicken it with a little flour and butter mixed, add pepper, salt, and a few drops of lemon juice; now add the mushrooms. Let them simmer a few minutes. Pour the sauce over the fillet of beef and serve.

95 Fish Sauce (Grand Hotel, Paris), Sauce Hollandaise.

Place in a saucepan the yolks of six eggs, and a little pepper; put them in a vessel of hot water, or over a very slow fire. Stir quickly, adding, little by little, one pound of the freshest butter to every six eggs. When the butter is melted and mixed, pass through a sieve; add the juice of a lemon, or a little vinegar. To keep it hot, return the saucepan to the vessel of hot water.

BEEF.

96 Roast Beef.

Wipe the joint dry; then place it on a pan, with the fat and skin side up; put into a hot oven, and when the heat has started enough of the oil of the fat to baste with, open the oven, and drawing the pan toward you, take up a spoonful of the grease and pour over the meat for a few times, closing the door immediately; this should be repeated four or five times during the process of roasting. When nearly done sprinkle with salt, and baste. Have ready a warm platter, and when the meat is dished drain off the grease, carefully keeping back the rich, brown juice which has exuded from the meat.

This remaining gravy leave in the pan, placing it on the stove and adding about a gill of water, or soup stock, let it come to a boil and then pour it over the meat. If a made gravy is preferred, more water should be added and a little flour. Salt hardens and toughens meat, therefore in beef and mutton it should not be put on till it is cooked. It is also necessary to have the oven hot in order that the heat may quickly sear the surface, which will prevent the juice from escaping. It is obvious, if water is put in the pan, this quick searing cannot be effected; water cannot be raised above a certain temperature (its boiling point), while fat is susceptible of a much greater degree of heat, and, therefore, as a basting agent, is preferable. Beef roasted before a fire has a flavor inexpressibly finer than that done in an oven.

[We recommend Yorkshire pudding to be cooked and eaten with roast beef.—ED.]

YORKSHIRE PUDDING.—One pint of milk, two-thirds of a cup of flour, three eggs, and one scant teaspoonful of salt. Beat the eggs very light, add salt and milk, and then pour about half a cupful of the milk on the flour, and when perfectly smooth add the remainder. This makes enough for six persons. Raise your roast of beef on bars or a stand, pour under it into the hot pan and dripping this pudding, let it bake under the beef thirty or forty minutes.

97 Fillet of Beef.

The fillet is the under side of the loin of beef, that portion from which porter-house steaks are cut. This under side or fillet is covered with skin or fat. Loosen the rib bones and leave a little of the fat on the opposite side, trim the thick sinewy skin carefully off. This operation is very simple, yet it requires great precision. Lard the beef with a fine larding needle and nice salt pork. After it is trimmed and larded, put it into a small baking pan, on the bottom of which is some chopped pieces of pork and beef suet, sprinkle some salt, pepper and flour over it, and put a large ladleful of hot stock into the bottom of the pan, or it may be simply basted with boiling water. Half an hour before dinner put it into the oven. Baste it often, supplying a little hot stock, if necessary.

Miss Parloa says this is one of the simplest, safest and most satisfactory dishes that a lady can prepare for either her own family or guests.

First remove from the fillet with a sharp knife every shred of muscle ligament, and thin, tough skin. If it is not then a good round shape, skewer into such. Draw a line through the center and lard with strips of pork from each side so that the lardoons meet in the center.

Dredge well with salt, pepper and flour, and put without water in a very small pan. Place in a hot oven for thirty minutes. Let it be on the bottom of the oven the first ten, then raise it to the upper grate to finish.

Serve with Mushroom, Hollandaise or Tomato Sauce, or with a garniture of roasted tomatoes and Saratoga or Julien potatoes.

98 Beef a la Mode.

Take the bone out of a small round of beef, cut some salt pork in strips, about the size of your two fingers, and the thickness of the beef; dip them in vinegar and roll them in the following seasoning: One grated nutmeg, one tablespoonful black pepper, one of ground cloves, one of allspice and two of salt; add parsley, thyme, sweet marjoram and summer savory; then cut openings about four inches apart all through the beef and insert them. Make a rich stuffing with bread crumb, etc.; lay it over the top. Put the whole into a covered pan, pour over it half a pint of vinegar and let it stand in the oven for five hours. The addition of vegetables, one large onion, four carrots and two turnips, chopped fine, is a great improvement. Half an hour before serving skim off the fat, take up the round and vegetables, and add a little browned flour to the gravy; this is as delightful a dish as a turkey when fowl is no longer in season.

99 A la Mode Beef.

Take a round of beef, from three to four inches thick, and pound well, make as many incisions in the meat as possible, mix thoroughly blades of onions with ground cloves, salt and pepper, and into each incision, put two blades of onions with one long narrow strip of pork. When the roast is filled in this way pack tightly in a jar and cover with vinegar. Let stand two days, turning twice in that time. To cook it, put butter and pork in a covered pan, lay in the meat, add a little water to prevent burning. Cover it closely and let it roast for four hours; season again with pepper and salt, and one pulverized laurel leaf, and dish when nicely browned. To make the gravy, add two tablespoonfuls of the vinegar in which the meat has been pickled to the liquid remaining in the pan, thicken with browned flour.

100 To Cook a Steak.

The choice of cut varies with the taste of a family— porterhouse, tenderloin, round or rump; the two latter require more beating with the steak-beater to break the tougher fiber. Break somewhat the fiber of the meat by beating with a steak-beater; lay the gridiron over bright but not too hot coals; place the steak on it, turn in two minutes, then again in two minutes. Take up the steak and press it into some soft butter on a warm platter; turn and press the other side; now lay again on the gridiron and finish by turning once or twice. A folding gridiron expedites and simplifies the cooking of steak. When sufficiently cooked place the steak on a warm platter on which is some soft butter, considerable salt and a dash of pepper; turn and press. Serve instantly. It is better to have the gentleman of the house wait for his steak than have the steak wait for the gentleman—be snubbed for having a thing good rather than have it poor. We decline to give a receipt for frying steak.

101 Miss Parloa's Method for Beefsteak.

Have it cut thick. It will never be good, rich and juicy if only from one-fourth to one-half an inch thick. It ought to be at least three-quarters of an inch thick. Trim off any suet that may be left on it and dredge with salt, pepper and flour. Cook in the double boiler before or over clear coals for ten minutes if to be rare, twelve if it is to be rather well done. Turn the meat constantly. Serve on a hot dish with butter and salt, or with mushroom sauce, *maitre d'hotel* butter or tomato sauce. Do not stick a knife or fork into the meat to try it. This is the way many people spoil it. Pounding is another bad habit. Much of the juice of the meat is lost. When, as it sometimes happens, there is no convenience for broiling, heat the frying pan very hot, then sprinkle with salt and lay in the steak. Turn frequently.

102 Maitre d'Hotel Butter.

Four tablespoonfuls of butter, one of vinegar, one of lemon juice, half a teaspoonful of salt, one-quarter of a teaspoonful of pepper, one teaspoonful of chopped parsley. Beat the butter to a cream and gradually beat in the seasoning. This sauce is spread on fried and broiled meats and fish instead of butter. It is particularly nice for fish and beefsteak.

To Boil Salt and Fresh Beef and Ham.

103 To Boil Pickled or Corned Beef.

Put on the fire in cold water; let it simmer slowly, allowing fifteen minutes to every pound; do not let it boil; keep skimming or it will look dirty; if it is left in the pot until the water is cold it will be much more tender.

104 Boiling Meat.

There is all the difference in the world between boiling meat which is to be eaten, and meat whose juices are to be extracted in the form of soup. If the meat is required as nourishment, of course you want the juices kept in. To do this it is necessary to plunge it into boiling water, which will cause the albumen in the meat to coagulate suddenly, and act as a plug or stopper to all the tubes of the meat, so that the nourishment will be tightly kept in. The temperature of the water should be kept at boiling point for five minutes, and then as much cold water must be added as will reduce the temperature to one hundred and sixty-five degrees. Now if the hot water, in which the meat is being cooked, is kept at this temperature for some hours, we have all the conditions united, which give to the flesh the quality best adapted for its use as food. The juices are kept in the meat, and instead of being called upon to consume an insipid mass of indigestible fibers, we have a tender piece of meat, from which, when cut, the imprisoned juices run freely. If the meat be allowed to remain in the boiling water, without the addition of any cold water to it, it becomes in a short time altogether cooked, but it will be almost indigestible, and therefore unpalatable.

105 Beef Stew.

This is a favorite dish with gentlemen. Two pounds of clear beef, from a nice, tender round, and cut an inch or an inch and a-half thick, one onion, two slices of carrot, two of turnip, two potatoes; put three tablespoonfuls of flour (in your dredging box), salt, pepper, and a generous quart of boiling water. Cut all the fat from the meat and put it in a stewpan; fry gently ten or fifteen minutes. In the meantime cut the meat in square pieces; dredge a plate with flour; spread the meat on it; dredge again; pile another layer of meat on this, and dredge again with flour, pepper and salt; cut the vegetables in fine pieces and put into the stewpan; with the fat fry them five minutes, stirring well, to prevent burning; now put in the meat and shake it about until it begins to brown; then add the quart of boiling water. Cover close and let it boil up once; skim and set back where it will just scald for one and a-half hours; then add the potatoes, cut in eight pieces, and a tablespoonful of flour mixed well with water; let the stew come to a boil and boil ten minutes; then add dumplings as per receipt dumplings for fricasseed chicken. Cover close and boil rapidly for ten minutes. Mutton, lamb and veal may be stewed in this way, except that you will use salt pork instead of the fat of these meats.

106 Remains of Roast Beef.

Take off with a sharp knife all the meat from the bones, chop it fine, take cold gravy without the fat, put it in the spider to heat; if you have not this, some of the water in which the bones were boiled; when it boils up, sprinkle in salt and put in the minced meat; cover it and let it stand upon the fire long enough to heat it thoroughly, then stir in a small piece of butter, into which you have rubbed a teaspoonful of browned flour, toast bread, and lay in a dish; put the meat over it; serve hot.

107 Kate's Monday Stew.

Take cold roast beef, cut it up in nice small pieces; the bones, fat and stringy pieces put into a soup digester with a quart of water (or more if the quantity of bones require it); let this boil for an hour; strain this liquor and add the meat prepared for the stew. Then put in two onions, two carrots, one turnip; let these boil half an hour or more; then about forty-five minutes before serving put in twelve potatoes, whole or cut in half; let these boil twenty-five minutes, then stir in two tablespoonfuls of flour mixed smooth, with water, pepper, salt and a tablespoonful of butter. The dumplings are made with the receipt for soda and cream of tartar biscuits, and dropped into the stew when the liquor is at a keen boil. Boil from fifteen to twenty minutes, with the pot well covered; serve in a hot platter with the dumplings on top.

108   To Bake a Ham.

Most persons boil a ham, but a first-rate Virginia housewife tells us it is much better if baked properly. Soak it for an hour or more and wipe dry. Next spread it all over with a batter made of flour and water; put it into a deep pan with muffin rings or bits of oak wood under it to keep it out of the gravy. When fully done—it will take from five to seven hours—take off the skin and batter crusted upon the flesh side and set it away to cool, or glaze it by the following receipt:

109   Glazed Ham.

Beat the yolk of two eggs very light. Spread them all over your ham; then sift over fine cracker crumbs, and set in the oven to brown. Currant jelly may be used instead of yolks of eggs, and is very nice.

110   To Boil a Ham as it is Done at the Parker House, Boston.

A ham weighing ten or twelve pounds should be boiled six hours. Wash and scrape the ham well. Put it into cold water enough to cover it well and stir into the water a teacupful of weak lye. Let it come to a boil gradually; keep hot water ready to fill up the boiler as it evaporates. If it is to be eaten cold, have ready a large pan in which to put your ham, and cover it with cold water, letting it stand an hour or two, or until it is cold. Take it up and remove the skin and ornament as you choose.

VEAL.

112 To Roast a Leg of Veal.

Take out the bone of the joint; then fill it with a stuffing. Dredge well with flour. (See receipt, No. 126, for turkey stuffing). Bind tight with skewers and cord, sprinkle over with pepper and salt, put two or three slices of pork in the bottom of the pan, with a teacupful of water. Baste well and often. Let a leg weighing twelve pounds cook three hours. Just before it is done sprinkle over a little flour and rub over a little butter.

For gravy, stir some brown flour in the pan in which the veal has been cooked, add a piece of butter size of a walnut, and a teacup of stock.

113 Veal Cutlets.

Veal cutlets should be cut one inch thick from the leg, divide into equal sized pieces, enough for a helping. Have ready a bowl of bread crumbs, seasoned with pepper, salt and a little summer savory, beat two eggs in a pie plate, dip the raw cutlets in the egg, crumb them well and lay into a frying-pan, containing a heaping tablespoonful of butter and the same of lard when it is at a keen boil, over a bright fire, lay in your cutlet and fry quickly on one side until a bright brown, turn and fry on the other. Let them cook until *well* done. Lay the cutlets on a hot platter, add to the butter in the pan a tablespoonful of browned flour, and let heat until quite dark; then pour in gradually a teacupful of milk or cream, and scald to a glaze. Pour around the cutlets and serve promptly.

SWEET-BREADS.

114 Veal Sweet-breads

Spoil very soon; the moment they come from the butcher's they should be put in cold water to soak for about an hour; lard them or draw a lardoon of pork through the center of each one; put into salt boiling water or stock and let boil for fifteen or twenty minutes; throw them into cold water for only a few moments, they will now be firm and white; remove carefully the skinny portion and pipes.

Mrs. Henderson.

115 Sweet-breads, Stewed.

Wash carefully, remove all bits of skin and fatty matter, cover with cold water and heat to a boil; pour off the hot water and cover with cold until the sweet-breads are firm. If liked, add butter as for frying before you put in the second water; stir in a very little flour the second time. When they are tender add for each sweet-bread a heaping teaspoonful of butter, a little chopped parsley, pepper, salt and a little cream. Let them simmer in this gravy for five minutes. Send to table in a covered dish with the gravy poured over them.

116 Sweet-breads Roasted.

Put into cold water for fifteen minutes; change to more cold water for five minutes longer; parboil; wipe perfectly dry, lay them in a dripping-pan and roast, basting with butter and water until they begin to brown; then withdraw them for an instant, roll in beaten egg, then in sifted cracker crumbs, and return to the fire for ten minutes longer, basting meanwhile twice with melted butter. Keep hot in a dish while you add to the dripping half a cup of hot water, some chopped parsley, a teaspoonful of browned flour and the juice of half a lemon. Pour over the sweet-breads and serve at once.

117 Sweet-breads, an English Method.

Wash the sweet-bread and remove all the adhering bits of skin, then soak in salt water for one hour, then parboil and skim; when half cooked take out and cut into small pieces, or, if you prefer, let it remain whole, and stew until tender, then add a bit of butter, a little salt, to your taste, a dust of pepper, and a teaspoonful of flour thickening. Boil up twice and pour over toast. Serve hot.

118 Broiled Sweet-breads.

Soak an hour in cold water. Parboil by putting them in hot water and keeping it at a fast boil for five minutes or longer, then plunging it into ice-cold water, a little salted. When the sweet-breads have lain in this ten minutes, wipe them very dry, and with a sharp knife split them each in half lengthwise. Broil on a clear, hot fire, turning every minute as they begin to drip. Have ready on a deep plate some melted butter, well salted and peppered, mixed with catsup or pungent sauce. When the sweet-breads are done to a fine brown, lay them in this, turning them over several times, and set covered in a warm oven. Lay toast upon a plate or chafing-dish and a sweet-bread on each, and pour the hot butter, in which they have been lying, over them, and send to the table.

MUTTON AND LAMB.

120 Mutton and Lamb.

To roast a leg of mutton or lamb is a very simple process, requiring simply to be put in a pan, and thoroughly basted and seasoned, baking twelve minutes for every pound of lamb and fifteen for every pound of mutton.

121 To Boil a Leg of Mutton.

Plunge the mutton into boiling water and let it scald fifteen minutes for every pound; in extremely cold weather, allow half an hour extra boiling. Serve with drawn butter, and nasturtions or capers.

122 Fore Quarter of Lamb, Roasted.

Have your butcher take out carefully the shoulder blade and fore leg. Stuff the cavity; close with a skewer or sail needle and twine; cook eleven minutes to the pound, basting often. Make a gravy by adding a little browned flour and half a teaspoonful of Harvey's sauce to the drippings and bastings left in the pan. Serve with mushroom pickles and boiled spinach, or mint sauce.

123 Saddle of Mutton.

It is not every butcher that knows how to cut a saddle of mutton, but insist upon its being cut and trimmed as for a saddle of venison. Hang it from six to ten days. Rub thickly with soft butter or lay thin slices of salt pork all over the top; lay the flaps under. Then fold around it a paste made of only flour and water, but of the consistency of pie crust. Lay slices of pork under it and put it in your pan with the flaps resting on the pork, that is standing in it like an arch. Roast an hour and a-half. Serve with a rich brown gravy made from the liquor in the pan; after the fat has been skimmed off and seasoned, a small slice of onion, six pepper corns, four whole cloves and two tablespoonfuls of currant jelly. After removing the paste cover, and while making the gravy, dredge the saddle with flour and let it brown in a hot oven.

124 Fore Quarter of Lamb, Broiled.

This is the most delicious method of cooking lamb. Choose a young and tender, but small fore quarter; have it well nicked by the butcher, and forty minutes before dinner place it on the gridiron over bright, but not too hot coals; every ten minutes baste it on both sides with a bit of butter and turn on the gridiron; send it to table just off the fire and well buttered; it will make its own gravy; it should be done thoroughly, that is, past the pink color demanded by French cooks, but not enough to dry the natural juices of the meat.

125 Mutton Cutlets, Breaded.

Season French chops with salt and pepper; dip them in melted butter and roll in fine bread crumbs; broil for eight minutes over a fire not too bright, as the crumbs burn easily. Serve with potato-balls heaped in the center of the dish.

PORK.

126 Leg of Fresh Pork, Roasted.

Score in crossed lines a leg of pork, run the knife around the bone until it is loosened, take out the bone and fill the place with a rich stuffing made of stale bread, seasoned with butter, salt, pepper and onion ; take a few stitches to prevent the stuffing coming out ; put it on the spit and baste it with fresh butter (it is more delicate than lard). Fresh pork requires longer cooking than any other meat. Serve with hot apple sauce and Irish potatoes, cut in quarters and fried. It will take from three to four hours to cook, according to size.

127 Pork Spare Ribs

Are best well broiled over a slow fire served with hot apple sauce.

128 Pork Tenderloins

Are either fried or broiled. In either case they require to be very thoroughly done and served without gravy, simply adding a tablespoonful of vinegar to the dripping from the gridiron or in the pan.

129 To Broil Salt Pork.

Soak some thin slices of salt pork in milk for two or three hours, lay on the fine double gridiron and turn quickly, so as not to scorch ; this makes a delicious supper if cooked and eaten promptly. It should not be taken off the coals till the family are seated at the table. Serve on a very hot dish.

130 To Fry Salt Pork.

Salt pork is greatly improved by soaking it in milk two or three hours, then rolling it in Indian meal before frying.

131 To Bake Salt Pork.

Let it soak over night in skimmed milk, then bake like fresh pork.

132 Pork and Beans.

One quart of beans soaked over night in tepid water, in which has been dissolved one teaspoonful of soda. Early in the morning pour this water off, add two quarts of boiling water and half a teaspoonful of soda, boil the beans two hours, until the skin cracks. Then drain, put into a bean pot, large tin or earthen dish, in the center of which is a pound of salt pork scored in small squares. Let the beans come up to the level of the rind of the pork, pour over this one quart of boiling water, in which two tablespoonfuls of molasses have been stirred. Cover and bake slowly from two to four hours. If necessary you may add a teacup more of boiling water. Baking in a Boston bean pot is a great improvement.

POULTRY AND GAME.

133 Turkey and Chicken Stuffing.

Three teacups of grated bread-crumbs (no crust and not a drop of water), one cup finely chopped suet, two-thirds of a cup chopped parsley, a tablespoonful of sweet marjoram and summer savory, one-half teaspoonful of pepper, one teaspoonful of salt, one or two eggs, beaten.

134 To Roast a Turkey or Chicken.

In England and on the continent, neither a turkey nor chicken is stuffed; but not only is the stuffing nice in itself, but it gives as well as preserves a fine flavor to the fowl. After drawing, washing, drying and singeing a fowl, stuff it according to the above recipe, craw and body; truss it well, tying down the legs and fastening the wings. Put into a dripping pan (or on to a spit) the bird thus prepared, and let cook till thoroughly done, but not dry. A fourteen-pound turkey will take three full hours; a ten-pound turkey will do in two. Save the giblets, consisting of liver, gizzard and heart, boil until tender, and mince fine. When you take up your turkey, add a little browned flour to the gravy in the pan, some hot water, and the minced giblets, a few sprigs of parsley about the dish adds greatly to its appearance. Many persons like fried sausages, or fried oysters, laid about the dish, and served with each helping.

135 To Boil a Chicken or Turkey.

It is not every housewife who knows how best to boil a chicken. Plain, artless boiling is apt to produce a yellowish, slimy-looking fowl. Before cooking, the bird should always be washed in tepid water and rubbed with lemon juice, then stuffed and trussed, and to insure whiteness, delicacy and succulence, should be boiled in a thin soup made of flour stirred into milk and added to the water; after being put into the boiling water it should be allowed to simmer slowly. This method is very effectual in preserving all the juices of the fowl, and the result is a more toothsome and nourishing morsel than the luckless bird which has been "galloped to death" in plain boiling water.

136 Broiled Chicken.

Singe the chicken and split down the back, if not already prepared, and wipe with a damp cloth; never wash it; season well with salt and pepper; take some soft butter in the right hand and rub over the bird, letting the greater part go on the breast and legs; dredge with flour; put in the double broiler and broil over a moderate fire, having the breast turned first to the coals. When the chicken is a nice brown, which will be in about fifteen minutes, place in a pan and put in a moderate oven for twelve minutes. Place on a hot dish and season with salt, pepper and butter. The chicken is improved by serving with *maitre d'hotel* butter. MISS PARLOA.

[NOTA BENA.—Of this receipt we can only say that in the main it is excellent, but for ourselves we prefer not to dredge with flour, and not to set in an oven to finish. Broiling is a fine art, and a chicken or quail should be rushed from the gridiron to the table without any *maitre d'hotel* butter, only its own rich, hot juices and the best of butter.]

137 Escaloped Turkey.

Take the remains of cold turkey, from which remove all the bones and gristle; chop the meat in small pieces. Place in an earthen dish a layer of powdered cracker, moistened with milk; then add a layer of turkey seasoned with pepper and salt, then another layer of powdered cracker, and then one of turkey, and so on until the dish is filled; over that pour the gravy you may have left, or a little hot water and butter, or cream. Finish the top with the powdered cracker, moisten with a beaten egg and sweet milk, bake one hour. Cover the dish for the first half hour, that the top may not become too brown.

138 Prairie Chickens, Partridges and Quail.

Clean thoroughly, using a little soda in the water in which they are washed; rinse them and drain, and fill with dressing, sewing them up nicely, and binding down the legs and wings with cord, or trussing with fine skewers. Then put them in a pan with a little butter, lay slices of thin pork over them, set them in the oven and baste frequently, until of a nice brown. The large bird ought to brown in about thirty-five minutes. Serve them in a platter with sprigs of parsley alternated with currant jelly.

139 A Nice Way to Cook Pigeons.

Stuff the birds with a rich bread dressing; place compactly in an iron or earthen dish; season with salt, pepper and butter (or if you like best, thin slices of salt pork over the top), dredge thickly with flour and nearly cover them with water. Then put over a closely fitting plate or cover, and place the dish in a moderate oven, from two to four, or even five, hours, according to the age of the birds. If the birds are *old* and *tough,* this is the best way they can be cooked, and they may be made perfectly tender and much sweeter than by any other process. If the gravy is insufficient add a little water before dishing.

140 To Pot Birds.

Prepare them as for roasting. Fill each with a dressing made as follows: Allow for each bird of the size of a pigeon one-half of a hard boiled egg, chopped fine, a tablespoonful of bread crumbs, a teaspoonful of chopped pork; season the bird with pepper and salt; stuff them, lay them in a kettle that has a tight cover. Place over the birds a few slices of pork, add a pint of water, dredge over them a little flour, cover and put them in a hot oven. Let them cook until tender, then add a little cream and butter. If the sauce is too thin, thicken with flour. One pint of water sufficient for twelve birds.

141 Fricassee Chicken.

Cut up, wash and dry a pair of chickens, and dredge them well with flour, salt and pepper; put into a stewpan a heaping tablespoonful of butter, let it boil; lay the chickens into this and shake them about, turning them and giving each piece a little *glazed* look; then add water enough to cover the fowls and let stew slowly from forty minutes to an hour. Just before serving let it come to a keen boil and stir in a teacupful of milk or sweet cream, in which a heaping tablespoonful of flour has been stirred. Let it cook five minutes and pour into a dish over which some freshly baked powder biscuits have been opened and spread. Season with salt and pepper. I butter my biscuits.

142 Fricassee Chicken, No. 2 (French Style).

Cut up a young chicken, dredge well with flour (even a grown one, if young and tender, will do), flavor well, put in a frying-pan one tablespoonful of hot lard, cut up a small onion, let it fry with the chicken, adding salt, red and black pepper. Do not cook entirely done, and be careful not to scorch; then pour into the frying-pan enough boiling water for the chicken to stew, which let it do for an hour, and just before taking it off add some chopped parsley.

143 Dumpling for Fricasseed Chicken.

If dumplings are preferred to biscuit there is no better recipe for them than Miss Parloa's.

One pint of flour measured before sifting, half a teaspoonful of soda, one teaspoonful of cream of tartar, one of sugar, half a teaspoonful of salt. Mix all thoroughly and run through a sieve. Wet with a small cupful of milk. Sprinkle a little flour on the board, turn the dough (which should have been stirred into smooth ball with a spoon) on it, roll to the thickness of half an inch, cut into small cakes and cook *ten* minutes. No more, no less.

By remembering that the soup should be boiling rapidly when the dumplings are put in, that they should not sink too deep in the liquid, and that the cover of the pot is shut tight, success will be insured.

144 Escalloped Chicken.

Cold chicken, chiefly the white meat, one cup of gravy, one tablespoonful of butter and one egg well beaten, one cup of fine bread crumbs, pepper and salt. Take from the chicken all gristle and skin, and cut, not chop, into pieces, less than half an inch long. Have ready the gravy, or some rich drawn butter in a saucepan on the fire. Thicken it well, and stir into it the chicken; boil up once, take it off and add the beaten egg; cover the bottom of a buttered dish with bread crumbs, pour in the mixture and put another thick layer of crumbs on top, sticking butter all over it. Bake to a delicate brown in a quick oven. Turkey may be used instead of chicken, also veal.

145 Chicken Pie, No. 1.

Dredge well with flour and stew until tender two chickens in just enough water to cover them. Make a nice crust, line a deep dish with it; when the chickens are done *remove all the bones ;* put the chickens in the dish in which they are to be baked; thicken the gravy with a little flour and cream; add a can of oysters; season with salt, pepper and butter; cover the pie with a crust, and bake quickly. This is very nice.

146 Rice and Chicken Pie, No. 3.

Boil a pint or more of rice; stir in a teaspoonful of butter, a little milk, two eggs and a little salt. Fricassee two chickens. Cover the bottom of a long dish with rice, then a layer of chicken, and so until it is full. Save out some of the gravy of the fricassee to eat on the rice. Cover the whole with the yolk of an egg and brown it. Curry powder may be put into the chicken if liked. One chicken makes a good sized dish.

147 Chicken Jelly.

Boil the chicken until tender, cut with a knife fine, put it in a dish, or mold; season with salt, pepper, a little summer savory, and a teaspoonful of vinegar; boil the bones in the broth awhile and pour over. When cold it will turn out.

148 Chicken Gumbo.

Fry one chicken; when about half done, slice with it four dozen ochras and three or four tomatoes; fry till all are done. Have ready some chopped onions (according to size), seasoned with salt and cayenne pepper, and a tablespoonful of flour. Fry this in one side of the frying-pan until brown, then mix with the chicken, ochras, etc.; pour on six cups of cold water, and let all boil two hours over a slow fire. Eat with boiled rice, unless used as a first course in place of soup. This is sufficient for six persons.

149 Chicken Pie.

Cut up and dredge well with flour, pepper and salt, two chickens; put them in a round-bottomed kettle where a heaping tablespoonful of butter has come to a boil; toss the chickens about for five or ten minutes, till their juice begins to start, then pour over them boiling water enough to cover them well; let them scald, but not boil, for one hour, then take out all the large bones, *i. e.*, legs, backs, neck-pieces, breast bones, etc., leaving only the wings and second joints. Cut the meat as little as possible, but in shapely pieces. Make a rich crust, roll it thicker than for ordinary pies. Line the bottom of the dish with a plainer under crust, lay the chicken in, season well with salt and pepper, pour over this the rich gravy in which the fowls were boiled with a teacup of cream and a heaping tablespoonful of flour braided with butter, and well scalded. Cover with rich paste and bake three-quarters of an hour. Many persons like three hard-boiled eggs cut in with the chicken.

150 Brunswick Stew.

Two chickens, whole, nine quarts of water; boil till tender, take out skin and bones, chop fine and return to kettle, adding six potatoes previously soaked an hour in cold water and chopped very fine, also one pint of sweet corn, one quart of tomatoes; boil two hours. Before dishing, add two hard-boiled eggs chopped fine, and one in slices, a piece of butter the size of a hen's egg, fourteen hard crackers, a little salt, very little red pepper, and three teaspoonfuls of Worcestershire sauce. To be served like soup.

VEGETABLES.

151 Potatoes a la Maitre d'Hotel.

Boil and peel the potatoes and let them become cold. Then cut them into rather thick slices. Put a lump of fresh butter into a stewpan, and add a little flour—about a teaspoonful for a middling sized dish. When the flour has boiled a litte while in the butter, add by degrees a cupful of broth or water. When this has boiled up, put in the potatoes with chopped parsley, pepper and salt. Let the potatoes stew a few minutes, then take them from the fire, and, when quite off the boil, add the yolk off an egg, beaten up with a little lemon juice and a tablespoonful of cold water. As soon as the sauce has set, the potatoes may be dished up and sent to the table.

152 Boiled Potatoes.—Miss Parloa.

The time of cooking the potato *does not vary* with age or freshness. Twelve medium sized potatoes, one tablespoonful of salt, boiling water enough to cover. Pare the potatoes, and, if old, let them stand in cold water an hour or two to freshen them. Boil fifteen minutes, then add the salt and boil fifteen minutes longer. Pour off every drop of water. Take the cover off and shake the potatoes in a current of cold air, at either the door or window; place the saucepan on the back part of the stove, and cover with a clean, coarse towel until serving time. The sooner the potatoes are served the better.

153 Mashed Potatoes.

Prepare as directed for boiled potatoes. Mash fine and stir into them a half a cupful of boiling milk and a tablespoonful of butter. Then take your pot stick or wooden spoon and stir with all your might, round and round, for a minute or two. This will give great lightness and delicacy.

154 Fried Potatoes.

Pare and slice the potatoes thin; if sliced in small flakes they look more inviting than when cut in larger pieces; keep in ice-water two or three hours, then drain them dry, or dry them on a crash towel, and drop them into boiling lard; when nearly done take them out with a skimmer and drain them. Let them get cold, and then drop them again into boiling lard, and fry until well done. This last operation causes them to swell up and puff out; sprinkle with salt and serve hot, our recipe says; but many like them cold, as a relish for tea or with cold meats.

155 Potato Puff.

Stir two cupfuls of mashed potatoes, two tablespoonfuls of melted butter and some salt to a light, fine and creamy condition; then add two eggs, well beaten (separately) and six tablespoonfuls of cream; beat it all well and lightly together; pile it in a rocky form on a dish; bake it in a quick oven until nicely colored; it will puff up quite light.

156 Potato Fritters.

Mash and rub through a colander six good boiled potatoes; add a little salt, two tablespoonfuls of sweet milk or cream, two tablespoonfuls of flour, one egg and the yolks of two others; beat the reserved whites to a stiff froth, and stir it into the other ingredients, after they are well mixed. Have ready a spider of hot lard, and drop by the spoonful, and boil as other fritters. This is a delicious breakfast dish.

157 Creaming Potatoes.

Slice cold boiled potatoes very thin, have ready a saucepan of boiling milk, in which place the potatoes, with salt, a good sized piece of butter, and while boiling, thicken with flour, mixed with water, stirring until delicate and creamy—when ready dish for the table. The goodness of this dish depends much upon catering, just when ready; ten minutes being sufficient time to prepare it.

VEGETABLES.

158 Salsify and Parsnips.

Grate a bunch or two of salsify as you would horse-radish, add a raw egg beaten, and a little bread crumbs or flour, and fry in a frying-pan, as you would oysters. Parsnips prepared in this way, are extremely nice.

Second way: Cut your salsify into round lozenges, parboil; throw it into a frying-pan with a little butter, and heat through, but do not fry brown; turn over this enough soup stock, or the boilings from steak or other bones, to cover it; thicken with a little flour and butter braided together, add pepper and salt, and you have a nice dish.

159 Oyster Plant.

Scrape the roots, dropping each into cold water as soon as cleaned. Exposure to the air blackens them. Cut in pieces an inch long, put into a saucepan with hot water to cover them, and stew until tender. Turn off the water and add soup stock or milk enough to cover them. Stew ten minutes after this begins to boil; put in a great lump of butter cut into bits and rolled in flour. Boil up once and serve.

160 Fried Salsify or Mock Oysters.

Scrape the roots thoroughly and lay in cold water ten or fifteen minutes. Boil whole until tender, and when cold mash with a wooden spoon to a smooth paste, picking out all the fibers. Moisten with one teacup of cream, a little milk, add a tablespoonful of butter, and three eggs for every two cupfuls of salsify. Beat the eggs light. Make into round cakes, dredge with flour and fry brown.

161 Cooking Carrots.

Cut the carrots in small pieces and stew in a little water till tender; pour off what water is left; put in milk enough to make a sauce, and a good lump of butter rolled in flour; boil up again all together, having added salt and pepper to taste. Celery is excellent prepared in the same way.

162 Asparagus.

Asparagus should be boiled in fresh water, and when thoroughly cooked taken out, salted, laid lengthwise upon pieces of toast in a deep dish; pour over a sauce for asparagus, made after this fashion: Take equal parts of flour and butter, a tablespoonful of each; mix thoroughly, add a pint of water and a little salt; cook in a stewpan; when done remove from the fire, and if you desire, stir in the beaten yolk of an egg. Some persons cut asparagus into inch-long pieces, but a genuine "*bon vivant*" prefers to eat only so much as glides off into his mouth from the four inch-long stalk.

163 A Dainty Way of Serving Asparagus.

Take the smallest Vienna breads and prepare them as in the receipt for croustade of oysters. When ready fill them with the heads of asparagus an inch long and which have been cooked according to the above receipt. This makes a nice and pretty course at a lady's lunch.

164 Radishes.

Prof. Blot says, cut off the root and all the leaves, *but the center one*, or stalk. This should always be left on and eaten, as it contains an element which assists in the digestion of the radish. Split the radish up into stems, and leave whole at the top; serve in fresh ice water.

165 Spinach.

To a peck of well washed and picked spinach take a gallon of water and three even tablespoonfuls of salt; boil for ten minutes or a trifle more, until tender; drain on a sieve, press a little with your hands or butter-ladle to extract the water; chop it up fine, put it in a stewpan with a tablespoonful of butter, a teaspoonful of salt, a half a teaspoonful of pepper, one tablespoonful of vinegar, and one or two of broth or beef stock; set over a bright fire for a few moments, stirring well; lay slices of cold hard-boiled eggs over it in the vegetable dish.

166 Tomatoes.

Plain stewed tomatoes perfectly done and seasoned with salt and pepper, need only a large lump of butter added, although it is quite common to stir in half a teacup of bread or cracker crumbs.

167 Escalloped Tomatoes.

Peel and cut across the tomato in slices a quarter of an inch thick, lay layers of tomato, then sprinkling of fine bread crumbs seasoned with pepper and salt, then bits of butter; repeat and end with bread crumbs and butter; bake an hour and a quarter.

168 Stuffed Tomatoes.

Choose large tomatoes; do not skin them, but cut a round off the top and scoop out the inside, which fill with a stuffing made of bread crumbs, minced onion, cayenne and salt; first fry the onions in a little butter, with what was scooped out of the tomatoes, add the bread crumbs, moistened with a little water or stock, and seasoned with a very little cayenne pepper, salt, and a little Worcester sauce. Fry these a moment; then fill the cavities, allowing the stuffing to project half an inch above the tomatoes and smooth it over the top. On this place a salt-spoonful of parmesan cheese and a bit of butter. Bake thoroughly.

169 Succotash.

Cut the corn from a dozen ears of corn, being careful not to cut into the cob. Boil one pint of Lima beans in three pints of water two hours; boil also, the cobs, as they contain much saccharine matter, with the beans. Take out the cobs and put in the corn. Just before taking up, mix a heaping tablespoonful of butter with one teaspoonful of flour, some salt and pepper. A cup of good cream is a great improvement. Let your corn boil only twenty-five minutes.

170 Green Corn.

Cut the center of kernels through lengthwise with a sharp knife; scrape the inside out with the back of the knife; put over and boil with a very little water. After cooking ten minutes, add milk, salt, a very little sugar, and plenty of butter, and let boil gently for twenty minutes more.

171 Corn Oysters, No. 1.

One dozen grated ears of sweet corn, three tablespoonfuls of cream, two do. of flour, one do. of melted butter, one egg well beaten; mix and bake in small cakes on a griddle, or in a frying-pan. These are very nice for tea when made from cold boiled ears of corn left over from dinner.

172 Corn Oysters, No. 2.

One teacup of milk, two eggs, two heaping tablespoonfuls of flour and a pinch of salt. Beat all well together and into this stir the corn cut from one dozen ears or more, according to the size, enough to make a thick mass, having just batter enough to bind it together.

Drop it by the tablespoonful into the frying-pan with enough hot butter or drippings to keep it from burning. Serve on a platter, hot.

173 Corn Oysters, No. 3 (Mrs. A. S.'s Lizzie).

One dozen ears sweet corn grated, one tablespoonful of melted butter, three eggs, two tablespoonfuls of flour, mix together and fry as for griddle cakes.

174 To Boil Turnips.

Peel, slice and boil three quarts of turnips till tender, then drain and mash as you would potatoes; put one teacup of cream with a teaspoonful of salt into a stew-pan, pour the mashed turnips into it, mix well, and let stew for twenty minutes or half an hour then add a tablespoonful of butter.

175 Egg Plant.

Slice the egg plant about a quarter of an inch thick, parboil in salt and water for ten minutes, or only soak in the same, for families have a choice; then take out and fry in part butter and part lard, or dip each slice (after drying it) into beaten eggs and then bread crumbs, and then fry. Or, slice the plant half an inch thick, soak in salt and water one hour, and wipe dry; dip in flour, then into beaten egg, then in flour again; fry light brown, serve hot.

176 Egg Plant.

Slice the egg plant about half an inch thick, soak in salt and water an hour; then take out, wipe dry, dip into flour, then in beaten egg, then in flour again, and fry in part butter and part lard.

177 Boiled Cauliflower.

To each half a gallon of water allow one heaped teaspoonful of salt. Choose cauliflowers that are close and white. Trim off the decayed outside leaves, cut the stalk off flat at the bottom. Open the flowers a little to remove the insects, and let lie in salt and water, with the head down, for an hour before cooking; then put them into fast boiling water with the addition of salt as above. Skim well and boil till tender. Serve with melted butter or delicate drawn butter poured over the yolk of an egg and stirred well. Serve this on the cauliflower.

178 To Stew Cabbage.

Parboil in milk and water and drain it, then shred it; put it into a stewpan with a small piece of butter, a small cupful of cream, and seasoning, and stew tender.

179 Cabbage Jelly.

Boil a cabbage in the usual way, and squeeze it in a colander till perfectly dry, then chop fine; add a little butter, pepper and salt; press the whole very closely into an earthenware mold, and bake one hour, either in an oven or in front of the fire.

YEAST, BREAD AND BISCUIT.

180 Old School Presbyterian Yeast.

Boil two liberal handfuls of *good* hops in three quarts of water. Strain. When cool stir in one quart of flour, one cup of sugar, and a handful of salt. Cover this in a stone jar, and let it stand three days in a warm place, stirring it occasionally. On the fourth day add one quart of nicely mashed potatoes. Let it stand until the day following, when it will be ready for use. A small teacup is sufficient for five loaves of bread.

This yeast, which has proved most reliable, needs nothing to start it, as it is self-raising, and if kept in a cool place will keep six weeks in the summer, and three months in cold weather.

It does not foam as do other kinds of yeast, so that one who had not used it would think it worthless; but if once used its excellency will not be doubted.

In making bread, a tablespoonful of white sugar to a quart of flour is a great improvement to all kinds of bread.

181 Joanna's Yeast.

Peel and wash five good sized potatoes, and boil in two quarts of water, then mash and add two small cups of flour, a handful of salt, and half a cup of sugar, white or brown; add potatoes and flour together, and mix slowly in the scalding water in which the potatoes were boiled, and strain all through the colander. Then add the sugar, salt, and a cup of yeast or an yeast cake; keep in a warm place until it rises, and then put away in an earthen crock.

Bread made with the above yeast: Sift two quarts of flour and add a little salt, boil three or four potatoes and mash in three pints of water and stir in with a cup full of yeast. Keep in a warm place over night.

182 Mrs. Isham's Potato Yeast.

Pare four potatoes and boil in one quart of water; when done mash them fine, and pour on them the water in which they were boiled, one teaspoonful of salt, one-half cup of brown sugar. When cold add half a teacupful of baker's yeast. Put in a warm place to rise.

183 Esther's Bread.

To make the yeast: Take ten or twelve potatoes from the dinner pot, wet two teacupfuls of flour with two cups of boiling potato water, add half a teacup of white sugar and one heaping tablespoonful of salt; raise twenty-four hours with a Twin Brothers or Capitol Yeast Cake. This will last a week or ten days. One cup and a-half is enough for four loaves of the bread. Scald skim milk; when cool enough sponge your bread at night; in the morning work it well, let it rise, then put it in a pan and let it rise again; bake in a quick oven.

184 To Sponge Bread.

Sift four quarts of flour into a deep pan, sprinkle a dessert-spoonful of salt over it. Make a hole in the center and add, by degrees, three pints of lukewarm water or skim milk; stir the flour into this till it reaches the consistency of a very thick cream; add one and-a-half cups of Esther's yeast, or one cup of Joanna's yeast, or two yeast cakes, or five cents' worth of compressed or German yeast, or three cents' worth of bakers' yeast, or two tablespoonfuls of brewers' yeast. German and brewers' yeast requires but two hours, the others all night, to raise them.

185 Brown Bread.

One quart of corn meal, one pint of rye or Graham flour, one quart of sour milk, one teacup of molasses, and one teaspoonful of soda. Steam four hours, or bake one hour. This quantity will make two loaves.

186 Corn Bread.

One quart of Indian meal, two ounces of butter, as much warm milk as will make a stiff batter, four eggs, a little salt. Beat the whole well together, and bake in shallow tins in a moderate oven.

187 Mrs. A.'s Corn Bread.

Two cupfuls of corn meal, two cupfuls of flour, one cupful of sweet milk, one cupful of sour milk, one-half cupful of sugar, two eggs, one tablespoonful of melted butter, one teaspoonful of soda, and a little salt.

188 Phillis' Corn Bread.

One pint of sour milk, one-half pint of sweet milk, one teaspoonful of saleratus, one teaspoonful of salt, one tablespoonful of lard or butter. White Indian meal stirred in to make a batter, thick, as for muffins. If the meal is perfectly sweet stir it in dry. If not, scald it first.

189 French Bread.

Mrs. Henderson, in her "Practical Cooking," gives this recipe which we copy in full, although it is very like the old Southern snap bread: Put a heaping tablespoonful of hops and a quart of water over the fire to boil. Have ready five or six large, freshly boiled potatoes, which mash fine; strain the hops, now put a pint of the boiling water in which the potatoes were cooked over three cupfuls of flour; mix in the mashed potatoes, then the quart of strained hop-water hot, a heaping teaspoonful of sugar and the same of salt; when this is lukewarm, mix in one-and-a-half Twin Brothers' yeast cakes that have been softened in a little warm water. Let this stand over night in a warm place.

In the morning a new process is in order. First, pour over the yeast a tablespoonful of warm water in which is dissolved half a teaspoonful of soda. Mix in lightly about ten-and-a-half heaping teacupfuls of sifted flour. No more flour is added to the bread during its kneading. Instead the hands are wet in lukewarm water. Now knead the dough, giving it about eight or ten strokes; then taking it from the side next to you pull it up into a long length, then double it, throwing it down snappishly and heavily. Wetting the hands again, give it the same number of strokes or kneads, pulling the end towards you again and throwing it onto the part left in the pan; continue this process until large bubbles are formed in the dough. It will take half an hour or longer. The hands should be wet enough at first to make the dough rather supple. If dexterously managed it will not stick to the hands after a few minutes, and when it is kneaded enough it will be very elastic, full of bubbles and will not stick to the pan; then put the pan away again in a warm place to rise. This will take one or two hours. Now comes another new process: Sprinkle plenty of flour on the board and take out lightly enough dough to make one loaf of bread, remembering that French loaves are not large nor of the same shape as the usual home-made-ones—draw it long so as not to spoil the grain of the bread, and with the rolling-pin roll it slightly out in the middle; take these middle flaps and fold, first one and then the other, into the center of the dough, draw it out long, turn the dough completely over and draw it long into the conventional shape. Turn a large dripping-pan bottom side up, sprinkle plenty of flour on it, upon which lay this and the succeeding loaves a little distance apart. Set the pan by the fire again to rise yet another twenty-five or thirty minutes longer; then bake.

190 Miss Parloa's Yeast Bread.

Ingredients for two loaves: Two quarts of flour, half a cupful of yeast, or one cake of compressed yeast, nearly a pint and-a-half of water, half a tablespoonful each of lard, sugar, and salt. Sift the flour into a bread-pan, and after taking out a cupful for use in kneading, add the salt, sugar, yeast, and the water, which must be about blood warm (or say 100 degrees, if in cold weather, and about eighty in the hot season). Beat well with a strong spoon. When well mixed sprinkle a little flour on the board, turn out the dough on this and knead from twenty to thirty minutes. Put back in the pan; hold the lard in the hand long enough to have it very soft; rub it over the dough closely that neither dust nor air can get in and set in a warm place. It will rise in eight or nine hours. In the morning shape into loaves or rolls. If into loaves, let these rise an hour when the temperature is between ninety and one hundred degrees; if into rolls, let these rise an hour and a half. Bake in an oven that will brown a teaspoonful of flour in five minutes. (The flour used for this test should be put on a piece of crockery, as it will have a more even heat.) The loaves will need from forty-five to sixty minutes to bake, but the rolls will be done in half an hour if placed close together in the pan, and if French rolls are made they will bake in fifteen minutes. As soon as baked, the bread should be taken out of the pans and placed on a table where it can lean against something until it is cool. It should then be put in a stone pot or tin box which has been thoroughly washed and scalded and dried, and be set away in a cool dry place.

Sticks.—Four cupfuls of flour, one tablespoonful of sugar, one-fourth of a cake of compressed yeast, one-fourth of a cup of butter, one cup of boiled milk, the white of an egg, one scant teaspoonful of salt. Dissolve the butter in the milk, which should be blood warm. Beat the white of an egg to a stiff froth. Dissolve the yeast in three tablespoonfuls of cold water. Add all the other ingredients to the flour and knead well. Let the dough rise over night and in the morning make into balls about the size of a large English walnut. Roll each of these balls into a stick about a foot long. Use the molding-board. Place the sticks about two inches apart in long pans. Let them rise half an hour in a cool place and bake twenty-five minutes in a very moderate oven. Sticks should be quite dry and crisp. They cannot be if baked rapidly.

Swedish Bread.—For this Miss Parloa took some of the dough left from the rolls or sticks; either will do, and rolled it very thin, then she spread over it one tablespoonful of cinnamon mixed with half a cup of sugar. First, moisten the sheet of bread with cold water, then sprinkle with the cinnamon and the sugar. Roll very tight, and cut into slices with a sharp knife. Place the slices on well greased tins. Let them rise one hour and a quarter, and bake them in a quick oven.

191 Parker House Rolls.

Scald a little more than a pint of milk, let it stand till cold; two quarts of flour; make a hole in the middle of the flour after rubbing into it a tablespoonful of lard or butter, then add a half teacup of yeast, a little sugar, salt, and the milk, and cover with the flour. Let it stand until morning, then work until smooth. When it is light roll out and cut with a pint pail cover; rub it over with a little butter and lap over like a turnover, then let them bake twenty minutes. They are splendid, and never fail if the directions are followed. This is an old receipt, and has been tried and endorsed by hundreds of cooks.

192 Miss Parloa's Parker House Rolls.

One and a quarter quarts of flour, one pint of cold boiled milk, one tablespoonful of sugar, one tablespoonful of butter, one teaspoonful of salt, half a cake of compressed yeast. Mix the dry ingredients together and then draw to the sides of the bowl; pour the yeast, which has been dissolved, in a third of a cup of water and the milk; cover the pan; let it stand all night; in the morning knead well; let this rise to a sponge and then roll down to about three-fourths of an inch thick; cut with an oval cutter; let these rise to twice their original size and bake about thirty minutes in a quick oven. It will be obsersed that these rolls differ from ours, by having no butter.

193 French Rolls.

One pint of milk, one quart of flour, whites of two eggs, one tablespoonful of white sugar, a piece of butter the size of an egg. First take the milk and flour, with a tablespoonful of yeast, and make a sponge. If made of bakers' or home-made yeast, it can be set at night. When the sponge is light, add the other ingredients and set to rise again; roll out to half an inch in thickness; cut with an oval cutter; bake in a quick oven.

194 Steamed Loaf.

Two cups of Indian meal, one cup flour, half-cup molasses, salt, one cup sweet milk, one of sour, teaspoon soda. Steam from three to four hours.

195 Ways of Baking Graham Flour.

By this time everybody knows how to make Graham "gems" by the usual method, which is simply to stir the batter just a little stiffer than griddle-cake batter, and bake quickly in a very hot oven. One thing is certain, the thinner the batter the hotter must be the oven. It is also the case that gems mixed with water require a hotter oven than those mixed with milk. So, if you can not have a very hot oven, either make the mixture of simple Graham flour and water quite thick, or mix the flour with milk. Skimmed milk is good enough, though new or creamy milk makes the bread more "short," of course. Have the gem pans very hot (I set them in the oven before filling them), and then a scrap of cloth with the least bit of butter upon it, rubbed over the irons, will prevent the gems from sticking.

196 Graham Gems.

One-and-a-half cupfuls of Graham flour, one cupful of sweet milk, one egg, one tablespoonful of melted butter, one tablespoonful of molasses, two scant teaspoonfuls of baking powder. Beat the egg, then put in the milk, then the flour, with the baking powder well mixed through, and last the molasses and butter. Bake in a very hot oven.

197 Graham Bread—Miss Parloa.

One pint of water or milk, one pint of flour, one large pint of Graham flour, half a cup of sugar, half a cup of yeast, or half a square of compressed yeast, one teaspoonful of salt. Have the milk or water blood warm, add the yeast to it; have the flour sifted in a deep dish, add yeast and milk gradually to the flour, beating until perfectly smooth; set in a rather cool place to rise over night. In the morning add the salt, sugar and then the Graham flour, a little at a time, beating vigorously all the time. When thoroughly beaten, turn into two bread pans and let it rise one hour. Bake one hour.

198 Graham Bread, No. 2.

One quart of Graham flour, three-quarters of a cup of yeast, one quart of water, warm, one cup of molasses. Let this rise over night. Mix with wheat flour in the morning into a stiff loaf; let it rise a second time, afterwards put into loaves to rise for baking. Very good.

CORN BREAD AND CAKES.

199 St. Michael's Corn Cakes.

One quart of corn-meal, one quart of flour, six eggs, one teaspoonful of soda, one tablespoonful of cream of tartar, one pound of white sugar, one quart of milk. Method: Mix corn-meal and wheat flour with two teacupfuls of home-made yeast and a little warm water four or five hours before baking, then mix all the above together and bake on griddle like scones.   Mrs. J. E. P.

200 Chrissie's Corn-Bread.

One cup white corn-meal, one cup flour, one-half cup white sugar, one cup cream and one egg, or one cup half milk and half cream, and two eggs; one teaspoonful of soda; dissolved in hot water; two teaspoonfuls cream tartar sifted in the flour; one saltspoonful of salt. Bake in two loaves, or several small tins.—*From "Breakfast, Luncheon and Tea," by Marion Harland.*

201 Steamed Corn Bread.

Three cups of flour, four cups of corn-meal, one egg, two-thirds of a cup of molasses, one quart of sour milk, soda and salt; steam three hours, and bake half an hour. If you do not have sour milk, use sweet milk and baking powder.

202 Corn Bread (Most Excellent).

One cup of corn-meal, one cup of flour, two teaspoonfuls of baking powder in the flour, one-half teaspoonful sugar, one tablespoonful of lard, two eggs, one cup of milk.   Mrs. G. M. D.

203 Corn Bread (Mrs. A. S.'s Lizzie).

One-half cupful of butter, one-half cupful of sugar, two eggs, one cupful of flour, two cupfuls of corn-meal, three teaspoonfuls of baking powder, two cupfuls of sweet milk. Beat the butter, eggs and sugar well together, add the milk, then the flour and meal. This will make two loaves.

204 Pone.

Boil one quart of milk, with which scald a pint of nice corn-meal; beat five eggs, whites and yolks separately; add a piece of butter, the size of an egg, and a teaspoonful of salt. Stir all together thoroughly and bake immediately, while it is still hot. This quantity makes two nice loaves, and should be baked half an hour in cast-iron pans or poured into small baking cups, and sent to the table in them after they are baked. Mrs. Isaac Lyons.

205 Miss Parloa's Spider Corn Cake (Most Delicious).

One and two-thirds cupfuls of yellow, coarse corn-meal, one-third of a cupful of wheat flour, two eggs, two cupfuls of sweet milk, one cupful of sour milk, one quarter of a cupful of sugar, a small teaspoonful of soda, one teaspoonful of salt, butter, half the size of an egg. Dissolve the soda in one cup of sweet milk; beat the eggs light; add the milk in which the soda is dissolved and the sour milk to the dry ingredients, then the beaten eggs; have a large spider, or two small ones, very hot; put the butter in the pan and grease the sides well; pour the mixture into the spider; now pour the remaining cupful of milk all over the batter in the spider, but do not stir it; put the spider into the oven and bake from twenty to twenty-five minutes.

N. B.—In making this cake the butter was accidentally rubbed into the corn meal, and more had to be substituted to grease the spider. Since then we have always repeated that mistake, as it made the cake much richer.

206 Rye and Indian Bread.

Three pints of sour milk, one cupful of molasses, one tablespoonful of salt, one even tablespoonful of soda, five cupfuls of rye flour, five cupfuls of Indian meal. Dissolve the soda in the sour milk, and mix with the other ingredients. Bake three hours in a moderate oven.

207 Old Recipe for Bannocks.

One pint corn-meal, pour in boiling water to wet it through. Let it stand a few minutes, then add salt, one egg, a little cream and melted butter, make into balls, and fry like doughnuts. A. N. C. W., 1850.

208 Brown Bread.

One quart of sweet milk, two quarts of Indian meal, one pint of Graham flour, one teaspoonful of saleratus, three-fourths of a cupful of molasses. Mix together the Indian meal, Graham flour, milk and molasses; dissolve the saleratus perfectly in one-fourth of a cupful of boiling water; beat this thoroughly into the mixture, pour into brown bread tins, and steam two and one-half hours, and then bake one half hour.

TEA AND BREAKFAST CAKES.

209 French Breakfast Rolls.

Take of good bread dough that is ready for its last rising what would make a large loaf of bread; cut from this pieces of dough about the size for a good biscuit, roll it under your hand till it is round; flatten it a little and then let it stand on your molding-board till the last of your rolls are finished; then let them remain five minutes "to prove." At the end of that time have a saucer of soft, nice lard ready. Dip the ball of your hand in the lard, and press the whole weight of "the heel of your hand" across the center of each roll so as to dent it almost through. Then fold it over and place in a pan so that they do not touch; let rise. Hop yeast will bring them up in five hours. They should then bake in twelve minutes. — *O'Neil's Receipt.*

N.B.—If you wish these rolls for tea or for the next morning's breakfast, set them in the refrigerator. They are perfectly delicious when treated in this way.

210 Galettes.

One pound of flour one half-ounce German compressed yeast, or one generous tablespoonful of home-made yeast, one teaspoonful of sugar; one-third of a teaspoonful of salt; one and one-half gills of sweet milk mixed with the yeast, four ounces of butter, three eggs. Mix one-half pound of the flour with the yeast, milk, sugar and salt, beat thoroughly, and set in a warm place to rise. When light, add the remaining half-pound of flour, the butter and the eggs. Beat well and set to rise again. When light, form into round cakes, handling the dough as lightly as possible. Set to rise again, and then bake fifteen minutes in a hot oven. Beat a dessert-spoonful of sugar with one egg. When the galettes are baked, and still very hot, brush them over with this mixture. These are the most delicious tea cakes imaginable. To be eaten hot, or when cold to be split and toasted.—*From Mrs. Welch's Book and National Training School of Cookery.*

211 Rusk.

Two cupfuls of sugar, one of butter, two of milk, one of yeast, three eggs; rub the butter, sugar and eggs together; add the milk and yeast and flour enough to make a thick batter; let this stand in a warm place until light, and then add flour enough to make as thick as for biscuits; shape and put in a pan in which they are to be baked, and let them stand two or three hours. Bake about forty minutes in a moderate oven.—MISS PARLOA.

N.B.—We prefer less sugar, and when within ten minutes of being done, we wash them over with an egg, into which a dessertspoonful of sugar has been beaten. They are best eaten cold.

212 Rusks.

One cupful of sugar, one of butter, two of milk, one of yeast, two eggs; rub the butter and sugar together; add the eggs, beaten separately, then milk and yeast and flour enough to make a stiff batter; let this stand in a warm place until light, then add flour enough to make as thick as for biscuits; shape and put in a pan in which they are to be baked; let them stand three hours; bake forty minutes in a moderate oven. It is always best to set the sponge at night, then it is ready to bake the following forenoon. If the rusks are wanted warm for tea, the sponge must, of course, be set early in the morning.

Mrs. A. S.'s "Lizzie."

213 Baking Powder Biscuit.

One quart of flour, one heaping tablespoonful of butter, (or lard), one salt spoonful of salt, three teaspoonfuls of baking powder, nearly two cupfuls of sweet milk or cold water—let all the ingredients be as cold as possible—sift the baking powder with the flour several times so that it will be evenly distributed, rub in the shortening as expeditiously as possible, then quickly add the milk or water. These and all biscuits raised with baking powder should be mixed just as soft as it is possible to handle them. Roll from half to three-quarters of an inch thick and bake at once in a quick oven. Success depends largely on speed and the oven—*Mrs. Welch's Cook Book.*

N. B. by the editor—We vary these biscuits by doubling the quantity of butter, rolling them thinner, pricking them with a fork and when nearly baked washing them over with milk. Soda and cream of tartar biscuits can be made as above by using one teaspoonful of soda and two of cream of tartar sifted through the flour.

214 Sally Lunn (Yeast).

One pint of milk, three eggs beaten separately, one tablespoonful of sugar, one teaspoonful of salt, and three pints of flour, one-half teacupful of yeast or half a cake of compressed yeast, and a piece of butter the size of an egg warmed in the milk. Mix it up in the morning if wanted for tea. When light stir down and pour into dripping-pans, and let Sally take another rise. Bake from three-quarters to one hour.

215 Sally Lunn, (Soda and Cream of Tartar.)

One quart of flour, one pint of sweet milk, two tablespoonfuls of sugar, two eggs, one cup of butter. Sift into and through the flour two teaspoonfuls of cream of tartar, add the mixed butter and sugar, and last, one teaspoonful of soda dissolved in the milk. Bake twenty minutes in a quick oven either in cups or shallow baking-pans.

MUFFINS.

Muffins are a very old-fashioned breakfast cake that has fallen from its first estate by the average cook baking it in an oven. Muffins should always be baked on a griddle in rings, and the batter should be thick enough to drop, not pour or string, from the spoon. Fill each ring two-thirds full; the batter will then rise to the top of the ring. You will see the bubbles form and stiffen into holes; the cake is then ready to slip your cake-turner under and turn ring and all. As it bakes stiff, slip the rings off and let them finish. A muffin should always be *torn* open.

216 Water, or English Muffins.

Into a quart of lukewarm water, in which three potatoes have been boiled and mashed, stir half a teacup of good hop or potato yeast, a teaspoon of salt, a tablespoonful of butter, and three pints of unsifted flour. This will, with ordinary flour, make a batter that will drop, not pour from the spoon. Set it in a warm place to rise; it will take from five to eight hours. Set over night for breakfast, and after breakfast for tea. Grease your muffin rings, put a tablespoonful of the batter in each ring and bake, turning as they require it. A griddle bakes nicer muffins than an oven.

217 Muffins.

One quart of sweet milk, three pints of flour, two eggs, a piece of butter the size of an egg, a little salt, one-half of a cup of yeast. Let the batter rise eight hours, and bake in muffin rings, on a griddle.

218 Indian Muffins.

One quart of milk, eight eggs, one and a-half cups of butter, one cup of flour, two cups of Indian meal, one teaspoonful of soda, two teaspoonfuls of cream of tartar, and a little salt; two teaspoonfuls of sugar. Beat well together and bake in muffin rings.

(This receipt is from a reliable source, but we can only recommend it to those who have eggs and butter in abundance).

219 Sweet Muffins.

Three eggs, beaten separately, one-half cup of sugar, two cups of flour, one cup of sweet milk, two teaspoonfuls of baking powder. Bake immediately in muffin rings.

220 Burlington Muffins.

Boil and mash four potatoes, rub them into one quart of flour, add one tablespoonful of butter, a little salt, half a teacup of hop yeast or its equivalent in German yeast, four eggs, half a teaspoonful of fine sugar, three teacupfuls of milk; mix at night; drop the dough from a spoon into muffin rings on a pan, and set it to rise till morning; bake half an hour, or on a griddle, turning to bake both top and bottom.

221 Rice Muffins.

Two cups of milk, four tablespoonfuls of yeast, one tablespoonful of white sugar, two tablespoonfuls of melted butter, nearly a cup of well-boiled rice, four cups of flour, or enough to make a good batter, salt to the taste, one-quarter teaspoonful of soda dissolved in hot water, added just before baking. Beat the ingredients well together, set to rise for six hours or until very light; put into muffin rings, let it stand fifteen minutes, and bake quickly; eat hot.

222 Potato Short-Cake.

Take six nicely mashed potatoes, add to this one pint of warm milk, a tablespoonful of lard, a teaspoonful of salt, and a quart of sifted flour. Let this be raised with a small quantity of compressed yeast or a portion of Twin Brothers' yeast cake, or a half cup of home-made. When ready to make up, which will be in about two hours, knead up to the consistency of biscuits, roll out to fill your pan, and score in diamonds; stand in a warm place till tea time. Will bake in fifteen minutes in a quick oven.

223 Potato Cakes.

Two pounds of mashed potatoes (one pound is a scant pint bowl), two tablespoonfuls of butter, a little salt, two pounds of flour; stir in milk enough to make a thick batter; add half a teacup of hop yeast or quarter of a cake of compressed yeast; set it before the fire to rise; when light, bake it in a large dripping-pan like a sally lunn or in gem-pans, the size of a muffin.

224 Stirred Bread.

One pound of flour, one teaspoonful salt, one tablespoonful of yeast; mix with one cup of milk and stir thoroughly, and set to rise. It will take about three hours to be light. When light stir in one egg, beaten light, and one teaspoonful powdered sugar, put in the pans, let rise and then bake. One egg is really enough for two pounds of flour.

225 English Crumpets.

One quart of lukewarm milk, half a cake of compressed yeast or Twin Brothers' yeast, a large quart of flour, an even teaspoonful of salt; make it into a batter as for muffins. When well risen stir into it a scant cupful of melted butter and let it rise a second time. Bake on a hot griddle in rings, double the size of muffin rings, very lightly on both sides. They will be thinner than muffins and cannot be split open. Are the better for being baked in the morning and toasted and buttered for tea. Send in on hot plates, serving them quickly and hot. They are a delightful change sometimes.

226 Puffets.

One quart of flour, one-half teaspoonful of salt, a piece of butter the size of an egg, two eggs, two even tablespoonfuls of white sugar, one pint of sweet milk, and three teaspoonfuls of baking powder, well sifted through the flour. Rub the butter in the flour, then add milk and yolk of eggs, and finish by stirring in the whites of eggs beaten to a stiff froth. Bake in gem-pans in a hot oven.

227 Breakfast Puffs.

One cupful of milk, one cupful of flour, two eggs beaten separately, a salt-spoon of salt, two tablespoonfuls of cream. Half fill the cups and bake three-quarters of an hour.

228 Pop Overs.

One cupful of milk, one cupful of flour, one egg, and one teaspoonful of salt. Let your gem pans get hot before putting in the batter; bake quickly and serve the moment they are done.

WAFFLES.

229 Good Ann's Receipt for Waffles.

A pint bowl of sour cream or buttermilk (I have known her in town to use *store* milk with about three ounces of butter in it, though, of course, the results were not quite the same), a pint bowl heaped with sifted flour, three eggs and a teaspoonful of soda, stirred well in a tablespoonful of hot water and then into the cream, and half a teaspoonful of salt. To be baked in an iron at just the right shade of heat (be sure and not have it too hot to start with); butter well and eat with powdered sugar, or sugar and cinnamon.

230 Yeast Waffles.

Three pints of milk, one heaping tablespoonful of butter; put them into a pan on the stove until the butter melts. Add the yolks of five eggs well beaten, one teaspoonful of salt, one and one-half tablespoonfuls of yeast, and about three pints of flour; let rise for six hours, then stir in the five whites of eggs beaten very light, and continue to rise for half an hour. Bake in a hot waffle iron.

231 Rice Waffles.

One teacupful of boiled rice (if cold, warm it a little), with one cupful of milk, a piece of butter the size of an egg, three eggs; add the yolks well beaten; stir in gradually one and one-half cupfuls of flour, with a little salt, one teaspoonful of soda, and two of cream of tartar (or three of baking powder) sifted through it just before baking; stir in the whites of the three eggs beaten to a stiff froth.

GRIDDLE CAKES.

232 Rice Griddle Cakes.

Can be made with above batter by adding from a half to three-quarters of a cupful of milk.

233 Three Receipts for Buckwheat Cakes.

1st. One pint of buckwheat; half-pint of sifted corn meal; two level teaspoonfuls of salt; four tablespoonfuls of yeast; one and-a-half pints of lukewarm water (or one pint water and one cup of milk); beat well and set to rise over night.

2d. One pint cup of very fine oatmeal, set to soak in the morning with one quart of water, into which two tablespoonfuls of yeast have been stirred; at night add one quart of buckwheat meal and one quart of water, three teaspoonfuls of salt; beat well and let rise till morning.

3d. One pint of buckwheat flour; three tablespoonfuls of yeast; one quart of lukewarm water. Stir well and let rise till morning.

If you use "a generator," and your cakes sour, add just before baking a half teaspoonful of soda dissolved in a quarter of a teacup of boiling water.

234 Dessert Pancakes.

One quart of milk, six eggs, a saltspoonful of salt, flour enough to make a thin batter. Fry brown in a spider, using an equal quantity of butter and lard. The cakes must be turned with great care; place one cake on the plate, and spread upon it a little butter, sifted fine; fine sugar and cinnamon or nutmeg over this; then another cake on top, and repeat until you have three or four; cut in segments like jelly cake.

235 Pennsylvania Flannel Cakes.

The yolks of five eggs well beaten, one quart of milk slightly warm, a little salt and flour enough to make a batter, add one cup of yeast. Keep warm and let rise seven or eight hours; just before baking add two tablespoonfuls of melted butter and the whites of the eggs beaten to a froth. Bake on a griddle.

236 Corn Batter Cakes.

One pint of corn-meal, a small teaspoonful of salt and one of soda. Pour on enough boiling water to make it like mush; let it stand a little to cool, then take four eggs, stir the yolks with the meal, a handful of flour (three-quarters of a cupful), two teaspoonfuls of cream of tartar, stir in as much milk or water as will make the batter suitable to bake on a griddle; whites last.

237 Pancakes of Rice.

Boil half a pound of rice to a jelly in a small quantity of water; when cool, mix with it a pint of cream, eight eggs, a pinch of salt, eight ounces of melted butter, and flour enough to stiffen or bind these rich ingredients; bake on a griddle with as little lard as possible.

Mrs. Gorton Arnold.

238 Pancakes.

Add enough flour to one quart of sour milk to make a rather thick batter. Let it stand over night and in the morning add two well beaten eggs, salt, and half a teaspoonful of soda dissolved in one-half cupful of warm water. Bake immediately.

239 Pancakes with Bread Crumbs.

To two cupfuls of bread crumbs soaked in milk, add one cupful of flour or corn-meal, two eggs, and milk enough to make a thin batter. If the milk is sweet add a teaspoonful of yeast powder; if sour, half a teaspoonful of soda, dissolved in a tablespoonful of warm water. Bake on a griddle and serve a griddle full at a time.

240 Wheaten Scones. (Scotch).

Take from your bread *dough*, when light in the morning before it has been kneaded, bits of dough the size of your fist; roll each one out thin (less than half an inch in thickness and the size of a breakfast plate in circumference), lay it on a *hot* but *dry* griddle—no grease whatever must be used; let it bake on one side, then turn and bake on the other; have a napkin warmed and lay the scone in it, covering, while a second scone is baking; when you have three baked fold your napkin close over them and send to table piping hot. Tear them open and butter. They are very nice.

MUSH, OATMEAL, RICE.

241 How to Make Corn-Meal Mush.

Very few people know how to make this dish as it should be. The ingredients for a dish of mush are water, salt and corn-meal. The water should be soft, and the salt fine, and the meal of the first quality; yellow meal gives the best color, but white meal is more easily cooked. The water should be boiling hot at the commencement, middle and end of the operation. The meal should be added very slowly, so as to prevent any lumps being formed, the cook stirring all the time, and should never be in such quantities as would bring down the temperature of the water below the boiling point. Herein lies the secret of making good mush. Mush should be thoroughly cooked. Proportions: To three pints of water, one pint of corn-meal, and one teaspoonful of salt. Cook one hour, and stir often.

242 Cracked Wheat.

Cracked wheat is very nice cooked just like oat-meal.

243 Boiled Rice.

To one-half pound of rice use about five pints of water. Let it simmer about twenty minutes. Handle carefully, not to break the kernels.

244 Cooking Oat-Meal.

Oat-meal is not usually liked, because its preparation is not properly understood. It requires very long and steady cooking. Take one teacup of oat-meal to five of water.

If your breakfast is early it does not hurt it to begin the night before by mixing the oat-meal smooth in cold water, then pour into boiling water, adding a little salt to season. Keep the water in the double boiler at a boiling point for two hours, and just before it is thoroughly cooked add a little milk to whiten and improve the flavor. Stir thoroughly at intervals.

245   Mrs. DeLand's Oat-Meal Porridge.

One coffee-cup of oat-meal, one pint of hot water. Put on the stove over night and cook in a double boiler; add half a pint of boiling water in the morning and cook one hour. If desired thinner, add more boiling water till adapted to wish or taste.

MACARONI.

246   Macaroni.

Throw the required quantity into salted boiling water, boil about twenty minutes, drain in a colander; then put in a porcelain lined kettle with half a teacup of butter (for seven or eight persons); toss about in the butter till it is all absorbed. Have a small dish of grated cheese for each to use at pleasure.   S. E. WETHERELLE, PER MRS. L.

247   Macaroni.

One-quarter of a pound of macaroni boiled in beef stock or milk and water, with a little salt, twenty or thirty minutes. When done, drain off the water and keep the saucepan covered; roll two tablespoonfuls of butter in two of flour; boil half a pint of cream, and one pint of milk, to which add the butter and flour and boil until it thickens. Stirring all the time, butter a dish, and put in a first layer of macaroni; then grate over this an ounce of parmesan or common cheese, and pour a portion of the sauce. Repeat this four times, which will fill your dish (use a quarter of a pound of cheese in all). Bake ten minutes. This is a very fine Hartford receipt, but in our family we prefer one quarter the cheese.

248 Macaroni de la Solferino.

To half a pound of macaroni boiled in water and well drained, add half an onion, a slice of raw ham chopped fine and then browned. Moisten the mixture with tomato sauce, or a layer of fried tomatoes; just before serving sprinkle the whole with grated cheese, and serve very hot.

249 Macaroni.

Scald a quarter of a pound of macaroni half an hour, in just enough water to cover it. Then put it in a buttered dish, add salt, butter and pepper. Grate over it about an ounce of cheese. Stir two eggs into one cup of milk, and pour over. Bake twenty minutes.

The appearance of macaroni is improved by laying strips of puff-paste cut with a paste jigger over the top, crossing them as you would for a tart.

Macaroni as a separate course, *a la fourchette*—in place of, or *after*, soup. Boil it as usual, and when sent to table pour over it a sauce made of cream or milk, with a little butter, flour, salt and cheese. It must not be entirely covered with the sauce.—MRS. ENDICOTT, PER MRS. L.

EGGS.

250 Boiled Eggs.

When the water is at a keen boil, lift the pot from the fire, and put the eggs in, and let them stay exactly four minutes. Serve pinned up in a warm napkin.

Another method is to keep the eggs in water at a keen boil for exactly two minutes and three-quarters.

A third and better method is to put your eggs in hot water and let them scald but not boil for ten minutes.

251 Poached Eggs.

Salt the water well, and when just ready to boil drop in the egg, which has been broken carefully into a saucer, and let stand till done, which can be seen by the white being cooked. Serve on buttered toast. Dust a litte salt and pepper on the top.

252 Scrambled Eggs.

Have your spider hot and buttered as soon as you are ready with six eggs broken into a dish, to which you add a little salt, a "shake" of pepper, a bit of butter the size of a nutmeg, and half a cup of rich, sweet milk. Beat them up a little, just enough to break up the eggs, then pour into the buttered spider. Scrape your spoon back and forth to prevent their adhering to the bottom of the spider. Do not cook too dry; a few minutes will cook them. This is nice for breakfast or lunch. Take them up while they are quite soft, as they harden a little after removal from the pan.

253 Egg Omelet (Very Nice).

Five well-beaten eggs, one-and-a-half cups of milk, three tablespoonfuls of flour; mix the flour in a little of the milk, and rub smooth, then add milk and flour to eggs, and beat well together; grease well with lard a frying-pan; put in, when not very hot, a large kitchenspoonful, it will cover about half; fold with a knife when light brown, and roll up as it browns.

254 Ham Omelet.

One-half pint of milk, two teaspoonfuls of flour, three teaspoonfuls of cracker crumbs, six eggs well beaten. Put thinly and evenly over the griddle; then immediately scatter over it finely minced ham. Double it one-third, then fold again.

255 Omelet.

Set a smooth frying-pan on the fire to heat; break five eggs into a bowl; put butter the size of an egg into a heated pan; give twelve strong beats to your eggs, and when the butter begins to boil, pour in the eggs. Draw up the eggs from the bottom of the pan, but do not stir, simply shake the pan. When the bottom is well done and the top a little soft, fold over and put on a platter. Serve immediately. This may be varied by the addition of three tablespoonfuls of milk.

256 Baked Eggs.

Six eggs, four tablespoonfuls good gravy, veal, beef or poultry; the latter is particularly nice; one handful of bread crumbs, six rounds of buttered toast or fried bread.

Put the gravy into a shallow baking-dish, break the eggs into this, pepper and salt them, and strew the bread crumbs over them. Bake for five minutes in a quick oven. Take up the eggs carefully, one by one, and lay upon the toast, which must be arranged on a hot, flat dish. Add a little cream, and if you like, some very finely chopped parsley and onion to the gravy left in the baking-dish, and turn it into a saucepan. Boil up once quickly, and pour over the eggs.

257 Eggs Sur le Plat.

Six eggs, one tablespoonful of butter or nice dripping, pepper and salt to taste. Melt the butter on a stone china or tin plate, or shallow baking-dish. Break the eggs carefully into this, dust lightly with pepper and salt; lay a bit of butter on each, and put into a moderate oven until the whites are well set. Serve in the dish in which they were baked.

258 Egg Vermicelli.

Boil three eggs twelve minutes. Separate yolks and whites; keep the former warm while chopping the whites fine, pepper and salt to taste (adding celery salt or celery powder), one heaping teaspoonful of flour, three tablespoonfuls of cream, butter the size of a walnut; boil the cream and butter, then add the whites of eggs. When thickened spread on toast or puff paste shells, and rub the yolks through a coarse sieve or strainer over the top.—
Maria Ames, per Mrs. L.

SALADS.

259 Chicken Salad

Is eminently an American dish, and Detroit is quite celebrated for its delicious chicken salads. Our entertainments may not be as showy as in other western cities, but *our* caterers understand that the stale salads of a previous party can never be freshened. Mrs. Henderson makes a suggestion which we have found works very nicely, that she calls "*marinating the chicken.*" Sprinkle upon the chicken a mixture in the proportion of three tablespoonfuls of vinegar to one of oil and one (level) of salt, a pinch—the smallest pinch—of cayenne, about what would lie on the point of a penknife, and a teaspoonful of mixed mustard. Let the chicken stand in this mixture an hour or two; drain off what may be in the bottom of the bowl; ten or twenty minutes before serving pour over a mild mayonnaise. Little strips of anchovy rolled up are used with pickles, hard boiled eggs, and lettuce-heads, or tender yellow celery tops to garnish.

We give as minute directions as possible for the various methods and tastes in mixing the dressing.

An eight-pound turkey, rubbed with a fresh lemon, and boiled in well-salted water (having two tablespoonfuls of raw rice in it), is used and preferred by many to a pair of chickens. The flavor is radically different, but quite delightful. Every one of the receipts given will make a nice salad. The colder your salad is the crisper and fresher it will taste, and the thicker and better will be your dressing.

260 Lobster Salad.

Use the "Mayonnaise Sauce," only adding to it two or three teaspoonfuls of anchovy sauce and a saltspoonful of Worcestershire sauce; celery or lettuce in less proportions than for chicken salad. Pickeled walnuts or olives make a nice garnish for this salad.

261 Shrimp Salad.

Take canned shrimps and use the dressing recommended for lobster salad. Put fresh lettuce in the salad dish, then the shrimps, and then pour over all the dressing.

262 Egg Salad.

Boil six eggs hard; chop the whites fine, and rub the yolks smooth. Take a cupful of finely chopped ham. Mix the whole carefully; sprinkle in a little salt, pepper and chopped celery, or celery salt; cover the whole with Mayonnaise dressing. Garnish with French peas, slices of lemon and hard-boiled egg. The whole can be served on nice leaves of lettuce if you have it.

263 Mrs. Henry Smith's Chicken Salad Dressing.

For the white meat of two chickens, take a coffee-cup of very strong vinegar; the yolks of five eggs, well beaten; butter the size of an egg; one tablespoonful of made mustard (thick); two teaspoonfuls of salt, a little white pepper. Cook the dressing over hot water, as you would a custard, until thick, stirring constantly; add the beaten whites. Have twice as much celery as chicken, and cut both up instead of chopping. Just before serving mix the meat and celery, then add to the dressing a cup of very rich sweet cream; beat well and pour over the chicken and celery, and stir it for a moment. N. B.—We double the mustard in this recipe.

264 Salad Dressing.

Four eggs, whites and yolks beaten separately, eight tablespoonfuls of vinegar, six tablespoonfuls of cream, one tablespoonful of corn starch, one teaspoonful of mustard, one teaspoonful salt, one teaspoonful pepper, two tablespoonfuls oil. Mix all the ingredients together except the oil and whites of the eggs; put on the fire and stir until it thickens; add the oil and beaten whites of the eggs the last thing and when very cold. N. B.—We do not like the whites of the eggs in this dressing, and put in four times as much mustard.

265 Miss Smith's Cream Dressing.

Five eggs, beaten separately; two tablespoonfuls of mixed mustard; butter the size of an egg; two teaspoonfuls of salt; one saltspoonful of red pepper; three tablespoonfuls of the finest table oil; one pint of thick cream. Scald the cream, stir in the yolks, and continue to stir until it begins to thicken; then add the mustard, salt, etc., and two or three tablespoonfuls of very strong vinegar; then let it cool, and add the whipped froth of the eggs. Beat all thoroughly together. Do not pour over the chicken and celery until just before using. N. B.—We double the mustard and double the oil, the latter we stir in when all is cold.

266 Mayonnaise Sauce.

Put the uncooked yolk of an egg into a cold bowl; beat it well with a silver fork; then add two saltspoonfuls of salt, and one saltspoonful of mustard powder; work them well a minute before adding the oil; then mix in a little good oil, which must be poured in very slowly (a few drops at a time) at first, alternated occasionally with a few drops of vinegar. In proportion as the oil is used, the sauce should gain consistency. When it begins to have the appearance of jelly, alternate a few drops of lemon juice with the oil. When the egg has absorbed a gill of oil, finish the sauce by adding a very little pinch of cayenne pepper, and one and-a-half teaspoonfuls of good vinegar; taste it to see if there is sufficient of salt, mustard, cayenne and vinegar. If not, add more very carefully. These proportions will suit most tastes; yet some like more mustard and more oil. Be cautious not to use too much cayenne. By beating the egg a moment before adding the oil, there is little danger of the sauce curdling; yet if by adding too much at first, it should possibly curdle, immediately interrupt the operation; put the yolks of one or two eggs on another plate; beat them well, and add the curdled mayonnaise by degrees, and finish by adding more oil, lemon-juice, vinegar, salt and cayenne, according to taste. If lemons are not at hand, may use vinegar instead.

267 Dressing for Salad.

FOR TWO CHICKENS AND TWELVE HEADS OF CELERY.

Four eggs beaten light, yolks and whites together; two tablespoonfuls of mixed mustard, one teaspoonful of salt, one teaspoonful of black pepper, or one-third of a teaspoon of red pepper, one tablespoonful of butter, and nearly one teacupful of sharp vinegar. Float the pan containing the ingredients in a pan of boiling water on the stove and stir until it is thick like custard. When cold pour over the salad, adding cold vinegar, if needed. N. B.—We add half a teacup of Gustier's salad oil when the dressing is cold.

268 German Salad Dressing.

The yolks of three hard-boiled eggs, put through a sieve, the yolks of three raw eggs, one teaspoonful of salt. Beat well together until cream-like, then add a pint of olive oil, one cup of vinegar, a little pepper and a little sugar. Beat all well together until light, cold and creamy. Add capers, if used for fish dressing.

269 Dressing for Mayonnaise.

The yolks of four eggs, beaten light with a silver fork; then add, drop by drop, a teacupful of the finest salad oil, two small onions, and a small bunch of parsley, minced very fine; pour this over a whitefish that has been boiled in salted water and flavored with a lemon (juice and rind); remove the bones from the fish; when cold, pile into a shape, and as it comes to table pour over the dressing.

270 Salad Dressing Made at Table.

The yolk of a raw egg, one tablespoon of mixed mustard, one-fourth of a teaspoon of salt, six tablespoons of oil; stir the yolk, mustard and salt together with a fork until they begin to thicken; add the oil gradually, stirring all the while. More or less oil can be used.

Miss Parloa.

271 Salad Dressing, No. 2.

The yolks of two hard-boiled eggs rubbed very fine with a silver spoon, one yolk of a raw egg, one small boiled or baked potato; to these add one tablespoonful of mixed mustard; blend the two thoroughly, then stir in one-half cup of thick, sweet cream and one tablespoonful of melted butter, or one teacup of the purest salad oil; a little salt and cayenne, and, if desired, a dash of anchovy or Worcestershire sauce. Last of all, add little by little, vinegar enough to make the whole a smooth, creamy mass, and pour it on the lettuce just before serving.

272 Salad Dressing—To Keep.

Two teacups of sweet cream, one teacup of vinegar, two tablespoonfuls of corn starch, two tablespoonfuls of sugar, one tablespoonful of mustard (dry), four eggs, yolks and whites beaten separately; put all over the fire together, vinegar last, and stir till the consistency of boiled custard; add the whites of eggs and bottle. The sugar may be omitted if not to the taste of the family.

273 Potato Salad—Good.

Can be made a delicious and rather complicated dish, like "the beggars' stone soup." Take six boiled potatoes steaming from the pot, cut them in slices, pepper and salt a little, lay over a shadow of very thinly sliced onion, a sprig of parsley or so cut very fine, some olives cut fine or left whole, as garnishes, two or three red beets sliced like the potatoes, some scraps of red herring or sardines, a cucumber pickle or two cut into small dice, and some pickled French beans. Over this pour the following:

274 French Dressing for a Salad.

Put into three tablespoonfuls of the purest salad oil a heaping saltspoon or level teaspoonful of salt, one even teaspoonful of scraped onion, one tablespoonful of vinegar, one teaspoonful of tarragon or pepper vinegar. Beat for a few moments with a fork, and pour over a vegetable salad.

275 Simple Potato Salad.

Boil your potatoes, then skin and slice while hot, into a covered vegetable dish; have all ready a dressing. One-third of a teacup of boiling water, one-third or more of vinegar, and a little more oil than vinegar; slice a small onion thin, and lay between the layers of potato; when the dish is full pour the dressing over it; cover, and put away to cool; just before serving, stir it with a salad fork or spoon. Mix the oil, vinegar, salt and pepper well together, and then add the hot water.

276 Fresh Tomatoes

Make a delightful salad sliced and having a tablespoonful of vinegar, a teaspoonful of oil, a saltspoonful of mustard, and a saltspoonful of salt beaten together and poured over them. Lobster served on tomatoes and covered with a mayonnaise dressing is a charming combination.

277 Tomato Mayonnaise

Is also nice, using the mayonnaise sauce very cold, and having the tomatoes very cold before the one is poured over the other.

PIES.

278 Pastry.

One pound and a quarter of flour, one pound of butter, or one-half butter and one-half lard, and if necessary a salt-spoon of salt, all cut together, sufficient ice cold water (less than a teacupful) to mix with; no more flour. Put upon the molding-board, roll out and cut in strips, put one upon another, then cut off in squares, roll out and put upon plates; bake at once in a quick oven.

279 Plain, but Good Family Pie-Crust.

One pound of flour, half a pound butter; mix thoroughly with a knife or spoon. Pour in very cold ice water, just enough to form a dough for rolling out; flour the board and rolling-pin, using a knife to handle the dough (the warmth of the hand makes it heavy); roll out the size of one plate at a time, so as to work it as little as possible. Bake in a quick oven.

280 Prof. Blot's Receipt for Pie-Crust.

One pound of flour, wet with water; then stir in one pound of butter, cut in small pieces, and roll out.

281 Plain Pie-Crust for Two Pies.

Three cups of sifted flour, one cup of lard, or half cup of butter and half cup of lard, a little salt, ice-water enough to wet it; stir with a knife and roll out. Roll butter in the upper crust three times, sprinkle a little flour over the butter, and roll out.

282 A Celebrated Puff Paste.

One pound of flour, one pound of butter, one egg. Mix the flour with a lump of butter the size of an egg, and the one egg to a very stiff paste, adding as little as possible of ice-cold water. Knead it well for a few minutes, perhaps ten or fifteen, divide the butter into six equal parts, squeeze any buttermilk out that may stand in the butter, roll the paste out thin, and put on one spreading of little bits of butter; dredge with flour; fold and roll out again; repeat this five more times, dredging, folding and rolling each time. Now place it on the ice, or in a very cold place, from one to four hours.

283 Tart Crust.

The white of one egg beaten to a stiff froth, one tablespoon white sugar, one cup of butter or lard, a little salt, five tablespoons of ice-water, three cups of sifted flour; roll quite thin for tarts; cut out with a cooky cutter—a scalloped one will look best; take an open-top thimble, make five holes in one, lay this on top of a whole one, which makes one tart; proceed with all the dough in the same way; bake lightly, when done split open the tart and lay a slice of nice jelly between the layers; squeeze up the jelly through the holes; place them on the table on a plate and you have a splendid-looking dish for the tea table, and something that will keep two months. Do not put your jelly in till you wish them for the table.

284 Rich Mince Pie.

Three pounds of beef, one fresh beef's tongue, four (or six) pounds of suet, three and-a-half pounds of raisins, three pounds of currants, three-quarters of a pound of citron, eight pounds of chopped apples, four and-a-half pounds of sugar, one pint of molasses, three ounces of cinnamon, two ounces of cloves, a nutmeg, one teacupful of the Mace compound, one-and-a-fourth ounces of salt, half an ounce of pepper, one gallon and-a-half of sweet cider. When mixed, put into a kettle and scald, stirring it all the time. Put it hot into Hero or Mason jars—two quarts or gallon jars—and the longer you keep it the nicer it will be. When making up your pies you can add a teacup of finely chopped apples for each pie.

285 Mince Pie.

Seven pounds of meat, six pounds of suet, four pounds of sugar, one gallon and-a-half of boiled cider, seven pounds of currants, seven pounds of seeded raisins, fourteen pounds of chopped apples. Boil together cider, apples and sugar, and when hot pour over the other ingredients; add one teacup of Mace compound, nutmeg and cinnamon to taste. If citron is liked, put in slices just before baking; the vinegar from pickled peaches is a nice addition—to this quantity use one pint.

286 Plain Mince Meat.

One pint bowl of meat and one of suet, chopped fine; two bowls of apples; one of boiled cider; one and one-half cups of molasses, one bowl of sugar, one teaspoon of cloves, two of cinnamon, two of allspice and one nutmeg. Let the mixture come to a boil.

287 Summer Mince Pies.

We do not recommend this, preferring fruit pies in summer, but the recipe is highly recommended. Two cups of dried apples soaked over night and chopped fine in the morning; four eggs boiled hard and chopped fine; one tablespoonful of butter, one cup of raisins, one cup of currants, a little salt, one cup of sugar, half a lemon, rind and juice, one cup of molasses; put in the water the apples soaked in; all kinds of spice; bake in a slow oven.

288 Mock Mince Meat.

This recipe is for "a last shift" for persons who have not "store privileges." It is not bad, but to our taste, not good. Two eggs, eight butter crackers rolled, one coffee-cup of raisins, one-half coffee-cup of vinegar, one coffee-cup of molasses, one of sugar, one of water, one-half of butter; spices to suit the taste.

289 Lemon Pie, No. 1.—Very Fine.

Grate the rind and squeeze the juice of two lemons; beat the yolks of three eggs with eight tablespoonfuls of granulated sugar, half a cup of water and two even tablespoonfuls of flour; stir the flour into the well-beaten yolks and sugar, then add water, juice and rind; bake with an under crust, have ready when it comes from the oven, the whites, beaten to a stiff froth, with four tablespoonfuls of pulverized sugar; spread over the pie, set in oven, and brown as quickly as possible, to avoid its being leathery.

I should like to add, for the benefit of many housekeepers who do not know, that a meringue should always be put on while the pudding or pie is hot, and browned as quickly as possible; if cold, it is apt to go back and taste of raw egg.—Mrs. D. A. L.

290 Lemon Pie.—No. 2.

One cup of white sugar, one tablespoonful of corn starch, one lemon, grate off the outside, and squeeze out the juice, two eggs. Wet the corn-starch with cold water, then fill the teacup with boiling water, a dessertspoonful of butter. When a little cold add the lemon and egg. Bake in a bottom crust with a meringue at the top.

291 Lemon Pie that will Keep a Long Time, No. 1.

One pound of sugar, half a pound of butter, eight eggs, the rind of two lemons, the juice of one; beat well and bake with an under crust in an oven not too hot, as it needs thorough baking, and must *not* have a soft or custard look when done. This recipe will make two pies, which, if not eaten fresh, will be equally good a week after with a fresh meringue and browned in the oven, and is recommended by a first-rate housekeeper.

292 A Substitute for Corn Starch.

Grate a large cooked potato, or its equivalent in small ones, as a substitute for corn-starch in a lemon pie, or sprinkle flour over it enough to thicken it a little. Some use raw potatoes, but I prefer cooked. Try it, if you have a good recipe; you will think your pies are delicious.

293 Lemon Pie, No. 3.

Take the juice and rind of one lemon, one cup of sugar, the yolks of three eggs, one teaspoonful of butter and one cup of milk; bake in a rich paste; beat the whites of three eggs to a stiff froth, with two tablespoonfuls of powdered sugar and spread over the top, return to the oven and brown slightly. If the pie is desired stiff, use a tablespoonful of grated potato.

294 Apple Lemon Pie.

One teacup of stewed apples, two eggs, one cup of sugar, lemon to suit taste. Use no upper crust.

295 Lemon Pie.

One large apple chopped fine, one lemon, chop the inside fine, just take off the thick white part, grate the rind first; one egg, one cup sugar, butter the size of a walnut. Bake with two crusts nearly an hour, or with a meringue and one crust. Delicious.

296 Cocoanut Pie.

One teacup of sugar, one-half cup of butter, three eggs, one grated cocoanut, one quart of scalded milk poured on the cocoanut, underlined with pastry.

297 Cocoanut Pie.

One cup of dessicated cocoanut soaked in one quart of milk, two powdered crackers or two tablespoonfuls of corn-starch, three eggs, a little butter and salt, add one cupful of sugar and grated rind of lemon. Very rich.

298 Orange Pie.

Rub the yellow of two oranges with lumps of sugar, add juice of three, and one cup of white sugar, one finely rolled and sifted cracker, a teaspoonful of butter, four eggs, one cup of sweet milk. Line pudding dish with paste, and bake until firm; nice either hot or cold. With or without a meringue.

299 Orange Pie.

Three oranges peeled with a knife, and sliced in rounds into a plate lined with paste. Sprinkle well (if sour) with sugar, and add two tablespoonfuls of water. If the oranges are sweet, add the juice of half a lemon. Cover with paste and bake. This is as nice as a peach pie. In early spring we have sometimes found the oranges turn bitter when cooked, possibly because they have been frosted.

300 Pie Plant or Rhubard Pie.

Peel a bunch of pie plant, put it into your chopping-bowl and chop into pieces the size of your little finger nail; grate the rind and squeeze the juice of a lemon over this, add sugar to taste; put this into a pie dish lined with paste, lay in a bit of butter, and cut strips of paste and lay them across the top, and bake. Or pour the chopped plant into a porcelain-lined basin with the sugar and give it a good scald. Bake with under and upper crust.

301 Strawberry Pie.

Make a nice puff paste, with which line a baking plate; half bake it in a quick oven. Have ready sugared strawberries to fill the plate, and the white of an egg beaten and sweetened as a meringue with which to cover the berries. Return to the oven long enough to brown slightly.

302 Pumpkin Pie.

Stir into a generous quart of boiling milk, one pint of well stewed and strained pumpkin; let it scald a moment, then add one and-one-half cupfuls of sugar, three eggs, one-half teaspoonful of salt, one even tablespoonful of ground ginger and one of ground cinnamon, a little nutmeg, and a tablespoonful of molasses. Bake in pie plates lined with good paste. Should be at least an inch thick. We have friends who prefer to use four eggs; this will make the pies a little stiffer.

Squash Pie may be made by the above receipt, but use less than a pint of squash, as it is dryer and of a finer grain than pumpkin.

303 Pumpkin or Squash Pie.

One quart of stewed pumpkin, which has been mashed and rubbed through a colander; then stir it into two quarts of boiling milk (or one quart of boiling milk, afterwards adding one quart of cream unboiled); let scald a moment and strain through a fine sieve; add five eggs, seven eggs or nine eggs, as suits your taste. The five makes a softer and more quaking pie; the latter a stiff pie. Spice with one heaping teaspoonful each of ginger, cinnamon and nutmeg, two cupfuls of sugar and two tablespoonfuls of molasses. Bake with one crust only; the pie an inches or an inch-and-a-half thick.

304 Cream Pie—Unsurpassed.

One pint of rich cream, one scant teacup of sugar, the whites of four eggs whipped to a stiff froth; beat all together and pour into a pie-plate lined with paste. Bake as you would custard pie and eat when very cold.

305 Peach Pie.

Line with paste a deep pie or soup plate, then skin the peaches (or if they are fair-skinned and tender, rub off with a crash towel the downy coat), and lay on the plate as many as will make one layer; cover with white sugar and lay on the top paste. Bake until the fruit is done. If the crust is likely to be overdone, leave open the oven door. Some prefer to have no under crust, in which case the upper crust should be somewhat thicker. To be eaten cold, and is delicious with the addition of cream.

306 Apple Custard Pie.

One pint of good stewed apples, quarter of a pound of butter, half a pint of cream, three eggs, beaten light. Sugar and flavoring to the taste. Bake on an under crust.

307 Sweet Potato Pudding.

Boil one pound of sweet potatoes very tender; let them dry a moment, add half a pound of butter and rub both through a sieve; then take a quart of milk, seven eggs, one heaping cupful of sugar; beat all together; add a little salt, the juice and rind of one lemon, and grated nutmeg; then beat again and pour into pie-plates, lined with nice crust. It may be baked without pastry.

308 Irish Potato Pudding.

May be made by exactly this receipt, except more salt and sugar.

309 Whortleberry Pie.

Pour just enough water on the fruit to prevent its sticking to the bottom of the preserving pan; add sugar; scald a moment, and pour into pie-plates lined with paste; dredge with flour, cover with paste and bake.

310 Apple Pie.

Pare and slice the apples; make a thick syrup of white sugar and a tablespoonful or more of water, into which throw a few cloves or mace. In this syrup scald a few apples at a time, taking them out and putting more in till all are slightly cooked; set aside to cool, then pour into pie-plates lined with paste; dredge with flour; put bits of butter about over the flour; dredge again, and cover with paste and bake.

311 Custard Pie.

One quart of milk, four eggs, five to eight tablespoonfuls of sugar; flavor with peach leaves or grated nutmeg; pour into a pie-plate, lined with paste, and bake slowly half an hour.

312 Washington Pie—A Ready Dessert.

Two cups of sugar, half a cup of butter, one cup of milk (if sour, stir in one teaspoonful of saleratus), add one egg; beat the butter and sugar together, then break in the egg and beat it light; then add the milk foaming, and three-and-a-half cups of flour (if the milk is sweet, use three teaspoonfuls of baking powder in the flour instead of saleratus). Bake in four tin plates, in a quick oven; then have ready some nicely stewed apples, sweetened and flavored with nutmeg or lemon, or other fruit like raspberry jam; spread a thick layer on one of the cakes and place another on the top, making two pies.

Or, make a custard of one-half pint of milk, one-half cup of sugar, one-half cup of flour, one egg; wet the flour with a little milk, and stir into the milk boiling; then add the egg and sugar beaten together. Boil up and take off; flavor with a pinch of salt and a teaspoonful of vanilla. When cold, spread between two layers of cake. This is very good for a dessert.

In an emergency, they may be made after the dinner is served if the fruit is at hand, or can be spread with custard, as in the following receipt: Juice and rind of one lemon, one cup of sugar, one egg, cooked together, then spread between cakes; frost the top. Jelly spread between is also nice.

PUDDINGS

In these days, when puddings are always "steamed in a mold," the temperature of the water is not a matter of such vital importance. We confess to being old-fashioned enough to prefer a pudding boiled in a bag. Take a half a yard of nice, new "Russia Duck," or strong unbleached drilling, or sail cloth, sew together so as to form a sausage; turn it inside out, dip it in boiling water, and rub it into a pan of flour, turn the bag so that the flour is on the inside, tie up one end tightly, and pour the the pudding into the other, leave room for it to swell; tie the other end. Put a plate in your pot, have the water boiling, and keep it boiling for three hours after you have plunged your pudding in. The flavor of a bag pudding is greatly superior to that of a mold.

Baking a pudding is a more simple process, but let us warn our students not to bake it to death. A bread or any custard pudding *should shake in the middle* when it is done. A rice pudding should be lightly baked; an Indian meal pudding will bear much longer baking. The boiled lemon pudding given at No. 329 requires a mold as it is so delicate.

313 Mace Compound.

Soak half an ounce of mace eight hours in one pint of lemon juice, add a teacup of boiling water and scald twenty minutes. An excellent substitute for objectionable flavorings.

314 Genuine English Plum Pudding.

Grate the crumbs of a ten-cent loaf of bread, boil a quart of rich milk, strain and set to cool; pick, wash and dry a pound of currants, stone and cut a pound of raisins; strew over the fruit three large tablespoonfuls of flour. Roll fine a pound of brown sugar and mince three-quarters of a pound of beef suet. Prepare two grated nutmegs, a large tablespoonful of powdered cinnamon, the grated peel of two large lemons or oranges, and one-half pound of cut citron; beat ten eggs very light and stir them gradually into the cold milk, alternately with the suet and grated bread-crumbs; add by degrees the sugar, fruits and spice, with half a teacup of the lemon and mace, and two teaspoonfuls of extract of nectarine, three dozen bitter and sweet almonds blanched and powdered, mix the whole very well, then pour it into a mold or a scalded and floured pudding bag, and put into boiling water and boil steadily five hours, replenishing the pot with boiling water.

315 English Plum Pudding Without Eggs.

Two bowls of grated bread-crumbs and three tablespoonfuls of flour, into which mix two teaspoonfuls of baking powder, one bowl of sugar, one bowl of suet, one scant bowl of milk, one bowl of fruit, one dessertspoonful of salt; cinnamon, cloves and nutmeg to taste. The fruit should be raisins, currants, and citron cut into strips, candied orange peel, and if desired, blanched almonds. Boil constantly for six hours, leaving room in the bag for it to swell. It should be boiled the day before it is wanted. Keep in the bag. Next day boil one hour. Eat with a rich sauce.

316 English Plum Pudding with Eggs.

Omit the flour, baking powder and milk, and substitute one bowl of eggs.

317 Phillis' Christmas Plum Pudding.

One pound of flour, half a pound of suet, one pound of currants, half a pound of brown sugar, eight eggs, half a teacup of milk, one nutmeg, four teaspoonfuls of mace compound, half a pound of citron. Boil ten to twelve hours.

318 Black Pudding.

Four eggs, one-half pint of molasses, one-half cup of butter, one-half cup of sugar, one-half cup of milk, one cup of sifted flour, one large teaspoonful of soda. Bake half an hour.

SAUCE.—Two cups of sugar, one tablespoonful of butter, one and one-half cups of boiling water, one lemon; grate the rind and squeeze in the juice.

319 Farina Pudding.

Stir into one quart of milk, while boiling, three large tablespoonfuls of farina, let scald five minutes, set it away to cool; then add three well-beaten eggs, three tablespoonfuls of powdered sugar, a little salt, and put into your pudding-dish that has been well buttered; set into the oven in a pan half filled with boiling water; bake for about half an hour, and then turn out upon a platter, and serve hot with a sauce made of butter and sugar beaten to a cream and flavored with nutmeg or vanilla. If the pudding-dish is oval-shaped of the size of the platter upon which the pudding is to be served, and the sauce put over the top of the pudding, a most tempting desert is before you.

320 Tapioca Pudding.

Put into one quart of milk a liberal half cup of tapioca which has soaked over night, in one pint of water, one saltspoon of salt; set it on the back part of the stove and simmer gently until the tapioca becomes clear; then beat the yolks of four eggs with one cup of sugar and the rind and juice of one lemon; stir this into the boiling milk and tapioca; of the whites of the eggs make a frosting with one cup of pulverized sugar. Add the juice of a lemon or other flavoring, spread over the top of the pudding in a baking-dish, and let it just brown to a cream tint in the oven. It is best eaten cold.

321 Sago Pudding

Is made like tapioca, except that the sago requires twice the time to soak and boil.

322 Very Nice Rice Pudding.

Put one-half cup of rice into one and one-half cups of water, or milk, and set it upon the stove until about done, then stir in a pint of milk and let it come to a jelly. Beat the yolks of three eggs with five tablespoonfuls of powdered sugar, and stir into it with a little salt while boiling. Beat the whites of two eggs to a stiff froth with five tablespoonfuls of sugar, spread over the top and bake a little. It may be flavored with lemon or vanilla, and eaten hot or cold.

323 Rice Pudding.

Half a teacup of rice in three pints of milk; set it in a tin pail in a kettle of boiling water; let it simmer till the rice is cooked soft; while hot, stir in two tablespoonfuls of butter; set it by to cool; beat five eggs; leaving out two whites, and a teacup of sugar; stir into the rice and milk when cold, and set in the oven to bake; take out as soon as it *forms* a custard; do not wait for the custard to set or it will whey; one-quarter of a pound of stoned raisins added to this is very nice. Make a meringue of the two whites of eggs and six tablespoonfuls of pulverized sugar beaten to a stiff froth; pile on the top and set in the oven just two minutes.

324   Rice Pudding.

Four spoonfuls of soft boiled rice to a quart of milk. While heating over the fire, stir in a small tablespoonful of corn-starch wetted with milk, add the yolks of two eggs, sugar, raisins, grate nutmeg on the top, then bake to the consistency of thick custard. When cold, make a meringue of the whites of the eggs, with two tablespoonfuls powdered sugar, cover it, return to the oven to brown, eat with sweet cream.

325   A Delicate Pudding—Cocoanut and Rice.

Half a teacup of rice in three pints of milk; set it, in a tin pail, in a kettle of water; let it simmer till the rice is cooked very soft; set it by to cool. Beat five eggs, leaving out two whites, one coffee-cup of sugar and one grated cocoanut; stir in the rice and milk when cold, and set it in the oven to bake; take out as soon as the custard forms; do not wait for it to *set*, or it will whey. Make a meringue of the two whites of eggs and six tablespoonfuls of pulverized sugar beaten to a stiff froth; pile up on the top and return to the oven for two minutes. Very nice hot or cold.

326 Poor Man's Rice Pudding.

Two quarts of rich milk, one teacup of raw rice well washed, one teacup, or more, of sugar, a piece of butter the size of an egg and a little salt. Flavor with nutmeg. Bake slowly from one and-a-half to two hours. Stir occasionally during the first hour to prevent the rice from settling in the bottom of the dish. Some like a few raisins added after the first forty minutes' cooking. This is very nice when cold.

327 Lemon Rice Pudding.

Boil one-half cup of rice in one quart of milk until very soft, add to it while hot the yolks of three eggs, grated rinds of two lemons, eight tablespoonfuls of sugar, and a pinch of salt. If too thick, add some cold milk. It should be a little thicker than boiled custard. Turn it into a pudding-dish, beat the whites of the eggs very stiff together with eight tablespoonfuls of white sugar, and juice of the lemons and brown on top. To be eaten icy cold.

328 Mrs. S.'s Boiled Lemon Pudding.

Rind of one and juice of three lemons, three cups of grated bread crumbs, one cup of suet (or one-half cup of butter), two cups of sugar. Mix well together and lay part of it in a tin mold, buttered twice. Make a custard of one pint of milk and three eggs, pour some of it over the bread crumbs, suet and sugar in the mold; then add the remainder of the ingredients and moisten them with what is left of the custard. Put the mold into a steamer and steam from one and one-half to two hours. Serve with a rich pudding sauce.

This pudding may be made richer by sprinkling through it a tablespoonful of chopped or grated candied orange peel, the same of citron, and the same of blanched and broken almonds; this fruit should be lightly dredged with flour. Great care should be exercised in putting in this fruit—LIZZIE'S FOAMING SAUCE OR KATE'S CREAM SAUCE.

329 Lemon Pudding.

Mix three heaping tablespoonfuls of corn-starch with cold water very thin; pour in three coffee-cups of boiling water, and boil till it thickens, stirring all the time; then add two coffee-cups of sugar, the grated rind and juice of two large lemons, two eggs well beaten, and salt to taste. Butter a pudding-dish and bake twenty minutes. To be eaten cold, and it is very nice with cream.

330 Apple Souffle Pudding.

Six or seven fine juicy apples, one cup of fine bread-crumbs, four eggs, one cup of sugar, two tablespoonfuls of butter, nutmeg and a little grated lemon-peel. Pare, core, and slice the apples, and stew in a covered farina kettle without a drop of water, until they are tender. Mash to a smooth pulp, and while hot stir in butter and sugar; let it get quite cold and whip in, first the yolks of the eggs, then the whites, beaten very stiff, alternately with the bread-crumbs. Flavor. Beat hard for three minutes, until all the ingredients are reduced to a creamy batter, and bake in a buttered dish, in a moderate oven. It will take about an hour to cook it properly. Keep it covered until ten minutes before you take it out. Eat warm with sauce.

331 Apple and Tapioca Pudding.

One teacupful tapioca, six apples, juicy and well-flavored pippins, pared and cored; one quart water, one teaspoonful salt. Cover the tapioca with three cups of lukewarm water and set in a tolerably warm place to soak five or six hours, stirring now and then. Pack the apples in a deep dish, adding a cup of lukewarm water; cover closely and steam in a moderate oven until soft all through, turning them as they cook at the bottom. If the dish is more than a third full of liquid turn out some before you pour the soaked tapioca over all. Unless your apples are very sweet, fill the center with sugar and stick a clove in each just before you cover with tapioca. Then bake one hour. Eat warm with sweet sauce.

332 How to Make a Cheap Apple Pudding—English.

In the first place select two deep earthen dishes, of the same size and shape, that will hold two or three quarts, according to the family. Then fill one with nice apples, peeled and sliced thin. Add a teacup of cold water. Cover the apples with a tender pie-crust, then turn the empty dish, after it has been well buttered, over the one in which you have the pudding, and place them both in a steamer. It will require about two hours and a-half. Let the pudding be just ready for the dessert, and do not remove the upper dish until the minute the pudding is to be eaten.

It is nice with sugar and butter, but with rich cream, sweetened, it is a very delicious dessert. This pudding can be varied by using canned peaches or apricots instead of apples.

333 Apple Pudding.

Make a pint of sour apple sauce, sweeten it a little, and put through a sieve; beat the whites of three eggs, stir half in the sauce and put the other half on the top as a meringue, brown in the oven; eat with a custard sauce.

334   Margie's Brown Betties.

One cup of bread-crumbs, two cups of chopped tart apples, one-half cup of sugar, one teaspoonful of butter. Butter a pudding-dish, put a layer of bread crumbs in the bottom, then a layer of chopped apples, with a sprinkle of sugar, cinnamon and small pieces of butter strewed on the top, a sprinkle of sugar and cinnamon if desired, then a layer of bread crumbs, and so on until the dish is full, having bread crumbs for the top. Cover the dish with a pan and bake three-quarters of an hour, then uncover and brown. Serve with sugar and cream or Fairy Butter sauce.

335   Apple Snow Pudding.

Take one-half pound of the pulp of roasted apple (about seven or eight good sized apples), one-half pound of granulated sugar, and the whites of two eggs. Beat the whites of the two eggs to a stiff froth, then put in just a little of the sugar, then a little of the apple, and so on alternately until the whole is mixed, and continue the beating for an hour, make according to receipt a soft custard; put in a dish and pile the snow on top. This is lovely, both to the eye and the palate, and the recipe, with one quart of milk, will serve an abundant dessert for a dozen people.

336   Fig Pudding.

Six ounces of suet, six ounces of bread crumbs, six ounces of sugar, one-half pound of figs chopped fine, four eggs, one teaspoonful extract nectarine, with one of water, half teacup of flour, one-half cup of milk, one nutmeg, one-half teaspoonful of soda, one teaspoonful of cream of tartar. Steam three hours and serve with Lizzie's foaming sauce.

337 Ginger Pudding.

Five eggs, two teacups sugar, one and one-half teacups of butter, four teacups of flour, after being sifted, one of molasses, one of sour milk, with a teaspoonful of soda dissolved in it, two teaspoonfuls ground ginger, a little cinnamon, a pinch of salt, unless the butter is salt enough; beat the eggs and sugar together, set the molasses and butter over the fire to melt the latter; mix alternately the eggs and flour; lastly, milk, soda and spice; bake slowly. Eat with the following sauce: One-half pint of molasses, one pint of sugar, lump of butter size of an egg, a teaspoonful of ginger, a little water. Let all boil and serve hot.

338 Cottage Pudding.

One egg, one pint of flour, one cup of milk, one cup of sugar, three tablespoonfuls of melted butter, one teaspoonful of soda, two teaspoonfuls of cream of tartar. Mix the cream of tartar in the flour, and the soda in the milk. Can be made in twenty minutes. Bake quickly, and eat with sauce. Square, shallow pans are better to bake it. Three teaspoonfuls of baking powder can be used.

339 Eve's Pudding.—Mrs. T.'s.

If you want a good pudding, mind what you are taught;
Take of eggs six in number when bought for a groat;
The fruit with which Eve her husband did cozen,
Well pared and well chopped at least half a dozen;
Six ounces of bread—let Moll eat the crust,
And crumble the rest as fine as the dust;
Six ounces of sugar won't make it too sweet;
Some salt and some nutmeg will make it complete;
Three hours let it boil without any flutter,
But Adam won't like it without sauce or butter.

One tablespoonful of flour, one even tablespoonful cinnamon, one even teaspoonful cloves.

340 Plum Duff.

Two cups of flour, saltspoon of salt, four eggs, two tablespoonfuls of sugar beaten in the eggs, one cup of sweet milk, or sour, two teaspoonfuls of baking powder for sweet milk, or one teaspoonful of soda for sour, a large cup of stoned raisins. Steam an hour and-a-half. Eat with sauce. This pudding is dry without one cup of finely chopped suet, or two tablespoonfuls of butter.

341 Sponge Pudding.

One quart of milk, scalded, and let grow cold, then take four ounces of butter, four ounces of sugar, stirred to a cream, four ounces of flour; mix all in the milk; add in the yolks of six eggs, then the beaten whites. Put in a pudding dish and set it in a pan of hot water in the oven, and bake half an hour.

342 Brown Bread Pudding.

Three cups of Graham flour, three cups of corn meal, one cup of molasses, one quart of milk, one teaspoonful of soda. Steam three hours in a mold.

343 Steamed Graham Pudding.

Two cups of Graham flour, one cup of milk, one cup of molasses, one cup of raisins, one egg, one teaspoonful of soda, one-half teaspoonful cloves and cinnamon each, a little nutmeg, a pinch of salt. Put the flour in a basin, then add all the other ingredients. Mix thoroughly. Flour the raisins, put the mixture in a greased pan, set in a steamer and steam three hours. (A very excellent pudding). MARGERY DAW.

344 Baked Indian Pudding.

Put half a pint of sweet milk and the same of water into a tin pan or basin, and when it boils stir in a cup of Indian meal, wet up with a little water and a teaspoonful of salt; remove from the fire and add a pint of cold, sweet milk, four beaten eggs, a cup of sugar, and any seasoning you like; stir well; bake in a deep dish half or three-quarters of an hour.

345 Mrs. Ward's "Corn-Meal Pudding."

One pint of milk, two large spoons of corn-meal, butter one-half size of an egg; boil three or four minutes. When cold add one egg, two tablespoons of sugar, salt and spice. Bake forty minutes.

346 Boiled Indian Pudding.

One quart of milk, one quart of corn-meal, one-half pint of molasses, two eggs, a little salt, one teaspoonful of soda. Mixed cold, put into a bag and boil four hours.

347 Sweet Corn Pudding.

Ten or twelve ears of corn, one tablespoonful of flour, one tablespoonful of butter, one or two teaspoonfuls of sugar, a little salt, a quart of milk, three eggs. Put the flour and butter into the corn, then the sugar and salt, then the eggs and milk, and bake.

348 Chocolate Pudding.

Half a cake of grated chocolate, vanilla to flavor, scant half pint of soda cracker crumbs, butter the size of an egg, one-half pint boiled milk, whites of six eggs, half cup of sugar, salt to taste. Boil in a mold for one hour; serve hot. Sauce.

349 Chocolate Pudding.

One quart of milk, three ounces grated vanilla chocolate, three tablespoonfuls of corn starch, two eggs, one cup of pulverized sugar. Boil the milk, stir in the chocolate, starch, sugar, and beaten yolks of the eggs, and then bake. When the pudding is cold, beat the whites of two eggs to a froth; stir in a half cup of pulverized sugar; place this frosting on the pudding and serve.

350 Chocolate Pudding.

One quart of milk, twelve tablespoonfuls of bread-crumbs, eight tablespoonfuls of chocolate, yolks of four eggs. Put the milk and bread crumbs on the fire; let them get moderately warm; beat sugar, yolks and chocolate, and stir them into the milk; one tablespoonful of corn starch; let it get boiling hot, then turn in a dish with the whites beaten with sugar on top, and bake a light brown.

351 Queen of Puddings.

One pint of bread-crumbs soaked from thirty to forty minutes in one quart of sweet milk; then add one cup of sugar, the yolks of four eggs, well beaten, the grated rind of one lemon, butter the size of an egg; bake till it looks like custard. When baked spread over the pudding a layer of fruit or jelly, and add a meringue made of the whites of the eggs, and one cup of powdered sugar. We prefer it without sauce, but it often is eaten with fairy butter. It ought to be out of the oven twenty minutes before eating it hot. It is also very nice cold. This recipe may be varied by spreading one cup of concentrated cocoanut instead of the jelly and covering this with the meringue.

352 Mountain Dew Pudding.

Three Boston crackers rolled fine, one pint of milk, yolks of two eggs, a little salt; bake half an hour; beat the whites of the eggs to a stiff froth; to this add one cup sugar; flavor with lemon or vanilla. Pour this over pudding and set it in oven until a light brown.

353 Delmonico Pudding.

One quart of sweet milk, three even tablespoons of corn starch, dissolved in cold milk; the yolks of five eggs, six tablespoons of white sugar, one cup of concentrated cocoanut; a little salt; boil three or four minutes; grease the baking-dish, and bake half an hour; after it is baked, beat the white of the eggs; to it add six tablespoons of white sugar, and season this with vanilla, and spread the whole over the pudding. Set in oven again and bake until it is a light brown.

354 California Bread Pudding.

Take four slices of bread and cut off the crust; put in a pudding-dish and pour over one pint of boiling milk. Beat the yolks of three eggs with another pint of milk, and one cup of sugar. Mix all together. Bake the pudding half an hour. Beat the whites of the eggs very stiff and add half a cup of powdered sugar. Put the icing on the top and brown.

355 Bread and Butter Pudding.

Take a loaf of bakers' bread, cut off "the heel," spread the end of the loaf with butter, cut a slice one-third of an inch thick, butter, and cut enough slices to fill your pudding-dish; sprinkle on each one a few raisins or dried currants, and then slips of citron; mix a cold custard of three pints of milk, the yolks of eight eggs, beaten light, a heaping cup or more of sugar; pour this over the bread; bake just enough; it is better underdone than overdone; let it stand to cool; make a meringue with the whites of two eggs and half teacup pulverized sugar, spread over the top, and brown a moment in the oven.

In old times it was baked without a meringue, and eaten warm with fairy butter.

356 Poor Man's Pudding, No. 1.

One cupful of chopped suet, one cupful of molasses, one cupful of sweet milk, four cupfuls of flour, one teaspoonful soda, one cupful raisins or currants, one-half teaspoonful of cloves, one teaspoonful of cinnamon, and half a nutmeg.

357 Poor Man's Pudding, No. 2.

One pint of fine bread-crumbs, one half cup fine suet, one cup of raisins, seeded and chopped, one cup of molasses, half a teaspoonful of soda.

358 Almond Pudding.

Half a pound of blanched almonds powdered to a paste, three half pints of cream, one-quarter of a pound of loaf sugar, half a pound of grated bread crumbs, yolks of eight eggs and whites of four; stir over the fire till quite thick; bake in a deep mold and serve with rich sauce.

359 Marrow Pudding.

Grate a large loaf of bakers' bread and pour on the crumbs a pint of rich milk boiling hot; when cold, add four eggs and three-quarters of a pound of beef's marrow, sliced thin, four tablespoonfuls of lemon juice, in which one teaspoon (level) of mace has been soaked and stirred, one teaspoon of extract of nectarine, and one tablespoonful of rose-water. Add two cups of raisins and one of blanched almonds, if you wish; boil three hours, or omit the fruit and use a pound of marrow instead of three-quarters, and bake it.

360 Vanity Fair.

One cup of sugar, half cup butter, half cup water, two cups flour, two eggs, two teaspoons baking powder; mix, and steam fifty minutes, and serve with foaming sauce.

361 Gipsy Pudding.

Cut stale sponge cake into thin slices; spread with jelly or sweet-meats, and put together like a sandwich; then lay them in a deep dish and pour over boiled custard hot; let it cool before serving.

362 Whortleberry Pudding.

One quart of flour, one heaping tablespoonful of baking powder, a little salt, mix with cold water, having the dough softer than for soda biscuit; roll out the paste and pour upon it one quart of whortleberries, then cover the berries by securely lapping the paste as for dumplings. The water must be boiling, the pot ample and well filled with the boiling water. Dip the pudding-cloth in hot water, then flour it well; tie the pudding very closely in the cloth and let it boil steadily one hour.

SAUCE.—One cup of sugar, a little less than half a cup butter, worked together until white and smooth; flavor with nutmeg; just before sending to the table pour in boiling milk until the whole is the consistency of thick cream. Stir the sauce when used, as it will settle a little.

363 Fried Bread Pudding.

One pint of milk, three eggs, a pinch of salt, and flour enough to make a very thin batter; cut a stale bakers' loaf in slices one inch thick; dip each slice one instant in milk, then lay them in the batter for fifteen or twenty minutes; remove carefully with a pancake turner when ready to cook, and fry brown on both sides, in hot batter, in a frying-pan; eat with sauce.

SAUCE.—Half a pint bowl of brown sugar, two heaped tablespoonfuls of butter, one teaspoonful of extract of nectarine, all stirred to cream; then dredge in about a tablespoonful of flour, and add a teacup of boiling water, stirring well for two or three minutes; grate half a nutmeg over the top, and use the moment it is done. The above is a delicious French dessert, though bearing so homespun a title.

364 Marlboro Pudding.

Nine tablespoonfuls of sweetened stewed apples; one-fourth of a pound of butter, six eggs, beaten seperately; flavor with lemon or vanilla; bake with an under crust. The whites of two eggs may be reserved and beaten to a meringue with one-half cup of pulverized sugar, spread it over the top when baked, and slightly browned.

365 Delicious Hasty Pudding.

Seven eggs beaten seperately, add to the yolks gradually ten tablespoonfuls of sifted flour alternately with a quart of milk and a half a teaspoonful of salt. Beat till perfectly smooth. Then add the whites poured into a buttered dish and bake twenty minutes. Eat with fairy butter.

366 Old-Fashioned Suet Puddings.

To make suet paste : Beat one egg, mix it with half a pound of suet, well chopped, add one pound of flour, well mixed, then add as much cold water as is requisite to bring it to a stiff paste; flour the pasteboard and rolling-pin and roll out and beat the paste till it puffs up; roll it out to the size desired and put in apples or other fruit, sprinkled with sugar or canned peaches without the juice, or spread with raspberry or strawberry jam; fold into a roll; roll in a floured cloth with room enough to swell. Boil an hour and a half.

367 Boiled Suet Pudding.

Three eggs well beaten, a teacup of chopped suet, two teacups of unsieved flour, a pinch of salt, a tablespoonful of sugar; sieve and stir the flour with the eggs and suet; grate in some nutmeg; thin down very smooth with half a teacup or more of cold water to a very thick batter; add a few raisins or citron, or boil without either for two hours in a pudding bag or two-and-a-half in a mold. This pudding has a far better flavor if boiled or steamed in a bag.

68 Quick Puff Pudding.

Stir one pint of flour, in which is mixed two teaspoonfuls of baking powder and a little salt, into milk until very t, place in the steamer well greased cups, put in each a spoonful of batter then one of berries, steamed apples or peaches, or raisins, cover with another spoonful of batter and steam twenty minutes. This pudding is delicious made with fresh strawberries and eaten with a sauce made of two eggs, half a cup of butter, and a cup of sugar beaten thoroughly with a cup of boiling milk and one of strawberries.

369 Pudding in Haste.

One egg, one cup milk, one cup flour, butter size of a walnut, a little salt. Bake in a very hot oven; serve with rich sauce. — Miss Field.

SAUCES.

370 Foaming Sauce.

One-half a cup of butter, one cup of sugar, one third of a cup of cold water, one tablespoonful of vanilla and two tablespoonfuls of orange flower water or lemon juice, or one of mace compound. Beat the butter and sugar to a cream, add the flavoring and water a few drops at a time, stirring all the time. It will become very light. Place it in a basin of boiling water on the back of the stove; let it simmer for one hour; do not let it boil. Do not stir until you are ready to serve, then give a good stir and serve. This is the most delicious sauce for all kinds of boiled and steamed puddings.—Mrs. Allen S.'s "Lizzie."

371 Katy's Cream Sauce.

One-half cup of butter, one full cup of pulverized sugar beaten to a cream. Have a pint of sweet cream whipped to a froth as for Charlotte Russe; whip both together and flavor with vanilla.

372 Pudding Sauce.

Beat well together a heaping tablespoonful of butter with two cups of pulverized sugar, add one egg, one gill of milk, and a tablespoonful of mace compound; if it curdles, place it in the warming oven for two or three minutes, stirring all the while.—MRS. N. D. LAPHAM.

337 Pudding Sauce.

Add to a coffee-cup of boiling milk, one tablespoonful of flour, wetted with two of cold milk, have ready a teacup of sugar, and half a teacup of butter, thoroughly stirred together, and when the flour and milk have boiled two or three minutes, add the sugar and butter; stir well but do not boil, flavor with lemon or vanilla.

374 Pudding Sauce.

Three tablespoonfuls of white sugar, one even of flour, a piece of butter the size of a hen's egg, stirred to a cream. Stir in gradually two tablespoonfuls of mace compound, add a teacup of boiling water. Then set into a kettle of boiling water, stirring it constantly, until the flour is cooked.

375 The Eyre Sauce.

Stew together for fifteen minutes half a pound of sugar, a piece of butter as large as an egg, and one pint of water; beat the yolks of three eggs; remove the pan from the fire and pour several spoonfuls of its contents into the beaten egg, stirring briskly; then pour all into a pan, place it over a slow fire and stir till it thickens; season with extract of nectarine (Burnet's) or vanilla.

376 Virginia Cold Sauce.

Whites of five eggs beaten to a stiff froth; sweeten to taste; pour in some *hot* melted butter, stirring well; season with almond or lemon.

377 Bath Lemon Sauce.

One cup of sugar, half a cup of butter, stirred to a light cream; add the yolks of two eggs, then pour over this half a pint of boiling water and the juice of one lemon; then the whites of the eggs well beaten.

378 Rappahannock Cold Sauce for Eight Persons.

One heaping tablespoonful of butter creamed till very light, adding sugar till as thick as you can stir; then add two tablespoonfuls of very rich milk or thin cream, a dozen pounded almonds or a teaspoonful of extracts of almonds and a little grated nutmeg.

379 Fairy or Nuns' Butter.

One tablespoonful of butter and three of powdered sugar stirred together till very light; grate a little nutmeg over the top.

380 Strawberry Sauce.

Omit the nutmeg in the above receipt and add a teacup of mashed strawberries.

381 Sauce for Sponge Pudding.

Two cups of sugar, one cup of butter, yolks of two eggs beaten to a cream; heat over the kettle top, add the beaten whites. Flavor to your taste.

382 Raisin Sauce.

Cut half a pound of raisins and stew them in three teacups of water, into which has been stirred three tablespoonfuls of imperial grits and one saltspoon of salt; let stew thirty-five or forty minutes, add half a teacup or six tablespoonfuls of sugar, and grate in half a nutmeg.

383 Molasses Sauce.

Half a pint of molasses, one pint of sugar, piece of butter the size of an egg, teaspoonful of ginger, half a teacup of water; let all boil and serve hot.

384 Virginia Molasses Sauce.

Moderately boil a pint of molasses from five to twenty minutes, according to its consistency, add three eggs well beaten, stir them, and continue to boil a few minutes longer; season with nutmeg and serve very hot.

385 Maple Sugar Sauce.

Make a rich syrup of one scant cup of water and one heaping cup of maple sugar; let boil from twenty to forty minutes. When ready to serve stir into the boiling sugar two tablespoonfuls of butter, braided with one teaspoon of flour.

386 Cream-Pudding Sauce.

One cup butter, two cups powdered sugar, one teaspoon extract nectarine, and four tablespoonfuls water; beat the butter to a cream, add the sugar gradually, when light add the juice of an orange, a little at a time. Lastly, place the bowl in a basin of hot water, and stir for two minutes; the sauce should be smooth and creamy.

Mrs. Dr. P.

FRIED CREAM, BATTER PUDDINGS, FRITTERS.

387 Fried Cream (Creme Frite).

Every one should try this recipe. It will surprise many to know how *soft* cream could be enveloped in the crust; it is an exceedingly good dish for a dinner course, or for lunch or tea. When the pudding is hard it can be rolled in the egg and bread-crumbs. The moment the egg touches the hot lard it hardens, and secures the pudding, which softens to a creamy substance, very delicious.

Ingredients: One pint of milk, five ounces of sugar (little more than half a cupful), butter the size of a hickory nut, yolks of three eggs, two tablespoonfuls of corn starch, and one tablespoonful of flour (a generous half cupful altogether), stick of cinnamon one inch long, one-half teaspoonful of vanilla. Put the cinnamon into the milk, and when it is just about to boil, stir in the sugar, the corn starch, and flour, the two latter rubbed smooth, with two or three tablespoonfuls of extra cold milk; stir it over the fire for fully two minutes, to cook well the starch and flour; take it from the fire, stir into it the beaten yolks of the eggs, and return it for a few moments to set them; now, again taking it from the fire, remove the cinnamon, stir in the butter and vanilla, and pour it on a buttered platter until half an inch high. When cold and stiff, cut the pudding into parallelograms, about three inches long, and two inches wide; roll these carefully, first in sifted cracker crumbs, then in eggs (slightly beaten and sweetened), then again in the cracker crumbs. Dip these into boiling hot lard (a wire basket should be used if convenient), and when of fine color take them out and place them in the oven for four or five minutes to better soften the pudding. Sprinkle over pulverized sugar and serve immediately.

388 White Puffs, Very Nice.

Marion Harland says: One pint of rich milk, whites of four eggs, beaten stiff; one heaping cup of prepared flour (or teaspoonful of baking powder in ordinary flour), one scant cup of powdered sugar, grated peel of half a lemon, a little salt. Whisk the eggs and sugar to a meringue and add this alternately with the milk, cream or half cream —half milk is better, if you have it; beat until the mixture is very light, and bake in buttered cups or tins. Turn out, sift powdered sugar over them, and eat with lemon sauce, or sauce flavored with lemon. These are delicate in taste and texture, and pleasant to the eye.

389 Cream Batter Pudding (Most Excellent).

Half a pint of sour cream, half a pint of sweet milk, half a pint of flour, three eggs, half a teaspoonful of soda. Beat the whites and the yolks of the eggs separately, and add the whites last. Bake in a moderately hot oven. This is the queen of batter puddings. Eat with half a cup of butter and one cup of sugar, stirred to a cream and flavored with a teaspoonful of extract of vanilla or half a teaspoonful of extract of nectarine—Burnet's.

390 Batter Pudding.

Six eggs, beaten light; six heaping tablespoonfuls of sifted flour; one quart of sweet milk; a pinch of salt. We use the cold method of mixing, and bake the little puddings in the iron-clads for forty-five minutes; serve with fairy butter sauce. Margery Daw scalds the milk, beats the eggs, and stirs into them the flour and mixture till smooth. Bakes half an hour. When in the oven stirs it from the bottom with a spoon.

391 Boiled Batter Pudding.

Four tablespoonfuls of flour, four eggs, one pint of milk; mix the flour in the eggs; add gradually the milk, and boil in a cloth or mold for one hour.

392 French Fritters.

One tumbler of water, a saltspoon of salt, a teaspoonful of sugar, quarter of a pound of butter. Put all together in a stewpan on the stove, and when well heated so that the butter is thoroughly melted, stir rapidly in one-half pound of flour; take it from the fire and break in one egg, blend it and break another, and then another, till five have been broken in; then in very hot lard and butter drop spoonfuls of this mixture and let boil slowly, as you do fritters; when they are taken out roll them in sugar and cinnamon, or eat with pudding sauce.

From a French Chef in Heidelberg.

393 Fritters Made with Yeast.

One quart of flour, three tablespoonfuls of yeast, five eggs, and one pint of milk; beat into a tolerably stiff batter; stir a cupful of boiled rice into the batter a short time (about an hour) before boiling. A great deal of lard boiling hot is required for frying the fritters. Drop the batter in with a spoon, which must be dipped each time into hot water. Set the fritters at breakfast time or just after.

394 American Fritters.

One cupful of milk, one and one-half cupfuls of sifted flour, two eggs, one teaspoonful of sugar, one small teaspoonful of baking powder; beat the eggs to a froth, then add milk and sugar. Lastly put in the flour with the baking powder stirred well through, drop them, a spoonful at a time, in boiling lard. Serve immediately.

395 Orange Fritters.

Take the above batter for American fritters; peel an orange, split it according to its natural divisions, as far as possible extract the seeds; dip each section of orange into the batter and boil in hot lard.

396 Apple Fritters.

Slice tender tart apples thin, mix in American fritters batter, and boil in hot lard.

397 Arrow Root Pudding.

One cup of milk, into which mix two heaping tablespoonfuls of arrow root stirred into three cups of boiling milk, add when nearly cold; have four tablespoonfuls of sugar beaten into two tablespoonfuls of butter and the yolks of four eggs stirred into the arrow root; flavor and bake twenty minutes.

398 Kissingen Pfannekuchen, very nice.

One cup of flour, one pint of milk, one tablespoonful of sugar, piece of butter, the size of a walnut (a heaping teaspoonful); scald the milk, butter and flour together. After the batter is cold stir in the yolks of eight eggs, and just before cooking add the whites beaten very light. Put into a frying or omelet pan a tablespoonful of butter; let it boil up, pour in one-sixth of this mixture, and let it fry as you do an omelet, but without shaking; fold over from each side of the pan and double in the middle, as you do an omelet. In Germany they sprinkle sugar over before folding up. We prefer sifting the powdered sugar on after it is folded. Raspberry jam is served with pfannekuchen. We prefer it without. It takes a little knack to make and bake pfannekuchen, but this receipt is right.

HOME-MADE EXTRACTS.

399 Almond Flavor.

Pound six bitter and twelve sweet almonds in a mortar, and add to pudding sauce, or add with this a teaspoonful of extract nectarine.

400 Mace Compound.

One teacup of lemon juice, one-half ounce of blade mace; let steep six hours, then add half a teacup of water and let it scald fifteen or twenty minutes; bottle and seal for use as directed.—O'NEIL.

401 Bitter Almond Flavoring.

From May till November three or four peach leaves scalded in milk make a delicious flavoring for cake, custard and ice cream.

402 Essence of Ginger and Vanilla.

We prefer to use Brown's Jamaica Ginger (Philadelphia maker), and Burnet's Extract of Vanilla.

403 Pickled Peach Vinegar

Is often a pleasant flavor to molasses or other sauces.

MERINGUES.

These have become an every-day addition to pastries, custards, and even charlottes. We therefore give two receipts for French and Italian meringues, as well as those interspersed throughout other receipts.

404 To Make a French Meringue.

To each white of an egg, beaten stiff as possible, take two heaping tablespoonfuls of pulverized sugar, sift it lightly and slowly into the whites, stirring till smooth; spread over your pie, pudding or fruit; sift a very trifle of sugar over the top and bake quickly. If the oven browns too fast shade the meringue with a paper that does not touch it.

405 Italian Meringues.

Boil four ounces of sugar slowly and steadily with two tablespoonfuls of water till it begins to crystalize, which can be told by its forming long threads as you give the skimmer a sudden jerk; then pour this onto the whites of two eggs, beaten to a very stiff froth, and stir for five or ten minutes off the fire; sprinkle the top with split and blanched almonds, and bake as you do French meringues.

CUSTARDS.

(*General Directions.*)

Eggs, milk and sugar of the best; a custard boiler or a tin pail set in a kettle of boiling water will answer the purpose, for boiled custards; bring the milk to a boil, stir your yolks of eggs and sugar together; pour a teacup of scalding milk on the eggs and sugar, blend all smoothly and then stir them into your scalding milk and keep your spoon moving around the boiler for a minute or a minute and-a-half, by the clock, till the custard begins to thicken and cling to the spoon; take quickly from the fire and continue to stir for a few moments after it has been removed. Never add flavoring till the custard is almost cold.

Baking custard can be accomplished by simply setting the pan containing the ingredients in the oven and baking twenty minutes; but a method that gives a more delicate flavor is to cover your pudding-dish or pan, set it in another larger pan, and two-thirds fill the latter with boiling water and let it bake till the center is like jelly and shakes.

As the foundation of most creams is a well-made boiled custard, and the main element of most puddings is "a baked custard with additions," it behooves every one desirous of being a dainty cook to make a study of custards.

406 Delicate Baked Custard.

Heat a quart of milk quite hot, that it may not whey when boiled, let it stand till cold; then beat six eggs very light (five will do very well), and add to the milk; sweeten to taste with white sugar, about a teacupful; flavor with lemon or vanilla, and a pinch of salt. Fill cups or bowls and set them in the oven in a dripping-pan filled with boiling water. When the water has boiled ten or fifteen minutes, take out a cup, and if the cup is the consistency of jelly, it is done. Cover the cups and they will bake better.

407 Boiled Custard, No. 1.

One quart of boiling milk, to which add the yolks of eight eggs and one heaping teacup of sugar, stir just one minute before taking off the fire; this is the genuine old-fashioned boiled custard; when cold, flavor with vanilla or bitter almonds or use no flavoring, but after it is poured into the cups grate a little nutmeg over each.

408 Cream Custards.

One quart of sweet cream, eight tablespoonfuls of white sugar, whites of four eggs. Stir the sugar into the cream, then add the whites of the eggs without beating them; stir all well and flavor with bitter almonds or vanilla; bake in cups set in a pan half filled with boiling water; put in the oven and bake till it thickens.

MRS. DR. STEWART OF DAYTON, OHIO.

409 Boiled Custard, No. 2.

Bring two quarts of milk to a boil, stir into them two even tablespoonfuls of corn starch and let cook till smooth and well done; add yolks of three eggs beaten very light with a cup and a-half of sugar; stir well for one minute by the clock; now stir in lightly the whites of four eggs beaten to a stiff froth, allowing it half a minute more over the fire to set the eggs. Flavor with vanilla or chocolate, or both. This is a particularly nice custard, and though it is comparatively inexpensive, it does not taste *cheap*.

410 Caramel Custard Pudding.

One small teacupful of brown sugar in a Charlotte Russe pan, in which it is to be baked, set in the oven five minutes or longer; prepare a custard of four eggs to one quart of milk and one heaping teacup of sugar; pour this gently into the pan and bake promptly.

411 Coffee Custard, Whipped Cream on Top.

Take a large cup of freshly ground coffee, break an egg into it and mix well; put it into a coffee-pot with a pint of boiling water, and let it stand ten minutes; turn it off very clear in a saucepan; add a pint off cream and give it one boil. Have ready eight eggs, well beaten, one and-a-half large cups of sugar; turn the coffee and cream boiling hot on the eggs, and finish in hot water till thick and smooth.

412 Lemon Custards that will Keep a Week.

Beat the yolks of eight eggs until they are white, then put to them a pint of boiling water, the rinds of two lemons grated, and the juice sweetened to your taste; stir it on the fire until it is thick, then add almond or nectarine flavoring, and after giving it one scald, put in cups to eat cold.

If it does not come thick enough a little corn starch can be added.

413 Custard to Turn Out.

Mix with the yolks of four eggs, well beaten, one pint of new milk, sweetened with sugar, about half a teacupful, and boil over the fire till it thickens; then add half a box of gelatine, previously dissolved by soaking one hour in half a teacup of cold water, then adding two tablespoonfuls of boiling water, and set it over the steam of the tea-kettle till needed. Pour into a dish and stir till a little cooler, then pour into cups to turn out when cold. Add flavoring to the eggs.

414 Chocolate Custard.

One pint of milk, three tablespoonfuls of grated chocolate boiled in the milk, three eggs beaten light, stirred into the boiling milk; let the whole come to a boil again. Sweeten to taste.

415 Cocoanut Custard.

To one pound of grated cocoanut allow one quart of scalding milk and one heaping cup of sugar. Beat well the yolks of six eggs and stir them alternately in the milk with the cocoanut and sugar. Pour this into a dish lined with paste and bake twenty minutes, or, if preferred, treat the milk, cocoanut, eggs and sugar as for boiled custard, and serve in cups.

416 Almond Custard.

One pint of new milk, one liberal half cup of powdered sugar, one-quarter of a pound of almonds blanched and powdered, two teaspoonfuls of rose or orange-flower water, the yolks of four eggs. Stir this in the double boiler as directed for boiled custards. When it is the thickness of cream take it from the fire, and when cool pour into custard cups. Beat the whites of the eggs with eight tablespoonfuls of pulverized sugar to a stiff froth, and lay on top.

417 Snow Custard (Winter Receipt).

For a three-pint mold put one-half box of gelatine in a bowl, soak it one hour with one pint of cold water, then add one pint of boiling water, stir until dissolved; then put to cool; sweeten with three-quarters of a pound of sugar and flavor with the juice of three lemons. Whip the whites of four eggs to a stiff froth; add them to the gelatine when it begins to stiffen or set; then whip the whole to a light froth, and when all begins to stiffen pour it into a mold. Take the four yolks of the eggs and make a rich custard, flavor it with the rind of one lemon and pour round. This pudding will keep for a day or two. This receipt is excellent in cold weather or where you can use plenty of ice.

418 Snow Custard (Summer Receipt).

Soak one-half a box of gelatine one hour in half a pint of cold water; add half a pint of boiling water, three-quarters of a pound of powdered sugar. Beat the whites of three eggs, add gradually the gelatine and sugar, when it begins to set then the juice of three lemons, grated rind of one; beat constantly, *hard* and *fast*, from half an hour to an hour, or until it is about as stiff as pancake batter; put it in the dish in which it is to be served, and set in a cold place or on ice; make the yolks into a soft custard, with a pint of milk, flavoring with the rind of the lemon. This pudding is good the second day, eaten with strawberries or canned fruit.

CREAMS.

In most Creams a well-made custard is the basis of their composition. This is also somewhat the case in Charlotte Russe. Nothing is more simple than to make a smooth, rich boiled custard, and we refer our readers to the "general instructions for making custards," which precedes Custards. The second thing in creams is the proper preparation of gelatine or isinglass. All gelatine or isinglass melts more smoothly and richly if soaked at least one hour in cold water, a scant teacup of water to an ounce of either. When all the water is absorbed, and the gelatine soft, add from two to four tablespoonfuls of boiling water, and set it on the back of the stove to melt. When it is a smooth glue stir it into your custard. Plan to have the gelatine ready to pour into the custard within five minutes after you remove both from the fire, and stir till it is so smoothly mixed with the custard as to be a part of it. The second and most important matter is *just when* to combine the custard, or simple gelatine, with the whipped cream. Your custard with the gelatine in, or the latter properly dissolved, *must be exactly at the point where it is ready to set.* You can easily tell this by the manner in which it begins to adhere to the bottom and sides of the bowl or pan. If the gelatine is not cold enough, and your cream is almost whipped, take a piece of ice as large as your two hands, fold it in an old cloth and beat it with a hammer or mallet till very fine; open the cloth stir a teacup of salt in the ice; pour it quickly into a pan, and set the lukewarm custard or gelatine upon it, stirring and beating till cold;

then the cream and custard can be blended quickly, but thoroughly. By neglecting these precautions, we have seen the most disheartening failure of the very best receipts; the mortified cook all the time protesting that she had done just what the book said. If you wish to make a charlotte or cream directly after breakfast, when you rise in the morning drop your gelatine into a tumbler, and cover it with the cold water; have your milk put on the stove to boil while you are breakfasting. When you go into the kitchen add the boiling water to the gelatine, and set it on to melt; break your eggs, add your sugar, et cetera, and in five minutes your custard is made. While it is cooling whip your cream, and in twenty-five minutes, if your plans are well arranged, you have made an elaborate dessert; and its preparation has been a pleasure rather than a toil.

Let us reiterate that the temperature in the combination of custard, cream and gelatine is the secret of success. Cold cream to whip, cold eggs to beat, cool custard to stir into the cream, will encourage you to believe that the art of cookery is yours.

Notwithstanding the best cookery books instruct you to "soak the gelatine in milk," and "boil the gelatine in milk," we can from our own experience give the advice of Punch to the young man about to marry, "Don't."

Gelatine and milk, either soaked or boiled, are very apt to curdle. In receipts for Spanish cream this boiling gelatine in milk and adding eggs afterwards, is always strongly urged. Our own plan is to boil the milk, scald the yolks of eggs and sugar in the same. Take them off the fire and cool five minutes; then stir in the gelatine which has been warmed, till it is a smooth liquid. Set away to cool, and when cold and just ready to set, stir in the well-beaten whites.

419 Charlotte Russe, No. 1 (Isinglass).

Sweeten and flavor to taste one quart of cold fresh cream; whip it to a froth with a whip churn, Dover egg-beater or wire spoon. Break up half an ounce of Cooper's isinglass into half a pint of cold water; let soak one hour, then set it over a boiling teakettle, or on the stove to dissolve. When thoroughly dissolved and cooled, pour it into the cream, stirring it until it begins to thicken. Line a mold with lady-fingers, and pour in the mixture.

420 Charlotte Russe, No. 2 (Isinglass).

Four sheets of Cooper's isinglass broken up and soaked in cold water till soft, then pour off the water and put the isinglass into half a pint of boiling water; set it on the stove to stew down to one-half. Beat the yolks of four eggs till very light, with three-quarters of a pound of sugar; stir these into one pint of boiling milk. Beat the whites separately; strain the isinglass into this custard as it cools and begins to stiffen; whip in the whites, flavor with two teaspoons of vanilla. Have ready a quart of creamed churned to a froth, which add when the custard is quite cold and commencing to thicken, stir very thoroughly but quickly, and put into molds lined with sponge cake.

421 Charlotte Russe (Katie T.'s, No. 3 (Gelatine).

Beat one pint of cream till thick and foamy; beat the whites of four eggs to a very stiff froth, soak two tablespoonfuls of gelatine in two tablespoonfuls of cold water one hour; then add two tablespoonfuls of boiling water; let it melt thoroughly and then cool, next put a scant teacup of pulverized sugar into a large bowl, add two teaspoonfuls of extract of vanilla; pour the eggs, cream, and last the gelatine, all into this bowl, and beat with an egg-beater till well blended. Pour this mixture into Charlotte molds, lined with lady-fingers, and put it away on ice for three or four hours to set. This is very pretty, made in a glass bowl, with lady-fingers at the bottom and sides, and two crossed on the tops. In summer double the quantity of gelatine if you wish it to turn out on a dish.

422 Charlotte Russe (Gelatine).

Three pints good cream, three-fourths of a pound pulverized sugar, one ounce of best gelatine, six eggs. Divide the sugar in half, sweeten the cream with one-half, flavor with Burnet's extract of vanilla, and whip with a Dover egg-beater. Beat the eggs to a stiff froth, add the rest of the sugar, beating hard. As soon as the gelatine is weighed, put it into half a teacup of cold water to soak one or two hours; then add half a teacup of boiling water, melt and strain, and keep warm. Put the eggs and sugar into a large bowl, pour over the scalding gelatine, stir well and quickly, and when it is well cooled, add the whipped cream, and with great dispatch to avoid congealing in lumps. Pour in glass bowls and ornament to suit the taste. If this receipt is closely followed, one need never fail in making this delicious desert.

423 :olate Charlotte Russe.

Soak in cold water for one hour one ounce of isinglass or Cox's gelatine; take three ounces of best chocolate, grate it, melt it in three tablespoonfuls of water and two of white sugar; let it cook smooth. Mix it into a pint of sweet cream, adding the soaked gelatine. Put all into the double boiler and let scald till the whole is melted. Then take off the fire and pour it upon the yolks of eight and whites of four eggs, which have been beaten light, with half a pound of sugar. Simmer the whole over the fire, but do not let it boil; then take it off and whip to a strong froth. Line molds with sponge cake, fill with the Charlotte and set on the ice.

424 A Charlotte a la Parisienne (Gateau Noyeau).

One large stale sponge cake, one cup of rich custard, one cup of sweet cream whipped, two tablespoonfuls of rose-water, one-half of a grated cocoanut, one-half pound of sweet almonds blanched and pounded, whites of four eggs beaten stiff, three tablespoonfuls of powdered sugar.

Cut the cake in horizontal slices the whole length of the loaf. They should be half an inch thick. Divide the whipped egg into two portions; into one stir the cocoanut with half the sugar; into the other the almond paste, with the rest of the sugar. Spread the slices with these mixtures, half with the cocoanut and half with the almond, and replace them in their original form, laying aside the top crust for a lid. Press all the sliced cake firmly together, that the slices may not slip, and with a sharp knife cut a deep cut out of the center down to the bottom slice, which must be left entire. Take out the rounds you have cut, leaving the walls an inch thick, and soak the part removed in a bowl with the custard. Rub it to a smooth batter, and whip it into the whipped cream, the rose-water in the almond paste will flavor it sufficiently. When it is a rich stiff cream, fill the cavity of the cake with it; put on the lid and then ice with the following: Whites of three eggs, one heaping cup of powdered sugar, juice of one lemon. Beat stiff, and cover the sides and top of the cake; set in a very cold place until needed. This is a delicious and elegant charlotte, which twenty-five years ago was called a "a Charlotte Polonaise."

425 Bavarian Cream (Our Own).

Take half a box of Nelson's or Cox's gelatine, pour over it half a teacup of cold water, let it soak one hour or more, then add two tablespoonfuls of boiling water and set the tin cup in which it is on the back part of the stove to thoroughly dissolve. Put a pint of rich milk or cream in your custard pail; let it come to a boil, add two heaping tablespoonfuls of pulverized sugar and the yolks of four eggs stirred together; beat and stir one moment over the fire; take off and pour into a bowl to cool, adding the half ounce of gelatine; then take one pint of very cold sweet cream, add to it one teaspoonful of extract of vanilla (Burnet's) and two heaping tablespoonfuls of pulverized sugar. Whip it to a froth, skim off the whipped cream and place it in a sieve to drain; whip and skim till it is all frothed. If by this time your custard is cold enough to begin to set, stir cream and custard rapidly together; if not thoroughly cooled set it on some ice broken up fine, and having half a teacup or more of salt sprinkled among it; the moment it begins to set stir quickly but delicately together the custard and whipped cream till well mixed; pour into a mold and set on ice or in a very cold place.

426 Mrs. Henderson's Bavarian Cream.

Sweeten with two heaping tablespoonfuls of sugar, and whip one pint of cream to a stiff froth, laying it on a sieve to drain.

Boil another pint of cream or rich milk with two heaping tablespoonfuls of sugar; take it off the fire and add half a box of Nelson's or Cox's gelatine (soaked for an hour in half a cupful of cold water in a warm place near the range; then add two tablespoonfuls boiling water and set over the steam of the teakettle till dissolved); when slightly cooled, stir in the yolks of four eggs well beaten; when it has become quite cold and begins to thicken, stir it without ceasing a few minutes until it is very smooth, then stir in the whipped cream lightly until it is well mixed. Put it into a mold or molds and set it on the ice or in a cool place. We prefer the preceding receipt, but as the effect is somewhat different, we give both as both are excellent.

427 Chocolate Bavarian Cream

Can be made as the preceding, by adding two sticks of chocolate grated (soaked and stirred smooth in two tablespoonfuls of boiling water) to the yolks of the eggs.

428 Spanish Cream.

Dissolve half a package of Cox's gelatine in half a pint of cold milk. Simmer a quart of milk; while hot on the stove pour in the gelatine, stirring till perfectly dissolved; add the beaten yolks of eight eggs, sugar and vanilla, as for a custard, and let them scald one minute or a little more. When done pour the mixture into a large dish containing the well-beaten whites of the eight eggs; stir briskly for one minute and pour into molds. It will fill two quarts and one pint. Our experience leads us to say that if milkman's milk and cream is used it is better not to soak the gelatine in milk, but water.

429 Spanish Cream.

One quart of milk, one and-a-half cups white sugar, one-quarter box shred gelatine, three eggs, one lemon, one gill of orange juice. Soak gelatine in one-half a coffee-cup of milk; boil one quart of milk and pour over the gelatine cautiously, a little at a time; turn the milk and gelatine on the sugar, yolks of eggs and orange (previously well beaten together) slowly, for fear of curdling stirring well. Beat the whites to a stiff froth, stir in a small one-half cup of sugar and the juice of one lemon. Spread this, like frosting, on top of the gelatine, milk, etc., with a wet knife, going round the rim of the dish first, covering gradually towards the center. Set in a quick oven only long enough to brown the frosting. It will be soft when taken from the oven, but quite stiff in a few hours or the following day, according to temperature. In winter it may be made two days before using. It is not stiff enough to turn out of a mold, but is set in a silver dish.

Mrs. J. E. P.

430 Almond Bavarian Cream.

Take three ounces of sweet and one of bitter almonds, blanch and skin them; put them into a pan on a moderate fire, stirring them continually. As soon as they have acquired a fine yellow color, take them off the fire, and when cold pound them into fine pieces; then add a pint of cream or rich milk nearly boiling and three or four heaping tablespoonfuls of sugar and half a package of gelatine, which has been soaked as before described. Put it upon the ice, and when about to thicken stir it until it is very smooth; then stir in lightly a pint of cream whipped and put it into a mold.

431 Riz de l'Imperatrice (Queen's Rice).

A large spoonful of rice, whitened in cold water; then put the rice in just enough milk to cook the rice properly. Take the yolks of four eggs and a cup of sugar, with a pint of milk, and cook like a custard. Mix the rice with the custard and set on the ice an hour and a half before dinner; add a pint of whipped cream and one-third of a box of gelatine and pour in a mold; before turning out of the mold, put some preserves in the bottom of the dish, and garnish the top with preserved cherries. This is the exact French receipt where something is preferred to rice: Use concentrated cocoanut, one teacup to the pint of milk; have the gelatine well dissolved and cool, but not cold, when added to the cream.

432 Bavaroise (Parisian Receipt).

A full pint of milk, four tablespoonfuls of ground coffee; cooked until well mixed, and strained through a jelly bag; add the yolks of four eggs, a cup of sugar, and cook as for a custard; set in the cold an hour and-a-half before dinner; add a pint of whipped cream, and gelatine one-half or a third of a box, the same amount as for Charlotte Russe.

Miss ANNE L.

433 Genoese Cream (Good).

One pint of milk, one tablespoonful of flour, four tablespoonfuls of sugar. Boil until it thickens slightly; add the yolks of three eggs and a piece of butter the size of an egg; flavor with lemon or vanilla. Cover the bottom of the dish with sponge cake, spreading one side of cake with currant or other jelly. Pour on the cream and dust the top with sugar.

434 Italian Cream.

Mix one pint of rich cream with half a pint of milk, sweeten to taste; add one teaspoon extract of bitter almond, one gill of rose-water. Beat these thoroughly together. Take one ounce of isinglass, break it small into a very little water and set it over a boiling teakettle until dissolved; strain and stir into the cream. Fill the molds and set in a cool place.

435 Her Majesty's Pudding.

One-third of a package of gelatine, yolks of four eggs, one quart of sweet milk, one cupful of sugar, one teaspoonful of vanilla. Soak the gelatine one hour in half a teacup of cold water. Beat the yolks of the eggs light with the sugar, stir them into the milk, letting it scald three minutes, but stirring constantly for fear of curdling; add the gelatine and vanilla, strain into molds and set aside four hours or more to thoroughly cool and stiffen.

SAUCES.—Whites of three eggs, four tablespoonfuls of cream and three of sugar. Beat the whites to a stiff froth, whip the cream light, add the whites of the eggs, and sugar and flavor with vanilla.—FROM MARGERY DAW.

436 Russian Cream.

One-half box of gelatine, cover it with cold water and let it stand one hour. Beat the yolks of four eggs and one cup of powdered sugar together; stir in the gelatine and pour all into one quart of boiling milk. Flavor with vanilla. Let it cool and then stir it into the whites of the eggs beaten to a stiff froth; pour into molds and let it stand four hours, when it will be ready to use.

437 Blanc-Mange.

This is an old-fashioned receipt, but after one has been cloyed on whipped cream, old-time blanc-mange will produce quite a new sensation.

Blanch four ounces of sweet almonds and half an ounce of bitter almonds; pound them in a wedgewood mortar, moistening them gradually with orange-flower water; mix this with one quart of fresh cream. Have the "largest half" of a box of Cox's gelatine soaking in half a cup of cold water one hour. Set your cream and almonds on the fire, stirring constantly; when it comes to a scald, pour in a scant teacup of sugar and the gelatine, and stir till it dissolves. Put in molds.

438 Cream a la Mode (Good).

Put half a pound of white sugar into a deep glass dish; the juice of one large orange and one lemon; to one ounce of isinglass add one pint of water; let it simmer down one-half, and when cool and beginning to set strain it on the above, and by degrees add one and a-half pints of cream, that have been well whipped; stir till cool and place it on ice to stiffen.

439 Tapioca Cream.

Three-fourths of one cup of tapioca; add to it sufficient milk to make it soft, say one pint, and soak eight hours; then take one quart of milk, let it boil for a few minutes; beat three eggs, whites and yokes separately, stir the yolks into one cup of sugar and then the milk, and, when it begins to boil, add the tapioca; let it boil up and make sure it is thoroughly cooked, then stir the whites very evenly through it. Flavor to taste; eat cold.

440 Peach Meringue.

Cut up peaches and put in the bottom of a dish; sprinkle them with sugar. Make an icing of the whites of three eggs and three-fourths of a cup of sugar, spread over the peaches and bake a few minutes. Canned peaches cooked in a rich syrup and then skimmed out of it and treated in this way, makes a pleasant desert.

441 Orange Souffle.

Two oranges peeled and cut in thin slices in your pudding-dish, with sugar sprinkled over them, and let stand an hour. Make a custard with the yolks of four eggs and one pint of milk, sweetened to taste, (about half a cup of sugar); pour over the oranges boiling hot. Beat the whites to a stiff froth with five tablespoonfuls of pulverized sugar, spread over the top of the custard; set the dish in a pan of water and put in the oven until it is a lovely brown.

442 Fruit Charlotte.

Line a dish with sponge cake, place upon the bottom, in the center of the dish, grated pine-apple; cover with a whipped cream charlotte. Keep back a little of the cream to pour over the top after it is turned out of the mold.

ICE CREAMS.

We have lived so much in the country that years ago we gave our mind to the simplification of making ice cream. We like a patent freezer; almost all are good, especially those that have not too much machinery, but we can make mighty good cream with a tall four-quart tin pail and an ordinary wooden bucket. Any of the receipts given are good. All cream is the richest—the flour, milk and whites of eggs with part cream is the next—the frozen custard is thoroughly digestible and an excellent and economical receipt. To freeze ice cream or water ices quickly and well: 1st. Have your cream or custard on the ice for two or three hours before you are ready to use it; flavor and sweeten the former when you are prepared to freeze it. 2nd. Take a fifteen-pound lump of ice, put it into an old bag or coffee sack, have at your hand three pints of coarse salt; then take the flat of the axe or a mallet, or, if you have neither, and are a woman, a great deal may be accomplished with a flat-iron, pound the ice *fine*, empty it out of the bag into an old dishpan or tub, pour over the salt, take your short-handled stove shovel or a scoop, mix all thoroughly and fill round the ice cream freezer after it has been properly placed in the tub, packing down with a wooden spade; then pour your cream into the freezer, stir and beat well while freezing; after it is pretty stiff, cover with a woolen cloth for one hour.

443 Ice Cream.

To one quart of cream take one heaping teacupful of sugar, grate in one-quarter of a vanilla bean, or two teaspoonfuls of extract of vanilla, strain it and put it into your freezer; add the whites of two eggs beaten very light, with three tablespoonfuls of powdered sugar to stiffen them. Freeze. N. B.—If your cream is not very rich, boil a little milk, sweeten it, beat two eggs very light and stir in and cook like soft custard. The flavor will perhaps be better if the vanilla bean is boiled a few minutes in a little milk, which may be added to the cream when cool.

In Pennsylvania the cream is always allowed to scald and cool before using, and this ought always to be done when the cream is for an invalid.

444 Ice Cream.

Three pints sweet cream, one quart of new milk, one pint of powdered sugar; put in a freezer till thoroughly chilled through, then add the whites of two eggs beaten light, and having three tablespoonfuls of powdered sugar in them, then freeze.

445 Ice Cream, No. 2.

Boil two quarts of milk, into which stir a pint of cold milk that has had four level tablespoonfuls of arrowroot or corn starch mixed smoothly into it, then scald, but not boil; when cold, add two quarts of cream, a tablespoonful of vanilla or other flavoring, and two pounds (or pints) of sugar; put in the freezer and whip till well chilled, then add the whites of six eggs, beaten to a stiff froth.

446 White Ice Cream.

Three pints of milk, whites of four eggs beaten light, three tablespoonfuls of arrowroot mixed in a little cold water and added to the eggs. Boil the milk and pour over the eggs, then set over the fire and stir till it thickens a little; when nearly cold, add a quart of cream, sweeten and flavor to the taste. We allow a cupful of sugar and a teaspoonful of vanilla, Burnet's extract, to every quart. If you have no arrowroot, use half a teacup of flour, let it boil well, and then strain well.

447 Vanilla Ice Cream—Miss Parloa.

This receipt is admirable if anyone likes so rich a combination, and can be made by a boy of twelve. The foundation given in this rule is suitable for all kinds of ice cream:

One generous pint of milk, one cupful of sugar, half a cupful of flour, *scant*, two eggs, one quart of cream, one tablespoonful of vanilla extract, and when the cream is added, another teacupful of sugar. Let the milk come to a boil. Beat the first cupful of sugar, the flour and eggs together, and stir into the boiling milk. Cook twenty minutes, stirring often, strain and set away to cool, and when cool add the sugar, cream and seasoning, and freeze.

448 Caramel Ice Cream.

Take two pints of brown sugar, put it in an iron skillet over a brisk fire until it is dissolved, stirring it constantly to prevent its burning; have a pint of milk at boiling point and stir a little of this at a time into the sugar, as it shows a disposition to scorch. Strain it, and when cool add it to three quarts of pure cream well beaten in the freezer, and freeze.

449 Norvell House Caramel Ice Cream.

Four quarts of pure cream, four heaping cups of powdered sugar, five tablespoonfuls of caramel; mix and freeze hard.

450 Caramel Custard Ice Cream.

Make two quarts of rich boiled custard, substituting for sugar one pint of brown sugar, treated as in caramel ice cream No. 1; freeze.

451 Biscuit Glace.

To half a pound of powdered sugar add the yolks of four eggs and vanilla flavor; beat well and then take two quarts of well whipped cream, and mix with sugar and yolks; color some of it red and spread on the bottom of paper capsules and fill up with the fresh cream. Then put them in a tin box, with cover, and pack well up on all sides with pounded ice and salt. Let stand for two hours; it is then ready for use.

The above receipt was procured from the French cook at the St. Nicholas Hotel, New York, where biscuits glace reach a perfection that cannot be excelled by any confectioner.

45   Chocolate Ice.

Grate four heaping tablespoonfuls of Maillard's triple vanilla chocolate; stir it smooth with two tablespoonfuls of hot water and the yolks of two eggs, put in a double boiler half a pint of boiling water, one teacup and-a-half of sugar; stir well for three or five minutes; then pour in a quart of milk that is at a keen boil; stir three minutes; take off the fire and add the beaten whites of the two eggs. Strain. Let get very cold and freeze.

453   Chocolate Ice Cream.

Six tablespoonfuls grated chocolate, one quart milk, two tablespoonfuls corn starch, two cups sugar, one quart cream. Boil the milk, add corn starch, boil five minutes, add sugar and chocolate, strain, and add cream.

454   Bisque.

One-half gallon of freshly turned bonny clabber or milk that has soured and set, one-half gallon of rich sweet cream, a vanilla bean boiled in a half pint of sweet milk; sweeten. Churn five minutes before freezing. One can of condensed milk can be used with less clabber. This is a Virginia receipt, our own is somewhat similar, except that six hours before making the bisque we take two quarts of fresh milk, add to it a scant teacup of sugar, a teaspoonful of vanilla, and set it by stirring in two scant teaspoonfuls of liquid rennet, prepared by Wyth, of Philadelphia.

WATER ICES.

455 Water Ices.

We wish to say a word on the subject of water ices. If you desire them to freeze promptly and be rich and smooth, be careful to obey these directions:

Know what quantity you need for your freezer, and make your calculations accordingly. Take the requisite amount of water and sugar, in the proportion of one pint of sugar to one pint of water, and let them boil till they form a rich syrup; it will take quarter of an hour if made with boiling water, and longer if with cold water. Then set it away to get thoroughly cold; add to this your lemon juice, pine-apple, orange, raspberry, currant, etc. Allow the whites of three eggs to every two quarts of the mixture; whip them very light, and when the ice has been frozen till it is just ready to stiffen, stir in the whites of the eggs.

Confectioners never use white of egg, nor gelatine. The latter is detestable. A good water ice can be made without either.

456 Lemon Ice.

Take the juice of four large lemons, add about three pints of thin syrup made with about one pint of sugar. Into every quart when it begins to freeze, stir the whites of two eggs beaten very light, with a little powdered sugar. This will make it smooth. The word "about" is used in this receipt, because you must have a strong, rich lemon flavor, be the quantity more or less.

Any kind of water ice may be made in this way, by mixing the strained juice of the fruit, currant, raspberry, strawberry, etc., with syrup flavored to taste, and add the white of egg when it begins to freeze.

457 Lemon Ice.—Margery Daw.

One pint of lemon juice, four pints of water, one tablespoonful of gum arabic, dissolved in water, the rind of two or three lemons, the whites of three eggs, sugar to make sweeter than lemonade. Mix the lemon juice, water, sugar, gum arabic and the grated rind of the lemon. Just as it is beginning to be very cold in the freezer, add the whites of eggs beaten light. Do not strain, but let the rinds of the lemons remain.

N.B.—We fear we would disobey this last.

458 Pine-Apple Ice.

Two juicy ripe pine-apples, peeled and cut small; juice and zest or rubbed peel of two lemons, two pints sugar made into syrup with two pints of water. Strew some sugar over the pine-apple and lemon juice, and let it stand an hour or more; mash all up together and strain out the syrup through a bag; add the boiled syrup and freeze.

459 Pine-Apple Ice, No. 2.

One pine-apple cut fine, one pound sugar made into syrup, with one pint of boiling water. Let the mixture stand six hours, then strain and add one quart thin syrup, white of one egg and juice of one lemon. Freeze.

460 Iced Coffee.

One pint of strong coffee; one pint of rich cream; one-half a pound of sugar; then freeze.

461 Tutti Frutti.

When a rich vanilla cream is partly frozen, candied cherries, chopped raisins, chopped citron, or any other candied fruit chopped rather fine are added; add about half the quantity of fruit that there is of ice cream; mold and imbed in ice and salt.

462 Currant Ice

Is a very nice and pretty country dessert. Make a syrup of one quart of water and one pint of sugar; let it boil down; skim, and when cold add a pint of currant juice. When partly frozen stir in the beaten white of one egg and a-half teaspoonful of extract of nutmeg.

463 Frozen Strawberries—Very Nice.

Two quarts of nice fresh berries, one pint of sugar, one pint of water, juice of two lemons. Let the berries and sugar stand for an hour or two, and then rub through a sieve; add the water and lemon juice, and freeze as you would lemon ice.

464 Orange Ice.

Cut and sugar well six oranges, press them through a coarse sieve, add the juice of two lemons and three tablespoonfuls of gelatine soaked and stewed till smooth; pour this into a quart of rich boiled syrup, made as in receipt No. 455; freeze; or you may omit the gelatine and substitute the whites of two eggs, or one tablespoonful of gum arabic.

FROSTING.

If made properly will prove "sure every time." The secret in boiling frosting lies in knowing just when to take it off the stove.

465 Frosting.

To one cup of sugar I take the white of one egg, just cover the sugar with water and let it boil without stirring till it *ropes;* have the egg beaten, and when the sugar has boiled sufficiently stir into the egg and continue stirring till cool. If boiled too much, and the frosting is inclined to dry before cooling, it can be remedied by adding a drop or two of hot water.

466 Confectioners' Icing.

Beat the whites of two eggs with eight large spoonfuls of white sugar, place in a small pan and cook over the boiling teakettle for five minutes, stirring constantly; spread it on the cake with a knife, and as quickly as possible, as it hardens immediately.

467 Boiled Icing.

Four tablespoonfuls of hot water, half a pint of granulated sugar, the whites of two eggs, a quarter of a teaspoonful of citric acid (finely powdered). Put the water and the sugar together into a small saucepan; stir well together to moisten the sugar all through, and set it on the stove, where it will simmer slowly while you beat the eggs to a stiff froth; boil the syrup until it will thread when dropped from a spoon (or begins to candy), then pour it over the beaten eggs, beating briskly all the time. Continue beating until the mixture is thick and light, and nearly cold, then stir in the citric acid. Flavor same as cake, if desired.

468 Old-fashioned Frosting.

Whites of three eggs, one pound of powdered sugar, one-half teaspoonful of cream of tartar, a little flavoring. Put the whites of the eggs in a bowl with a little of the sugar, and beat with a wire spoon to a froth, then add the sugar and the cream of tartar, a little at a time, beating constantly until when the frosting is dropped from the spoon the drops retain their form, add the flavoring. If the quantity of sugar given is not sufficient, add more. This receipt is enough for two cakes. One or two drops of boiling water makes icing smoother for the outside coat.

Pink frosting is very effective on some cakes; it can be obtained by adding a few drops of cochineal syrup to plain frosting.

CAKES.

General Directions for Mixing Cake—From Mrs. Welch's Book.

First, get everything that will be needed ready before the mixing begins—the pans lined with paper and greased—bowls, spoons, egg-beater, grater, sifted flour, weighed or measured ready for use, milk, eggs, sugar, etc., should be close at hand. The oven, too, should be at the proper temperature and all things so arranged that when once the eggs are broken and the mixing actually begun, nothing need interrupt or delay proceedings until the process is complete and the cake in the oven. Flour should be sifted before measured, unless the contrary is expressly advised; if baking powder is to be used, that should be sifted with the flour; soda and cream of tartar should both be added dry to the flour, and perfectly distributed through it by several siftings; cups or measures should not be heaped. When all things are ready, the order of mixing, is, in general, as follows:

1. Cream the butter.
2. Mix with it the sugar, and blend both together until they make a smooth, light paste.
3. The beaten yolks of the eggs are next added.
4. Stir in a little flour, then add a part of the milk, then flour, then milk, until all the milk has been added. This process should use at least half the flour.
5. The flavoring extracts come next.
6. Sift in gradually a part of the remaining flour; add the whites of the eggs well beaten, and at the same time the remainder of the flour.
7. All cake should be put at first into a moderate oven, so that it may have a chance to rise before the crust begins to form.

N. B.—Two-thirds of the art of cake making is in the management of your oven, and to attain that knowledge requires patience, perseverance, and practice.

469 Black Wedding Cake.

Thirteen pounds raisins, five pounds currants, three pounds candied lemon, three pounds citron, four pounds butter, six pounds sugar, thirty-six eggs, one pint molasses, four pounds flour, two ounces mace, half ounce nutmeg, half box cinnamon, half box cloves, two and-a-half pints strong coffee.—Mrs. Lewis Davenport.

470 Excellent Fruit Cake.—Good.

One cup of brown sugar, one-half cup of butter, one cup of molasses, one-half cup of sour milk, two and one-half cups of flour, yolks of four eggs, cloves, allspice, cinnamon and nutmeg, each one-half teaspoonful, and one teaspoonful bicarbonate of soda added to the milk. Then stir in one pound of raisins, one pound of currants, one-quarter of a pound of citron, all well dredged with one teacup of flour.

471 Mrs. H. M. D.'s Reliable Fruit Cake.—Good.

One pound of light brown sugar, ten ounces of butter, eight eggs, broken into the butter and sugar, after it has been stirred to a cream; one tablespoon rose-water, one teaspoonful ext. bitter almonds (Burnet's), one teaspoonful of baking powder in one pound of flour and two pounds of raisins, mace and nutmeg; pour into a pan till half the quantity required is in, then cut slips of citron, dredge them with flour, sprinkle on the top of the batter, put in another layer, and repeat, this being an excellent way of putting in the citron; finish with a layer of the cake batter and bake forty-five minutes, or more.

472 Imperial Cake.

One pound of sugar and one pound of butter, stirred to a cream, then beaten yolks of ten eggs, grated rind and juice of one lemon, then one pound of flour and the stiff whites of the eggs; have prepared beforehand one pound of almonds, blanched and split (or if you prefer, pounded), one-half pound of raisins stoned and halved, and one-half pound of citron cut in thin slips; have these well dredged with two tablespoonfuls of extra flour, one tablespoonful of extract of nectarine in one teaspoonful of water, and one tablespoonful of rose-water and one of orange-flower water. This is a delicious cake, and when cut is very distinguished-looking; will keep a long time.

473 White Fruit Cake—Very Nice.

One cup of butter, two cups of sugar, one cup of milk, four cups of flour, whites of six eggs, four very small teaspoons of baking powder, two coffee-cups of raisins, boiled, drained dry, and stoned, and then rolled in flour, citron, if you like. After all is mixed, beat very hard.

Miss Carrie S——.

474 Loaf or Bread Cake.

Two pounds of light dough, one pound of sugar, one-half pound of butter, three eggs, and one teaspoonful of saleratus. Rub the butter and sugar together, then add the eggs, well beaten, and the saleratus. Work the mixture thoroughly into the dough, until it is entirely smooth. Flavor with one teaspoonful of ground mace and one grated nutmeg, three teaspoonfuls of molasses, a coffee-cupful of seeded raisins. A few thin bits of citron are an improvement. Put it to rise as soon as mixed and bake in a slow oven, and bake about one hour. This will make two ordinary sized loaves; and if frosted is nearly as good as the old-times Connecticut election cake. Use extra flour for dredging the fruits, and add half a teacupful if the dough seems soft.

475 Rich Bread Cake.

Four cups of light dough, two cups of sugar, one cup of butter, three eggs, one cup of raisins, well floured, a little nutmeg, half a teaspoon cloves and the same of cinnamon, half a teaspoonful of soda dissolved in hot water. Let it rise a short time before baking; then put in the raisins and bake in a very slow oven.

476 Aunt Fanny's Loaf Cake.

Six teacups of bread dough, five eggs, three teacups of sugar, one cup of butter, two teaspoonfuls of ground cloves and cinnamon mixed, half a nutmeg, one and-a-half pounds of raisins. Bake in a moderate oven.

477 Short Bread—The True Scotch Receipt.

Four pounds of flour, two and-a-half pounds of butter, one and one-quarter pounds of sugar, one wine-glass of rose-water, one-half pound of caraway comfits and one-half pound of citron. Rub the butter and sugar to a cream, add the rose-water and then the flour, roll out to rather less than half an inch in thickness, and strew over the top the candy comfits and the citron cut in thin pieces the size of your thumb nail, pass your rolling-pin over this and then cut out into squares and diamonds with a paste-jigger, and bake in a dripping-pan; it will keep nice and fresh two or three months. This receipt has been in an old Scotch family for more than three-quarters of a century, and has always been the New Year's cake in the old-fashioned Knickerbocker visitations on that day. The candy and citron make it a very handsome-looking cake, as well as delightful in flavor.

478 Election Cake.

Eight coffee-cups of flour, three pints of milk, three cups shortening (two of butter, one of lard), four cups of sugar, six eggs, two oranges, one and-a-half pounds of raisins, half pound citron, one yeast cake or one cup of liquid yeast, four nutmegs, one tablespoonful of salt. If a yeast cake is used dissolve it well, make a sponge of it (do the same with liquid yeast), and some of the flour about noon. Beat part of the butter and sugar to a cream, and when the sponge is light add it to it, and let it rise until very light. About nine o'clock add the rest of the butter and sugar, well beaten, and other ingredients (like other cake, only using the hands and beating thoroughly), saving out part of citron and raisins until morning, then add them, put into pans (seven) and stand until very light. Bake about one hour.   COUSIN ANNIE DWIGHT.

479 Good Pound Cake—Miss Beecher.

One pound powdered sugar, one pound sifted flour, three-quarters of a pound of butter, eight eggs and one nutmeg; rub sugar and butter to a cream, then add yolks, spice, and part of the flour; add the whites with the rest of the flour.

480 Delicate Cake.

One cup of butter beaten to a cream, with two of sugar; add the whites of eight eggs beaten to a stiff froth, and three and one-third cups of unsifted flour, in which has been mixed one teaspoonful of baking powder; then sieve the flour twice, add one teaspoonful of essence of bitter almond.

481 Delicate Cake.

One cup of butter, one cup of corn starch, two cups of sugar, two cups of flour, one cup of sweet milk, the whites of seven eggs, three teaspoons of baking powder, and flavor with almond.
   MRS. GERTRUDE MANNING DELAND.

482 Mrs. Henderson's Delicate Cake.

Of this receipt Mrs. Welch says: "I have tried it many times, and always with success. The cake is mixed contrary to the usual rules."

INGREDIENTS.—Whites of six eggs, scant three-quarters of a cupful of butter, one and one-quarter cupfuls of pulverized sugar, two cupfuls of flour, juice of half a lemon, one-quarter of a teaspoonful of soda. If soda is used, mix it well with flour and pass it through the sieve several times to distribute it equally. Beat the butter to a light cream, and add the flour to it, stirring it in gradually with the ends of the fingers until it is a smooth paste. Beat the whites of the six eggs to a stiff froth, and mix in them the pulverized sugar; now stir the egg and sugar gradually into the flour and butter, adding also the lemon juice, and mix it smoothly together with the egg whisp. As soon as it is perfectly smooth put it into the oven, the heat of which should be rather moderate at first. When done, and still hot, spread over it a frosting made in the following manner: Use a heaping teacupful of fine pulverized sugar to the white of each egg, or say a pound of sugar to the whites of three eggs. Beat the eggs until they are *foaming* only; do not beat them to a froth. The sugar may all be poured on the egg at once, or if considered easier to mix, it may be gradually added. Either way, as soon as the sugar and eggs are thoroughly stirred together, and flavored with a little vanilla or lemon, the icing is ready to spread over the cake. The icing made with the white of one egg is quite sufficient to frost an ordinary sized cake. This cake may be made with one teaspoonful of baking powder, or with prepared flour, or with one-quarter teaspoonful of soda, and one-half teaspoonful cream of tartar, when the essence of lemon should be used instead of lemon juice.

483 Angel's Food.

Whites of eleven eggs, one and one-half tumblers granulated sugar, one tumbler sifted flour, one teaspoonful of extract of vanilla, one teaspoonful cream tartar. Sift the flour four times, then add cream of tartar, and sift again, but have only one tumbler after sifting; sift the sugar and measure; beat the eggs to a stiff froth, add sugar lightly, then the flour very gently, then vanilla. Do not stop beating till you put all in the pan. Bake forty minutes in moderate oven, try with straw; if too soft let it remain a few minutes longer. Turn pan upside down to cool, and when cold take out by loosening around the sides with a knife. Use a pan that has never been greased. The tumbler for measuring must hold two and three-quarters gills. Beat eggs on a large platter, and mix the batter on same platter.

484 Angel's Food.

Whites of eleven eggs, one and-a-half tumblers granulated sugar, one tumbler of sifted flour, one teaspoonful cream of tartar, one teaspoonful vanilla extract, sift flour once, beat the eggs to stiff froth, add the sugar, stir as little as possible, then half of the flour, reserving the other half to stir the cream of tartar into; add vanilla, then the cream of tartar and flour. The trouble with this cake is that people are under the impression that after the ingredients are added, it requires a great deal of beating, which is very apt to make it tough. The less you stir it, the more ft and spongy it will be.

Mrs Allan S.'s " Lizzie."

485 Angel's Food.

Half a pint of sifted flour, one even teaspoonful of corn starch, three even teaspoonfuls of cream of tartar, four tablespoonfuls of hot water, one cup and-a-half of granulated sugar, the whites of eleven eggs, half a teaspoonful of salt, one teaspoonful of flavoring; sift the flour, corn starch, and cream of tartar together through a *very fine* sieve; put the water and sugar in a saucepan, stir well together; put it on the stove and let it simmer slowly while you beat the eggs; sprinkle the salt over the whites of the eggs and beat them to a stiff froth. Boil the syrup until it will thread, and pour it slowly over the beaten eggs; beat all briskly until the mixture is light and cool; then sift the flour over it, little at a time, and stir it gently until all the flour is in and the batter is free from lumps; stir in the flavoring, and pour the batter into a three-quart pan with a tube in the center; bake in a moderate oven about forty minutes. Stick a straw into the cake, if it comes out clean, the cake is done. Turn the pan upside down and let it rest on the table until the cake is nearly cold, then remove it from the pan and place it bottom up on a large flat plate. Cover with boiled icing.

N. B.—In making the Angel's Food, the beating and mixing must all be done with a wire-spoon egg-beater (not a Dover). The eggs must be very cold. Grease the pan very slightly—do not use a piece of butter larger than a pea; do not cut this cake until it is ten or twelve hours old. Better when two days old. *Saw* the cake with the knife when cutting it. Mrs. Pitkin, Chicago.

486 Sunshine Cake.

The whites of ten eggs, the yolks of seven eggs, one tumbler of flour, one and one-half tumblers of granulated sugar, one teaspoonful of cream of tartar, juice and rind of one lemon, or one teaspoonful of extract of lemon, one-half teaspoonful of carbonate of ammonia. Beat the yolks and one-half tumbler of sugar very light; beat the whites to a stiff froth, beating in lightly the remainder of the sugar, then add the beaten yolks and sugar and flavoring; stir in the flour lightly, adding the ammonia last. Bake in a tin the same as Angel's Food, without greasing it; sift the sugar once and the flour four times; turn the tin upside down to cool, as in Angel's Food.—MARGERY DAW.

N. B.—Carbonate of ammonia can be powdered fine and dissolved in the lemon juice, or sprinkled over and stirred into the batter the last thing.

487 Queen Cake—A Delicious Cake.

One heaping cupful of butter, two and-a-half teacups of sugar, four teacups of unsifted flour, one teacup of sweet cream, two teaspoonfuls of baking powder, yolks of five and whites of three eggs.

488 Miss Eliza Horner's Queen Cake.

Two teacupfuls of butter, three teacupfuls of sugar, one teacupful of sweet cream, five teacupfuls of flour, six eggs, three teaspoonfuls of baking powder.—MARGERY DAW.

LAYER CAKES.

The following receipts for Layer Cakes are arranged so that the cake maker can select the style of cake wished.

Cakes Nos. 1 and 2 are made with butter, and the whites and yolks of the eggs, or what we might call a Pound Cake basis.

Cake No. 3 has a Delicate or White Cake basis of butter, sugar, and the whites only of the eggs.

Cake No. 4 has an Angel's Food basis, that is, no butter, and only whites of eggs, sugar and milk.

Cake No. 5, a Sponge Cake basis of whites and yolks of eggs, and sugar; no butter.

The appropriate fillings follow each cake, and the cake maker can select whichever one she prefers.

489 Chocolate Cake. No. I.

One full cup of butter, two cups of sugar, three and-a-half cups of flour, one scant cup of milk, one-half teaspoonful of bicarbonate of soda, one and one-half teaspoonfuls of cream of tartar, five eggs, leaving out the whites of two. Rub your butter and sugar (which, if pulverized, makes the best cakes), to a cream, and add the eggs, then two-thirds of the milk, then the flour, having the cream of tartar mixed with it; then the remainder of the milk in which you have dissolved the soda. Pour into two dripping-pans and bake so that the cake is an inch thick. While hot, and as soon as turned out on a cake-box, tray, waiter, or any other flat surface, spread with an icing.

Mrs. L.

490 Icing. No. 1.

Beat the whites of two eggs to a stiff froth, adding a cup and-a-half of pulverized sugar, six tablespoonfuls of grated chocolate, and two teaspoonfuls of essence of vanilla, lay one cake upon another, or else bake the batter in thin layers, spreading the icing between the layers and over the loaf.

Mrs. L.

491 Layer Cake. No. 2.

One-quarter of a pound of butter, one pound of granulated sugar, one pound of flour, less three tablespoonfuls, five eggs, one cup of milk, three teaspoonfuls of baking powder, flavor according to the filling used. Cream the butter, add the sugar, then the eggs, well beaten, then the flour, in which have the baking powder mixed, and then the milk. Bake in layers, spreading between them any of the following

FILLINGS

Which may be used with either of the above recipes.

492 Chocolate Icing. No. 2.

Whites of four eggs, beaten very little (they must not become white), add four ounces of grated chocolate, then add gradually fourteen ounces of pulverized sugar, mixing it well; flavor with vanilla.

493 Jelly. No. 3.

Spread currant or other jelly between layers and cover the loaf with icing.

494 Cream Filling. No. 4.

One pint of milk, three-quarters of a cup of granulated sugar, two eggs, three tablespoonfuls of corn starch. Let the milk come to a boil, reserving enough cold in which to mix the corn starch. Beat the eggs, add the sugar and beat very light; then add them to the boiling milk, add the corn starch and cook until thick enough. When cold flavor with vanilla. Spread between layers and cover the loaf with chocolate icing.

495 Orange Filling. No. 5.

Whites of three eggs beaten to a stiff froth; add one pound and-a-quarter of powdered sugar, the grated rind, soft pulp and juice of two sour oranges and one lemon (there should be one gill of juice). This will make it the right thickness for spreading the layers, but for covering the loaf sugar must be added to make it the thickness of ordinary icing. Then the top of the loaf may be decorated with quarters of an orange.

496 Cake No. 3.

One-half cup of butter, one and-a-half cups of granulated sugar, three cups of flour, one-half cup of sweet milk, whites of eight eggs, two teaspoonfuls of baking powder. Flavor; bake in layers and spread with any of the following fillings:

497 Almond Filling. No. 6.

One-half pint of sweet milk, one-third of a cup of granulated sugar, one egg, one and one-half tablespoonfuls of corn starch; beat eggs and sugar very light; add to the boiling milk, then add the corn starch, which must be mixed in a little of the cold milk. Cook until thick, then add half a cup of almonds blanched and chopped fine. When cold flavor with bitter almond and spread between the layers. Cover the loaf with plain icing flavored the same, and decorate the top with almonds.

498 Fig Filling. No. 7.

Brush the top of the layer with white of eggs, then spread it with chopped preserved figs and cover the loaf with plain icing; trim the top with wafers cut from the figs.

499 Cocoanut Filling. No. 8.

Whites of four eggs beaten to a stiff froth, add enough powdered sugar to make it as stiff as ordinary icing. Spread this and grated cocoanut between the layers, and cover the loaf with the same, or spread layers with chocolate icing No. 2, and cover loaf with the cocoanut.

500 Cake No. 4.

Whites of eleven large eggs, one tumbler of granulated sugar, one and-a-half tumblers of flour, one teaspoonful of cream of tartar, one teaspoonful of vanilla, a small pinch of salt. Beat the eggs very stiff, sift flour and sugar, in which have the cream of tartar mixed, six times, and add gradually to the eggs, then the vanilla. Stir very lightly. Bake in unbuttered layer-tins, and when cool spread icing between the layers and over the loaf, or else use either of the following

501 Almond Custard Filling. No. 9.

One-half pint of milk or cream. Boil and stir in the well-beaten yolks of three eggs, two tablespoonfuls of sugar, one teaspoonful of corn starch, dissolved in cold milk. Boil until thick. When cool, add one-half pound of blanched almonds, chopped fine, saving out two dozen to decorate the top. After putting the cream between cakes (which must be flavored with almond), ice the top and sides of the loaf, decorating the top with the whole almonds.

502 Charlotte Russe Filling. No. 10.

Spread between the layers Charlotte russe, and then ice the loaf with plain icing. This will be found very delicious.

503 Cake No. 5.

Make a plain sponge cake according to No. 515. Bake in layers and use fillings Nos. 5, 6, 9, 10, or the following

FILLINGS:

504 Orange Filling. No. 11.

Take the juice of two large oranges, coffee-cup of pulverized sugar, one egg. Mix the yolks of egg, sugar and juice together. Beat white of egg to stiff froth; stir in and spread between layers and ice the top and sides of loaf.

505 Marmalade Filling. No. 12.

Spread orange marmalade between layers of sponge cake and ice the loaf.

506 Ambrosia Cake.

Three-quarters of a cup of butter, two cups of sugar, one-half cup of milk, three cups of flour, four eggs, one teaspoonful of soda, two of cream tartar. Bake in layers.

FOR THE FILLING.—Mix together one cup of grated cocoanut, one cup of whipped cream, half the rind and juice of one orange, one well-beaten egg and half a cup of sugar. Spread this between the layers and on top of the loaf.

507 Pineapple Cake.

Two-thirds of a cup of butter, two cups of sugar, one-half cup of sweet milk, six eggs, three cups of flour, three teaspoonfuls of baking powder. Bake in two sheets. Put together with one pint of grated pineapple, and one grated cocoanut bound together with frosting.

508 Hickory Nut Cake.

One cup of butter, two cups of sugar, three and one-half cups of flour, white of four eggs, one cup of milk, two teaspoonfuls baking powder and one cup of chopped nut meats. Bake in layers and put together with chopped meats and frosting.

509 Minnehaha Cake.

One and one-half cups of sugar, half a cup of butter, three eggs, two teaspoonfuls of cream of tartar, one teaspoonful of soda, two heaping cups of flour, half a cup of milk or water. Mix the cream of tartar in the flour and the soda in the milk or water. Bake in three jelly cake pans.

FILLING FOR THE ABOVE.—One cup of sugar, two tablespoonfuls of water; boiled together until brittle when dropped into water; remove from fire and stir briskly into the well-beaten white of one egg, add to this one cup of stoned raisins chopped fine, or a cup of nuts. Spread between layers.

510 Ice Cream Cake.

Two and one-half cups of powdered sugar, one cup of butter, one cup of milk, four cups of flour, whites of nine eggs, three heaping teaspoonfuls of baking powder.

ICING.—Four cups powdered sugar, eight tablespoonfuls of water. Boil until it candies without stirring. Beat whites of four eggs to stiff froth, pour over them the candied sugar and beat until cold. Spread this between layers and over the loaf. Flavor cake and icing with vanilla or lemon, or bitter almond.   KALAMAZOO.

511 Delicate Fruit Cake—Very Nice.

Whites of five eggs, three-fourths of a cup of butter, two cups of sugar, one cup of milk, two and one-half cups of flour, three teaspoonfuls of baking powder, flavor with vanilla. Ordinary jelly cake tins are not deep enough for this cake. For the fruit cake two large baking spoons of this batter, one-half cup of chopped raisins, one-third of a cup of currants or citron, one-half cup of flour; put a teaspoonful of extract of nectarine in your cup, and molasses enough to half fill it, one teaspoon of mace, cinnamon and cloves mixed. Bake in three deep jelly tins, two white, one dark; put together with jelly, the dark cake in the middle.

512 Iowa Chocolate Cake. (Delicious).

One cupful of sugar, half a cupful of butter, half a cupful of sweet milk, two eggs beaten separately, two cupfuls of flour, one even teaspoonful of soda; for the chocolate two-thirds of a cup of grated chocolate, one cup of sugar, one-half cupful of sweet milk, yolk of one egg; flavor with one teaspoonful of extract of vanilla; cook as thick as cream; when cool mix this preparation with the dough. Bake in layers and put together with boiled frosting.

513 Mrs. Millard's Almond Cake.

Six eggs, two cups of sugar, one cup of butter, one cup sweet milk, two cups flour, two cups corn starch, two teaspoons baking powder. Flavor with vanilla.

CUSTARD—Blanch and pound one pound almonds, mix with them one cup thick sour cream with sugar to taste; take two eggs, beat the yolks very light, add them to cream and almonds with one tablespoon of corn starch. Flavor with vanilla. Beat the whites and sweeten to taste. Mix all well and spread between layers of cake, which must be cold. The custard must be very sweet.

514 Winnie's Caramel Cake.

Two cups of sugar, three-fourths of a cup of butter, three cups sifted flour, three-fourths of a cup of milk, the whites of six eggs, two teaspoonfuls baking powder. Bake in jelly cake tins, and put frosting between.

FROSTING.—Three large tablespoonfuls of grated chocolate, one cup of sugar, two tablespoonfuls of water; melt and thicken on the stove; spread between the layers and on top of the loaf. Flavor with one teaspoon of vanilla.

515 Maria's Jelly Cake.—Good.

Two cups of sugar, whites and yolks of six eggs, beaten separately, two cups of flour, three even teaspoonfuls of cream of tartar, one teaspoonful of soda dissolved in six tablespoonfuls of water, grated rind and half the juice of one lemon. Bake and spread with jelly in layers.

516 Custard Cake.—Good.

One cup of sugar, three eggs, three tablespoonfuls of melted butter, one and-a-half teaspoonfuls of baking powder, a half cup of sweet milk, one and-a-half cups of flour; baked in jelly tins; let it cool.

DRESSING.—One cup of milk, one teaspoonful of flour, two teaspoonfuls of corn starch, one egg, six teaspoonfuls of sugar; flavor to taste; spread like jelly. See Lemon Cocoanut Cake. MRS. L., 1856.

517 Jelly Roll.

Three eggs, one cupful of sugar, one cupful of flour, one teaspoonful of cream of tartar, half a teaspoonful of soda dissolved in milk. Bake in oblong "pie tins," turn out and spread with currant or grape jelly, then roll up compactly as possible.

518 Chocolate Eclairs.

Make a batter as for Boston cream cakes receipt; form it with the spoon on the baking pan in cakes four inches long and one and one-half inches wide; leave a space between. When baked and cold make an opening in the side and put in the cream, which must also be cold. Make the cream as follows: Break, dissolve and mix smoothly one ounce of chocolate with three tablespoonfuls of boiling water in a pint basin, set over a boiling teakettle, add gradually half a pint of milk, and leave it to scald; beat one egg and add it to one gill of sugar, and two even tablespoonfuls of corn starch; mix well and stir into the scalding milk; then put the whole into the basin over the boiling water, and stir till it is much thicker than boiled custard; add salt half as large as a pea, and half a teaspoonful of vanilla; after filling the cakes with the custard, frost with hot icing with two ounces of chocolate dissolved in it. Frost the top only.

519 New York Cream Cakes.

Two cups of flour, one cup of butter, one-half pint of water; boil the butter and water together, stir in gradually the flour while it is boiling. Let it cool, then add five eggs, one-quarter of a teaspoonful of soda. Drop from a spoon on buttered pans and bake in a quick oven.

For the dressing take one pint of milk, one-half cup of flour, one cup of sugar and two eggs. Wet the flour with a little cold milk and put with the eggs and sugar, and stir into the milk while boiling, until it thickens; open the cakes and fill with it.

520 Calico Cake.

Three cups of sugar, one and one-half cups of butter, six eggs, two-thirds of a cup of milk, one half teaspoonful of soda, one teaspoonful of cream of tartar, four cups of flour. Make half of the above with brown sugar, adding a little ground cloves, cinnamon and nutmeg, and one-half pound of dried currants. Make the other half with white sugar and the whites of the eggs. Put into your pans for baking alternate tablespoonfuls of the dark and light, and the effect will be novel and the cake palatable.

521 Honour K. Cake (Good).

One cup butter, two cups powdered sugar, three cups of flour, one cup sweet milk, four eggs, one-half teaspoon soda, one of cream tartar sifted with the flour.

When the cake is mixed, take out about a teacupful of the batter, and stir into this three great spoonfuls of grated chocolate; wet with a scant tablespoonful of milk. Fill your mold about an inch deep with the yellow batter, then drop upon this a spoonful of the dark mixture, spreading it in broken circles upon the lighter surface; proceed in this order till all is used.

522 Marble Cake.

LIGHT—One cup of sugar, half a cup each of butter and milk, the whites of three eggs, two cups of flour, one and a-half teaspoonfuls of baking powder.

DARK—Half a cup each of brown sugar and molasses, one-fourth cup each of butter and milk, two cups of flour, the yolks of three eggs, one and-a-half teaspoonfuls of baking powder, three teaspoonfuls of mixed spices; put the batter into the tin in alternate layers.

523 Watermelon Cake.

For the white part take two cups white sugar, two-thirds of a cup of butter, the same of sweet milk, the whites of five eggs, a heaping teaspoonful of baking powder sifted into three cups of flour, and any flavoring you prefer. For the red part, or the core of the melon, take one cup of red sugar sand, half a cup of butter, two-thirds of a cup of sweet milk, two cups of flour, one teaspoonful of baking powder, the whites of five eggs, and half a pound of raisins, or English currants, for the seeds. In filling the cake pan, put the white part outside and the red part inside. Just before putting it in the oven drop in your seeds here and there, where they belong.

524 Choice Fig Cake.

A large cup of butter, two and one-half of sugar, one of sweet milk, three pints of sifted flour with three teaspoonfuls of baking powder, whites of sixteen eggs, a pound and a quarter of figs well floured and cut in strips like citron; no flavoring.

525 Aunt Eliza's White Cake.

Two cups of sugar, a small half cup of butter, one cup of milk, three scant cups of flour, the whites of three eggs, three teaspoonfuls of baking powder; if in the season, boil three peach leaves in the milk, or add half a teaspoonful of extract of bitter almond, and one teaspoonful of water.

526 Coffee Cake.

Four eggs, two cups sugar, one cup of molasses, one cup of butter, one cup of hot coffee, four and one-half cups of flour, one teaspoonful of soda, two teaspoonfuls of cream of tartar, one-half cup of chopped raisins, cloves, nutmeg and cinnamon to the taste.

527 Coffee Cake—Excellent.

One cup of molasses, one cup of sugar, one cup of butter, one cup of strong hot coffee, one egg, one teaspoonful of saleratus in the molasses, one teaspoonful of cloves, two teaspoonfuls of cinnamon, and four and one-half cups of unsifted flour. Bake in loaves, or gem irons, or by the spoonful in a dripping-pan.

528 Leopard Cake.

Two cups white sugar, four eggs, one cup of butter, half a cup of sweet milk, half a teaspoonful of soda, one of cream of tartar. Stir with flour sufficiently, then take nearly half the mixture into another dish and add half a cup of molasses, three tablespoonfuls of milk, half a cup of flour, one cup of raisins or English currants, and cinnamon, cloves and nutmeg to suit the taste, and put in a spoonful of the dark and light alternately. Bake in a moderate oven.

529 Almond Cake.—Very Fine.

One-half cup of butter, two of sugar, two and-a-half of flour, three-quarters of a cup of sweet milk, one-half a teaspoonful of soda, one teaspoonful of cream of tartar, whites of eight eggs beaten to a stiff froth, one pound of soft shelled almonds blanched by steeping in boiling water till the skins are loose enough to remove, and then sliced or rolled, adding while crushing them, the juice of an orange, or two tablespoonfuls of orange-flower water; flavor with essence of bitter almond. Bake in a pan two inches deep.

530 Hickory Nut Cake.

Two teacups of white sugar, half a cup of butter, three cups of flour, three-quarters of a cup of sweet milk, a half teaspoonful of soda, dissolved in the milk, a teaspoonful of cream of tartar, put into the flour, the whites of eight eggs. Just before baking, add two teacupfuls of hickory nut meats.

531 Cream Cake.

Two eggs beaten in a coffee-cup; fill the remaining space up with rich sweet cream; one cup of sugar, one and-a-half cups flour. If the cream is sour, two teaspoons of baking powder; if sweet, three teaspoons of baking powder. Bake in two layers, and put jelly or chocolate between.— MISS CARRIE S.

532 Cream Cake.

One cup of sour cream, one and-one-half of sugar, two eggs, two tablespoonfuls of milk, two and-a-half cups of sifted flour, and one teaspoonful of saleratus. Beat the eggs and sugar together till very light; then dissolve the saleratus in the cream and stir it in with the flour. Add extract of nectarine, one teaspoonful of ground mace, and one grated nutmeg. Bake in shallow tins. Very nice baked in layers and put together with frosting.

533 Cold Water Sponge Cake.

Seven eggs, three cups of sugar, three cups of flour, three-quarters cup of water, two teaspoonfuls of baking powder, juice of one-half fresh lemon. Beat yolks and sugar together, light and creamy. Stir in water, then add flour with the baking powder mixed in. Lastly, whites of eggs and lemon juice.

534 Sponge Cake—Good.

One pound of sugar, half a pound of flour, ten eggs, the juice of one lemon and grated rind and a pinch of salt.

The yolks of the eggs, the sugar and lemon juice should be stirred hard together five minutes, the whites beaten separately, until they stand stiff. The whole should then be stirred slowly together, adding at the last the flour, and do not beat after it is mixed. No soda or cream of tartar should go into sponge cake, as they make it dry. The lemon is very essential, not only for the flavor, but to make it light. The oven should be pretty hot.

We give Mrs. Welch's process as differing from our own, and doubtless giving a little variety to the combination: Beat both yolks and whites very thoroughly; blend them lightly and quickly together; add the sugar gradually, then the lemon juice and rind and salt, and lastly the flour. Do not beat it after the flour is added. Bake in a moderate oven.

535 Delicious Sponge Cake.

Yolks of nineteen eggs, fifteen ounces of sugar, eight ounces of corn starch, whites of nine eggs, one teaspoonful extract of bitter almond or nectarine. Beat the yolks of the eggs till very light and white; add the sugar, stir till very smooth, then very gradually the corn starch, and lastly the well-beaten whites. Butter the pan for baking the cake, sift or sprinkle finely rolled cracker crumbs over the butter, pour in the cake, which, with this management, will never stick.

536 Hot Sponge Cake.

Two large cups of coffee sugar, eight tablespoonfuls of cold water, put on the stove and boil; six eggs, the whites and yolks beaten separately and then together in the boiling syrup, stirring briskly all the time; when cool add two cups of sifted flour and the rind and juice of a fresh lemon.

537 Hot Water Sponge Cake.

One cup of sugar and two eggs well beaten together, one teaspoon of baking powder sifted with one cup of flour; stir well together, then stir in one-third cup boiling water or milk; bake quickly in a buttered tin. If these directions are followed carefully, the cake will be "just lovely."

538 Boston Cream Cake.

One-half pint of water, one-quarter of a pound of butter, six ounces of flour and five eggs. Boil the butter and water together, adding the flour while the above is boiling. When thoroughly stirred take it from the fire, and when it is cold add the eggs, one at a time, beating the mixture until it is entirely free from lumps. Dissolve soda in the proportion of one teaspoonful to one cup of water, with which wet the baking-pan, on which the mixture is to be dropped in round places the size of a cream cake. Bake twenty minutes in a hot oven; avoid opening the oven door while baking. When cool, open them on one side and fill with the following mixture: One cup of sugar, one-half cup of flour, two eggs and one pint of milk. Beat the eggs, sugar and flour together and stir them into the milk while it is boiling, stirring constantly until it thickens. When it is cold flavor to suit the taste. We like extract of nectarine.

539 Jamaica Plains Lemon Cake.—Try.

Five eggs, three cups of sugar, one cup of butter, one of milk, five of sifted flour, one lemon rind grated, half a teaspoonful of soda dissolved well in the milk, and one teaspoonful of cream of tartar in the flour; after all is well beaten, add the juice of the lemon and bake immediately.

540 Mrs. B.'s Receipt for Washington Cake.

Two-pounds of flour, one and one-half pounds of sugar, three-quarters of a pound of butter, one scant pint of milk, to which add one teaspoonful home-made extract lemon, five eggs, two large teaspoonfuls of baking powder, and two pounds of raisins, upon which scatter spices and flour well rubbed upon the fruit.

541 Composition Cake.

One and three-fourths pounds of flour, one and one-half pounds of sugar, three-fourths pound of butter, one pint of milk, five eggs, two nutmegs, two pounds of raisins, two pounds of currants, one teaspoonful of soda. This will make four or five loaves.

542 Mother's Rich Cup Cake.

Five cups of flour, two and one-half cups of sugar, one and one-half cups of butter, one cup of milk, six eggs, one teaspoonful of soda, two teaspoonfuls of cream of tartar. Flavor with lemon or vanilla.

543 Burwick Sponge Cake.

Six eggs beaten five minutes, three cups sugar beaten five minutes longer, two cups flour first. Then add one cup of cold water, juice of one lemon in the water, and rind grated, two cups more of flour, two heaping teaspoons of baking powder.—L.

544 Jumbles.

One-half cup butter, one cup sugar, two eggs, one-half teaspoon soda, one-half teaspoon extract of lemon, flour enough to roll out.

545 Dora's Cake.

Mix together two teacupfuls of white powdered sugar, one-half cup of butter, then add the whites of four eggs, beaten to a stiff froth; add to this one teacupful of cold water. After it is well mixed, stir in three teacupfuls of flour, in which has been thoroughly mixed two teaspoonfuls of baking powder.

546 French Cake.

One cup of sugar, one-quarter of a cup of butter, one-half a cup of sweet milk, two eggs well beaten, one and-a-half cups of flour, one teaspoonful of cream of tartar, one-half teaspoonful of soda, one cup of currants, a few slices of citron and a little mace. Bake in a shallow pan; frost and cut in square pieces.

547 Water Sponge Cake.

Three eggs, one and-one-half cups of sugar, two cups of flour, one-half cup of cold water, one teaspoonful of cream of tartar and one-half teaspoonful of saleratus. Beat the sugar and eggs together until very light, then add the water, then the flour in which mix the saleratus and cream of tartar. Flavor with lemon and bake in a quick oven twenty minutes. This will make two sheets of cake.

Miss MAY T.

548 Spice Cake.

Three-quarters of a pound of butter, one pound of brown sugar, one pound of flour, one cup of sour milk, one teaspoonful of soda, five eggs, one tablespoonful of cinnamon, one-half teaspoonful of cloves, half a nutmeg, one pound of stoned raisins and one pound of currants.

549 Clove Cake.

One pound of brown sugar, one pound of flour, one pound of raisins, one-half pound of butter, one cup of milk, two large teaspoonfuls of baking powder stirred well in the flour, one tablespoonful of cloves, one tablespoonful of cinnamon, one tablespoonful of nutmeg, four eggs; chop the raisins.

(For lesser quantity, divide proportionately).

550 Golden Pound Cake.

One pound of flour, one pound of sugar, three-quarters of a pound of butter, yolks only of fourteen eggs, the juice and rind of two lemons. Cream the butter and sugar, add the yolks, well beaten and strained; now add the grated rind of the lemon and flour, dissolve one teaspoonful of carbonate of ammonia in a little hot water, taking care to cut it well and beat it into the mixture, add the lemon juice just before putting into pans, beating thoroughly.

N. B.—This is an excellent counterpart for Angel's Food, as it utilizes the yolks of the eggs and makes a pleasant contrast. MARGERY DAW.

551 Hickory Nut Macaroons.

One pound of powdered sugar, one pound of nut meats, chopped fine, whites of five unbeaten eggs; one tablespoon of flour, two small teaspoons of baking powder.

MARGERY DAW.

552 Grove Cake.

Two and-a-half cups of sugar, one cup of butter, one cup of sweet milk, four and-a-half cups of flour, eight eggs, omitting the yolks of four; two teaspoonfuls of Snowflake baking powder.

553 Zucker Kuchen (Sugar Cake.)

Take bread dough, as large as a good-sized loaf; one pint of milk, a small cup of butter, two handfuls of sugar, and a teaspoonful of cinnamon. Mix the butter in the milk, on the stove; make a hole in the dough, put in the sugar and two eggs; then add the warm milk and butter, mix well, add flour enough to make a light dough; let it rise again. Roll it out one and one-half inches thick; put in a dripping pan; beat light one egg and spread it over the top; lay on pieces of butter, raisins and chopped almonds, and sifted cinnamon and sugar on the top. Bake in a hot oven fifteen or sixteen minutes.

554 Berlin Kaffee Kuchen.

One pound of light raised dough, one ounce of sugar and three of butter, one egg; cream the butter and beat well with the sugar and the egg; add the dough and mix thoroughly with the hand; put it in a warm place to rise; when light pour it in a small dripping-pan (when baked it should not be more than two-thirds of an inch thick), and let it stand ten or fifteen minutes; put in the oven, and while baking prepare the icing. Blanch two dozen almonds and shred them; add to the beaten whites of two eggs about half the usual quantity of sugar, stir in the almonds, and when the cake is baked cover it with the icing and let dry in the mouth of the oven. The almonds may brown a little if liked.

555 Coffee Cake (for either Breakfast or Tea).

Three cups of light sponge of bread dough before flour is added for the first molding, one cup sugar, one cup of half lard and half butter, one cup currants, teaspoonful soda; add a few raisins, if wished. Put it in a long cake-pan to rise, when light have melted some butter and sugar, cover the top of the cake and sprinkle over it thickly ground cinnamon. Omit the raisins and currants for ordinary use.

556 Gold and Silver Cake.

A simple but good recipe. One-half cup butter, one cup sugar, one and one-half cups of sifted flour, one-half cup of sweet milk, one and one-half teaspoons baking powder, vanilla for flavoring, whites of four eggs; beat the butter and sugar to a cream, then add the flour and milk, then the flavoring, and lastly the whites of eggs beaten to a stiff froth. The golden cake made the same, only substituting the yolks for whites, and lemon for vanilla flavoring. This makes two nice loaves, and is a really delicious cake.

557 Currant Short Cake—Good.

We like better than strawberry. String and sugar a quart of currants, take a quart of flour, mix well in it a large tablespoonful of butter, a tablespoonful of Snowflake baking powder, and a little salt; add milk enough to make a soft biscuit dough, roll it out three-quarters of an inch thick, and put it into dripping-pans eight by twelve inches, as this is a good size to cut. Bake immediately, when partially done, brush over with milk, and the moment it is baked, turn out on to a platter, and with your carving knife open right through the center; spread well with butter the top and bottom crust, then put in your currants, strawberries or raspberries, sprinkle some more sugar over, put on the top crust, and return to the oven for ten minutes to soak.

We consider sweet cream essential for eating with these short cakes, but many people do not mind its absence.

Strawberry short cake is made as above, except that you mash one-half the strawberries and leave the other half whole.

558 Lemon Hasty Cake—Good.

Three eggs, whites and yolks separated; stir the yolks into a teacup of pulverized sugar till the mixture is very light, add half the grated rind and all the juice of one lemon, the three whites beaten to a stiff froth, one heaping teacup of sifted flour, into which a teaspoonful of baking powder has been well mixed; stir the flour in very slowly, and bake in a quick oven; slack baking makes it richer.

559 Quick Loaf Cake.

One-half pound butter, one teacup of milk, one pound of flour, one nutmeg, three-quarters of a pound of sugar, one teacup of raisins, three eggs, citron to taste, two and-a-half teaspoons of baking powder, a little salt, two tablespoonfuls of strong coffee. Mix and bake immediately in two loaves.

560 White Mountain Cake.

One cup of butter, two cups sugar, four cups of flour, one cup milk, whites of five eggs, three teaspoonfuls of baking powder. Miss May T.

561 Lemon Cocoanut Cakes.

Two cups sugar, one cup butter, one cup sweet milk, four eggs, three teaspoonfuls baking powder, four cups flour, and bake in layers. To put between the layers: one cocoanut grated fine, one-half pound sugar, rind and juice of one lemon, and two eggs beaten together. Mix and cook until the eggs thicken; stir all the time; spread as for jelly cake. Mrs. G. M. D'L.

562 Cocoanut Drops.

One pound of sugar, three eggs, three tablespoonfuls of flour, two grated cocoanuts, two tablespoonfuls of milk. Flour the pans on which you bake them.

Cousin Annie Dwight.

563 Shrewsbury Cake.

Quarter of a pound of butter, quarter of a pound of granulated sugar, six ounces of flour, one teaspoonful of powdered cinnamon and mace, one egg. Roll out thin; cut and bake.

564 Jumbles.

One cup of granulated sugar, one cup of butter, one egg, two cups of flour; use as little flour as possible when rolling out; roll very thin; cut out with common cake cutter; cut out the center of each in order that they may keep shape when baking. Flavor with vanilla; bake a light brown, and when done sprinkle with powdered sugar. These are very nice. You may add two tablespoonfuls of sweet cream and roll the jumbles on a board sprinkled with pulverized sugar.

565 Cinnamon Wafers.

One pound of sugar, quarter of a pound of butter, three eggs, half a teaspoonful of saleratus dissolved in as little milk as possible, two or three tablespoonfuls of ground cinnamon, flour enough to roll out; roll thin and bake quickly.

Mrs. Romeyn.

COOKIES.

566 Cookies. No. 1.

One cup of sugar, one half-a-cup of butter, one egg, one quarter of a cup of milk, one teaspoonful of baking powder; flour enough to roll; flavor to suit the taste, roll very thin.

567 Cookies. No. 2.

Break one egg in a coffee-cup, one tablespoonful of sour cream or milk, two tablespoonfuls of melted butter, half a teaspoonful of soda, dissolved in one tablespoonful of hot water; fill the cup up heaping with sugar, grate in a nutmeg, stir all to a cream and add flour. From this one cup can be made five pans of cookies.

568 Cookies. No. 3.

One and-one-half pounds of flour, one pound of white sugar, one half pound of butter, three eggs, one half teaspoonful each of soda and cream of tartar, a little nutmeg. Roll out, using as little flour as possible, cut round, and bake on flat tins.—Mrs. J. E. P.

569 Drop Cookies.

Two cups of sugar, three-fourths of a cup of butter, four cups of flour, one cup of milk, four eggs, two teaspoonfuls of cream of tartar, one teaspoonful of soda, caraway seeds. Drop in pan and bake in quick oven.

570 Brown Sugar Cookies.

One cup of sugar, one cup of molasses, one cup of butter, two eggs, two teaspoonfuls of soda in the molasses in a tablespoonful of hot water; mix soft, spice to taste, cloves, ginger and cinnamon, or either one of these spices.

571 New Year's Cookies.

Six cups of sugar, three of butter, one and-a-half of sour cream or milk, six eggs, one teaspoonful of saleratus, one ounce of caraway seeds; make them stiff.

572 Chocolate Cookies—Very Fine.

One cup of butter, two cups of sugar, two cups of flour, two eggs, two cups of grated chocolate, two dessert-spoonfuls of extract of vanilla. Roll very thin and bake in a quick oven.

GINGER CAKES.

573 Drop Ginger Cakes—Mrs. D.'s.

One cup of boiling water, one cup of butter, one egg, one cup of brown sugar, one cup of molasses, in which is dissolved two teaspoonfuls of saleratus (*not soda*), five cups of flour, two tablespoonfuls of ginger, two tablespoonfuls of cinnamon, and one teaspoonful of cloves.

Process.—Pour your boiling water into a pan, set it on the stove, add the butter and sugar, then the molasses. Take it off the stove and stir in the flour, spice and egg. Drop it by the spoonful on a dripping-pan or into iron cake bakers.

574 Ginger Snaps.

One cup of brown sugar, one cup of molasses, one cup of lard (or drippings), one egg, a little salt, one tablespoonful of ginger, two teaspoonfuls of soda dissolved in a little hot water, flour enough to roll out easily. Lay a little apart on tins that they may not run together in baking.

575 Lulu's Ginger Snaps.

One cup sugar, one cup butter, one cup molasses, one tablespoonful ginger, one tablespoonful cinnamon, one teaspoonful soda, one teaspoonful vanilla. Let all boil together fifteen minutes, then add, while hot, four cups of flour, and an extra cup for molding.

576 Soft Ginger Bread.

One cup of molasses, one cup of brown sugar, one tablespoonful of ginger, one small teaspoonful of soda, one egg, one cup of boiling water, six tablespoonfuls of butter, four and one-half cups of flour. Mix butter, sugar and egg first, then add molasses and boiling water. Bake fast.

577 Ginger Cookies.

One cup sugar, one cup molasses, one cup good fryings or butter, two beaten eggs, one teaspoon soda dissolved in four tablespoons buttermilk, and one teaspoon of cloves in two tablespoonfuls of vinegar, one tablespoonful of ginger. Stir with a spoon until stiff enough to mold with the hand, roll and bake in a quick oven.

578 Gingerbread (Delicious).

Into a coffeecup put one tablespoonful of butter, three tablespoonfuls of boiling water, one teaspoonful of soda, one teaspoonful of ginger, one teaspoonful of cinnamon; fill up the cup with molasses. Beat two eggs very light, add the mixture in the cup and one and one-half cups of sifted flour.—Mrs. WELCH.

579 Molasses Sponge Cake.

One pint of molasses, three tablespoonfuls of butter, two eggs, three teaspoonfuls of soda, dissolved in a teacupful of hot water, one quart of flour, a little ginger; beat the eggs separately.—Mrs. D.

580 Molasses Pound Cake.

One cup of butter, one cup of sugar, one cup of molasses, one-half cup of milk, four eggs, one teaspoonful of soda, one-half teaspoonful of cinnamon, one teaspoonful of ginger, four cups of flour.

581 Hard Gingerbread.

One pint of molasses with one teaspoon saleratus, beaten in until light, piece of butter the size of an egg worked into the flour, three teaspoons of ginger. Mix as hard as possible with flour; roll out.

Mrs. AMES, per Mrs. LOTHROP.

582 Gingerbread.

One cup of brown sugar, one cup of butter, one cup of sour milk, two cups of molasses, five cups of flour, five eggs, one dessertspoonful of soda, one teaspoonful of cinnamon, one-half teaspoonful of cloves, and the same of ginger. Bake in a very slow oven.—Mrs. HICKOX.

FRIED CAKES.

583 To Prepare the Yeast for Doughnuts.

Take from the potato pot at dinner time, two good-sized boiled potatoes, two heaping tablespoonfuls of flour, and a teacupful of the scalding potato water; mash and beat the whole smooth. Add a tablespoonful of white sugar and set it by till lukewarm, then add a Twin Brother yeast cake, and let it ferment from two till eight or nine o'clock P. M.

584 Cup Measure Doughnuts.

One cup of lukewarm milk, four tablespoonfuls of butter, three eggs beaten light, half a nutmeg grated, a pinch of salt, half a teacup of yeast, as above, and one quart of flour; let rise over night. Mold up at 9 A. M. with as little flour as possible; set near the stove till 2 P.M., and fry. This receipt is excellent without yeast, substituting two teaspoonfuls of baking powder, or one of bicarbonate of soda, and two of cream of tartar.

585 Raised Doughnuts.

Three-quarters of a pound of butter, one and one-half pounds of white sugar, five eggs, one pint of milk, one cup of fresh yeast, as above, and flour enough to make them of the consistency of bread dough; one nutmeg and one-half teaspoonful of salt.

PROCESS.—Mix the butter warmed in the milk, the sugar

and eggs; stir it into the flour until it is a soft sponge, then add the yeast and more flour; set it to rise over night.

In the morning roll out and cut into diamond shapes or twists, lay them on the paste-board, set them in a warm place, let them rise again until very light, say till two or three o'clock P.M.; then drop them into hot lard, turn them over in the pot once, promptly but not hurriedly. Should the lard incline to burn, throw in an apple skin, or a pared potato, which will clear it of any scorching propensity.

BRIDGET MEE.

586 Delightful Raised Doughnuts.

Beat one egg very light, in one cup of sugar; add one tablespoonful of butter (sweet lard will do as well), and work it in one quart of raised dough; roll out, cut in fancy strips and fry in boiling lard. Doughnuts are much lighter and nicer if let rise before adding the eggs and sugar. Nice and easy as these doughnuts are, we regret to say they dry in two days.

587 Queen of Doughnuts.

One-half pound of butter, one tablespoonful of lard, three-quarters of a pound of sugar, five eggs, one and one-half pints of milk and one coffee-cupful of home-made yeast. Heat the milk and sugar together, mix with them flour enough to make a stiff dough, heat the butter and lard, pour over the dough when very hot and work it well in with the hands, add the eggs beaten separately, cinnamon or nutmeg, and then the yeast thoroughly kneaded in; let stand until light, from eight to twelve hours; pinch off pieces about as large as a walnut, roll into balls, let rise, and fry in hot lard. While hot, sprinkle powdered sugar over them.

588 Fried-Cakes.

Six tablespoonfuls of sugar, three tablespoonfuls of melted butter, two eggs, one cup of sweet milk, three teaspoonfuls of baking powder, one-half teaspoonful of extract of vanilla, as little flour as possible.—Mrs. J. M. B. S.

589 Mrs. Mays's Doughnuts.

One coffee-cup of light brown sugar, two eggs, beaten beforehand; one and one-half cups of milk; two tablespoons melted butter; two teaspoons of cream of tartar, one teaspoon of soda; flour to make a soft dough.

590 Crullers.

Dissolve a teaspoonful of saleratus in four tablespoonfuls of milk, strain it onto half a pint of flour, four tablespoonfuls of melted butter or lard, and a teaspoonful of salt. Beat four eggs with six heaping tablespoonfuls of rolled sugar, work them into the rest of the ingredients, together with a grated nutmeg, add flour to make them stiff enough to roll out easily. They should be rolled out about half an inch thick, cut with a jagging-iron or knife in strips about half an inch wide, and twisted so as to form small cakes Heat two pounds of lard in a deep kettle; the fat should boil up as the cakes are put in, and they should be constantly watched while frying. When brown on the under side turn them; when brown on both sides they are sufficiently done.

SANDWICHES.

591 Sandwiches.

Take well-boiled ham, one-third fat and two-thirds lean, chop it until it is as fine as paste, then stir in the yolk of an egg. To one teaspoonful of made mustard mix one teaspoonsul of Worcestershire sauce. Use this or more, in such proportions as you may require.

592 Egg Sandwiches.

Boil eggs very hard, plunge them in ice-water and let them get very cold and dry. Spread slices of bread, lay them out on a nice white paper, or fresh towel, and grate the eggs through a coarse grater on each slice; mix pepper and salt, and with it dust them (two heaping spoonfuls of salt to a level spoonful of pepper); then lay two slices gently together. This sandwich may also be varied by grating a layer of cold smoked tongue or ham over the egg on one slice and not on the other. These require a light and dexterous hand to keep the egg from being crushed.

593 Sardine Sandwiches.

Open a can of sardines, remove the skin and bones, lay bits of the fish on well-spread bread and butter; squeeze lemon over it; lay a slice of buttered bread on top.

594 Croquette Sandwiches.

Make croquettes according to receipt, also French rolls. Open the rolls, scoop out the crumb, spread the inside with butter; lay in a croquette.

595 Egg Sandwiches (Children's School Lunches).

Beat three eggs, three tablespoonfuls of milk, saltspoon of salt, and a dash of pepper; fry it as you would a griddle cake, and lay between buttered bread or biscuit, or slice hard-boiled eggs or cut rissole balls or nice stewed codfish left cold, and lay between slices of bread and butter.

596 Potted Ham and Tongue Sandwiches.

It is well to keep an unopened can of each in the house, and then it is ready for any emergency that may arise. Spread a thin layer on well-buttered bread, and fold together.

597 Oyster Sandwiches.

Chop raw oysters very fine, season with pepper, salt, a little nutmeg, and four crackers pounded and sifted; the white of an egg beaten, cream and butter. When all is mixed, heat them over steam in an oat-meal boiler, or over the fire until a smooth paste; set them away to get very cold, cut and lay between buttered slices of bread. A quart of solid meats, a half teacup of melted butter, the same of rich cream, whites of three eggs and eight crackers. Pie paste biscuit, with slices of oyster sandwiches, are nicer than bread and butter.

598 Tongue or Ham Sandwiches.

Chop fine the lean of cold boiled tongue or ham, season with prepared mustard and black pepper. Add melted butter and sweet cream until smooth like a paste, then spread between buttered slices of bread. A teaspoonful of Worcester or Harvey sauce to every pint gives a pleasant flavor.

599   To Carry Sandwiches.

A nice and dainty way of carrying delicate sandwiches, such as oysters, lobsters or egg, is to make little bags of tissue paper. There is a rather strong white tissue paper that can usually be got for this purpose. Put one or two sandwiches into each bag. They can be folded in papers, such as come for paper napkins. On all pic-nics it is a good plan to carry one or two substantial towels.

600   Small Roll with Salad Filling.

Cut off the end of a French roll, remove the inside crumb, prepare a filling of cold tongue, chicken and celery, that have been mixed with a mayonnaise dressing; cover the top with the piece that was taken off.

601   Fried Cream

Makes a rather nice pic-nic dish eaten cold.

BREAKFAST AND TEA RELISHES.

602   Bichamelle or Minced Veal.

Mince your cold roast veal fine in a chopping-bowl, leaving out the stringy part; put into your frying-pan a teacupful (or more as the quantity requires) of milk or sweet cream, into which stir, when hot, a teaspoonful of butter and one of flour, braided together; then add your veal heat it thoroughly through, grate a little nutmeg, or sprinkle fine mace over it, and pour it into a dish that has a border of puff paste leaves spread around it (you can make your leaves when you are making pies, and just heat them in the oven a moment); then squeeze the juice of a lemon over the top of the minced veal, laying five or six leaves of paste on it, and serve. This was from old Mammy Wood, and is delicious for breakfast. You can make veal patties of it by grating cold ham over it and then inclosing it in a paste and baking it.

603 Chopped Beef.

Take two pounds of the round of beef, chop raw, heat the spider, put in a small piece of butter; add meat, season with salt and pepper, add a large spoonful of flour, then pour in a cup of milk or stock; season well.

604 Beef Collops.

A pound and a half of lean beef, chopped into square pieces the size of a large bean; put a tablespoon of butter into your frying-pan and pour the meat into the boiling butter; cook through, stirring frequently; add at the last a teaspoonful of brown flour, a little water, pepper, salt, and a tablespoonful of vinegar.

605 Hash.

This dish by any other name might make a more welcome impression. Our receipt is for a sweet and wholesome breakfast relish. Take two pint bowls of cold roast beef, or corned beef, chop it quite fine, then chop double the quantity of potatoes much coarser; put into a frying-pan a tablespoonful of butter, and a scant teacup of stock or boiling water; let 'it boil up, put the hashed meat and potatoes into it and stir it from time to time, till the liquid dries away and leaves a skin on the bottom of the pan.

606 Hashed Mutton

Is not pleasant with potatoes. Chop the mutton fine, put some gravy into your pan, heat the meat very thoroughly through, and pour it on well buttered slices of toast.

607 Corned Beef to Serve Cold,

Mrs. Henderson gives a receipt of her friend, Mrs. Gratz Brown, that we know will prove useful. If your corned beef is very salt, soak it an hour or more in cold water, then put it over the fire, cover with fresh cold water, four or five cloves for each six pounds of beef, and three tablespoonfuls of molasses; in an hour change the water, add another five cloves and three more tablespoonfuls of molasses. In two hours more press the beef into a colander and put a flat-iron or any heavy weight upon the cloth you spread over it; let it stand all day.

608 Dried Beef—Breakfast Dish.

Here is another nice breakfast dish. Take about half a pound dried beef; first slice thin, then pulled in small pieces. Have a quart of milk boiling, into which put the beef with a good piece of butter and a little pepper. When it comes to a boil, thicken with a little flour or corn starch, then toast bread, a slice for each member of the family, and poach in hot water an equal number of eggs; place one on each slice of toast; put all on a large platter, and pour over the above dressing and send to the table hot; lean ham may be used in the place of the beef.

609 Persilade.

Cut any nice cold meat in very thin slices; take two tablespoonfuls of finely chopped parsley, one small onion; then beat two tablespoonfuls of vinegar, one teaspoonful of oil, one teaspoonful of salt, a teaspoonful of pepper vinegar or tarragon vinegar improves this; pour this over the slices half an hour before serving.

610 Stewed Kidney.

Soak and then parboil the kidney, cut it off in inch pieces, roll in flour, add butter the size of an egg, and water enough to stew till tender; add, of you like it, a tablespoonful of mushroom catsup, or walnut pickle vinegar.

611 Liver.

Cut a calf's liver into half-inch slices, dredge them with flour, lay them on a gridiron and broil slightly; then put them into a frying-pan with a tablespoonful of butter or some slices of bacon, and fry for a few moments; cut the slices of liver into pieces the width of your finger; add a tablespoonful of flour, brown and add water; stew ten minutes.

612 Spanish Toast.

Beat three eggs to a foam, toast a few slices of bakers' bread; dip them in the egg and fry to a light brown.

613 To Make Milk Toast.

First toast nice slices of stale bread (*i. e.*, one or two days old); put in a saucepan or spider a quart of milk, with a piece of butter the size of an egg, a little salt and pepper. When the milk and butter are hot, but not quite boiling, dip your slices one by one and lay them in your tureen. When all are dipped just enough to moisten, but not break them, set your saucepan where it will come to a boil. Have ready a large tablespoonful of flour, made smooth with milk, and as soon as the milk boils stir it in till it is thickened. Turn it over the toast, raising the slices a little so that all may receive a share. This for a family of four or five. A richer toast is made by buttering the slice of toast and adding a quarter of a pound of butter to the milk instead of the flour.

614 Pressed Beef.

Three pounds round steak, raw, chopped fine, six crackers rolled fine, three eggs beaten, one-half nutmeg, two small teaspoons of pepper and a little more salt, one cup of water. Put into a small-sized bread-pan and bake till tender when tried with a fork; baste frequently with the dripping from the beef. The original receipt calls for three hours' baking, but less can be given with judgment.

615 Beef Loaf.

Two pounds of steak and one pound of fat pork, chopped fine, two and-a-half cups of rolled crackers, five eggs, two teaspoons of pepper, two teaspoons of salt; mix all together and bake three hours in a moderate oven.

616 Ham Toast.

One-fourth of a pound of lean ham, chopped fine ; beat well the yolks of three eggs; one tablespoonful of melted butter, two tablespoonfuls of cream or good milk; stir over the fire till it thickens; spread on hot toast.

617 Veal Loaf.

Three pounds of fresh veal and two pounds of salt pork, chopped fine; three eggs, six crackers, rolled; one teaspoonful of salt, one of pepper, and a little parsley. Roll into an oblong form and baste with butter while it is baking. This makes a nice relish, sliced cold for tea.

618 Breakfast Bacon.

If old and a little strong, soak thin slices of bacon or pork in milk, dip them in a nice fritter batter and fry. Breakfast bacon is very nice cut in thin slices and fried quickly over a bright steady fire and served dry.

ENTRÉES, CROQUETTES, ETC.

619 Chicken Croquettes—From a Celebrated Chef.

To one good-sized chicken (after having been boiled and finely chopped), add one pint of rich cream, four eggs, butter the size of an egg, and a handful of flour. Flavor with nutmeg, cayenne pepper and salt. Cook over a slow fire until it is of the consistency of paste, then put into the refrigerator until thoroughly cold; mold into oval patties. Paint the croquettes with the yolks of three eggs and roll into bread crumbs, after which brown them nicely in a little butter and serve hot, or lay in the frying-basket and plunge them into boiling lard. With two sweet-breads added this receipt makes two dozen croquettes.

620 Chicken Croquettes.

One pint of milk or cream, one tablespoonful summer savory, three cups of finely-chopped cooked chicken meat, two ounces of butter, half cup of sifted flour, five eggs; stir flour and butter to a smooth paste; boil milk, salt and summer savory together; add butter, flour, meat and eggs, well beaten; cook all together a few minutes and set to cool; when cold form in balls and fry in boiling lard to a delicate brown; serve hot.

621 Fricatelles.

Take chopped parsley and salt and pepper, a small onion, one pound and-a-half of cold veal, chopped very fine, one tablespoonful of butter and two of flour, mixed perfectly smooth, adding by degrees two tablespoonfuls of boiling water, and beat till very light; stir into this one cup of cold milk; into this mixture stir the meat and half a teacup of fine bread crumbs, and cook well; then form into oblong rolls (like little mice without any heads or tails). Roll these in egg and very fine sifted cracker crumbs, and boil in lard as you do doughnuts.

622 Friteurs.

Put in a saucepan a little butter, two tablespoonfuls of flour with soup stock if you have it, if not, a little water, until it thickens, then add minced turkey, chicken or veal, with a little salt. Take off the fire and cool. Then make in any shape you please, say like small sausages half a finger long. Roll in egg and then in cracker or brown bread crumbs and drop into boiling lard until a delicate brown.

623 Chicken or Beef Rissoles.

Take a cold chicken (roast or boiled), or cold roast beef or veal, mince it very fine or it will not adhere, moisten it with the gravy, season with pepper, salt, thyme or onion, a slice of cold ham, an equal quantity of fine bread crumbs, a bit of sage, parsley or thyme. Chop well together, add one egg or more, a little melted butter, pepper and salt. Make up in flattened balls, dredge with flour and fry in hot lard. They are very nice.

624 Pickled Fowl—Marinade.

After removing the skin of a chicken, cut it in pieces, wash it in cold water, and clean and prepare the giblets; cook these slowly for three or four hours in a pickle made of vinegar and chicken soup stock in equal parts, adding salt, pepper, parsley, onions, then add the pieces of chicken and scald thirty minutes. Then drain them, dip them in eggs well beaten, roll them in flour or fine cracker crumbs, fry them, and serve with garniture of parsley.

625 To Cook Canned Salmon and Lobster.

Open the can by taking the top off, drain away the liquor, take a tablespoonful of butter, a teaspoonful of vinegar and a teacup of boiling water; pour over the salmon, set the can in a pot of hot water and let cook for twenty or thirty minutes; again drain off the liquor, let the salmon cool and pour over it a mayonnaise dressing. Lobsters should be drained in a colander and left to air two hours.

626 Salmon in a Mold.

One can of salmon, four eggs, beaten light, four tablespoonfuls of butter, melted, but not hot, half a cup of fine bread crumbs; season with pepper, salt and minced parsley; chop the fish fine, then rub the butter in till smooth; beat the crumbs into the egg and season before working together; put into a buttered mold and steam one hour.

SAUCE FOR THE SAME.—One cup of milk heated to a boil, thickened with one tablespoonful of corn starch and one tablespoonful of butter rubbed together, the liquor from the salmon, one raw egg, one teaspoonful of tomato catsup, pinch of mace, pinch of cayenne; put the egg in the last and very carefully.

Lobster may be prepared in the same way.

SAVORY JELLIES.

627 Savory Chicken Jelly.

Take a chicken, cut it in small pieces, lay it in a saucepan and just cover with cold water; cook slowly until very tender, taking off the scum as it rises. Take up the chicken and boil the liquor to a cupful; remove all the bones and pick the meat to pieces. Season with salt and pepper, sweet herbs and a little butter; mix with the gravy and put into a mold, well buttered. Set in a cool place until perfectly firm. Cut in slices for the table.

628 Jellied Tongue.

One large boiled tongue (cold), two ounces of gelatine, dissolved in one-half pint of water; one teacup of browned veal gravy, one pint of liquor in which the tongue was boiled, one tablespoonful of burnt sugar for coloring, three tablespoonfuls of vinegar, one pint of boiling water; put together the gravy, liquor, sugar, vinegar and a tablespoonful of burnt sugar dissolved in cold water. Add the dissolved gelatine and mix well, then the boiling water, and strain through flannel. Cut the tongue in slices as for the table. Let the jelly cool and begin to thicken. Wet a mold with cold water, put a little jelly in the bottom, then a layer of the tongue, more jelly, and so on until the mold is full; cover and set in a cool place. To turn it out set the mold in hot water for an instant, invert upon a dish and garnish with celery sprigs and nasturtion flowers. Cut with a sharp knife perpendicularly. This is a handsome and delicious dish, and easily made.

CHEESE.

629   Cheese Fondu.

One cup of bread crumbs, very dry and fine; two scant cups of milk, rich and fresh, or it will curdle; one-half pound of dry old cheese, grated; three eggs, whipped light, one small tablespoonful of melted butter, pepper and salt, one pinch of soda dissolved in hot water, and stirred into the milk; soak the crumbs in the milk; beat in these the eggs and butter, seasoning, lastly the cheese; butter a baking-dish, pour the fondu into it, strew dry bread crumbs on the top, and bake in a rather quick oven until delicately browned. Serve immediately in the baking-dish, or it soon falls.

630   English Welch Rarebit.

One-quarter of a pound of cheese, yolks of two eggs, five ounces of grated bread, a quarter of a pound of butter, one tablespoonful of mustard, a little salt. Mix with a quarter of a pound of grated cheese, five ounces of bread crumbs, and a quarter of a pound of good butter. Add a tablespoonful of mustard and a little salt. Mix all well together, and then beat it smooth in a mortar. Lay the mixture neatly on slices of toasted bread, and place them in a Dutch oven before the fire to become thoroughly hot and slightly brown. Placing a thick white paper over the dish until hot, and then removing it, prevents the cheese from becoming brown or dry. Time, ten minutes.

N. B.—This receipt is from Warne's celebrated book. Our method adds to this half a teacup of milk, and gives it a thorough heating in a frying-pan, then pour it on toast.

631 Cheese Balls (for Dessert).

Grate three or four tablespoonfuls of cheese, give them a dash of red pepper, press it into balls the size of a nutmeg, roll them in yolk of egg, lay in your frying-basket and boil in hot lard. The flavor can be varied by stirring a saltspoonful of dry mustard into the egg. To be served cold for dessert.

PICKLES AND CATSUP.

632 The Very Best Brine for Cucumber Pickles.

Five gallons of water, three quarts of salt, one pound alum, heat and skim well. When cool add one gallon of good vinegar. This will make brine for half a barrel of pickles. For smaller quantity, take ten quarts water, three pints salt, one-half pound alum, two quarts vinegar. I will warrant that your pickles will keep hard and good.

N. B.—We highly recommend this brine; it is by far the best we have ever used. In the autumn we make a five-gallon jug of this and have it ready for every sort of pickle. You may leave pickles in it six months and then do them up.

633 Cucumber Pickles.

To a hundred good sized cucumbers, put a cup of barrel salt; pour on boiling water enough to cover them; cover tightly to keep the steam in; let them stand twenty-four hours; take them out, drain and wipe them dry, being careful not to break the skins; put them in the vessel in which they are to be kept, heat enough pure cider vinegar to cover them. For every three hundred pickles take one ounce of allspice, one of cinnamon, one of mustard seed; use them whole. Boil the vineger and spices together; while boiling pour it on the pickles and cover tightly. Let them stand three weeks and they are ready to eat. Mother used to put alum in them. Sometimes I put in wild grapes and a large piece of horse-radish; this gives the vinegar something to live on; also put in a few string beans, onions and cauliflower. These pickles will keep for years, and we have used the recipe in the family for forty years.

N. B.—This recipe answers admirably for the pickles which have been kept in the salt, alum and vinegar brine.

634 Cucumber Pickles—Mr. H. M. D.'s Favorites.

I usually freshen four quarts of cucumbers at one time, and when sufficiently fresh scald them in weak vinegar, with a lump of alum the size of a hickory nut dissolved in it; let them stand in it twenty-four hours, then drain it all off. I then take enough sharp cider vinegar to cover them; add a coffeecup three times even full of brown sugar, five or six sticks of cinnamon, let it heat slowly, and when boiling pour over the cucumbers and cover tightly. If when you come to use them you should find them not quite suited to your taste, you can remedy this by heating the vinegar over, and adding more sugar as you see fit. Have tried the above receipt and find it better than any I have ever used before. Do not be afraid of the quantity of sugar used; it is just right if your vinegar is sharp enough. The one kind of spice is better than different ones, as we usually use them.—FANNIE P. D.

N. B.—The sugar in the above receipt does not seem to taste, but nevertheless we omit it in our household. It makes a different, but none the less delightful, pickle.

635 Sliced Cucumber Pickles.

Twelve large cucumbers, six small onions, salt, half teacup salad oil or more, half cup black mustard seed, one tablespoonful celery seed and one quart of vinegar. Slice cucumbers thin with the skin on, onions same. Place alternate layers of cucumbers and onions in a deep dish, sprinkled well with salt; let them stand three hours, and then pour off the water; add the oil, half cup white mustard seed, with the black and celery seed, put in a jar and pour on the vinegar and cover tight.

Mrs. Gertrude M. D'Land.

636 Tomato Catsup (Best in the World).

Take sound ripe tomatoes, slice and cook until done enough to pass through a sieve; then to every gallon of the tomato pulp and juice add one teacupful chopped onion, one half cup black pepper, four pods red pepper cut fine, one-half teacup ground ginger and dry mustard (English), mixed, one ounce celery seed, one-half teacup allspice, nutmeg and cinnamon mixed, one-half teaspoonful of cloves, two teacupfuls of sugar and sufficient salt to taste distinctly, one pint *strong cider* vinegar. Put all on together and cook two hours, or longer if not thick enough. It must not be thin or watery. Bottle and seal while hot, and in a cool cellar it will keep for years. Spices should all be the best. Do not use the ground spices purchased from druggists, as they are not strong enough.

637 Cucumber Catsup.

Late in September take a bushel of full-grown cucumbers, peel and slice them, sprinkle them with salt, and let them stand over a sieve two hours, that the salt may drain off, then chop them fine. Add two dozen onions cut up small, one pound of white mustard seed, one pound of black mustard, one-fourth of a pound of black pepper, ground. Mix all together very thoroughly with the best vinegar, making it the consistency of a thick catsup, and fill your jars, tying up closely. It requires no cooking.

638 Plum Catsup.

To three pounds of fruit put one and three-quarter pounds of sugar, one tablespoonful of cloves, one tablespoonful of cinnamon, one tablespoonful of pepper, and very little salt. Scald the plums and put them through a colander, then boil until about the same consistency as the tomato catsup.

639 White Pickle.

Two quarts of vinegar, one-quarter of a pound of ground mustard, one-quarter pound of white mustard seed, two ounces of black mustard seed, one teaspoonful of root ginger, one teaspoonful of celery seed; tarragon and mace to taste; green and red pepper to taste; a lemon or two cut into this quantity improves the flavor, as also does a root of horse-radish. Scald the vinegar before adding the above ingredients, and pour all, when cold, over sliced green tomatoes that have stood in salt one day and scalded. It is equally good over beans, cucumbers, etc.

640 Mustard Pickle.

Fill a three-gallon jar with small green tomatoes, cucumbers, nasturtions, onions, cauliflowers, horse-radish, and a few small green peppers. Let them stand in salt and water twenty-four hours. Drain off this water. Put the mixture in a brass or porcelain kettle with fresh water, and boil ten minutes; then drain thoroughly, and put back in the jar.

Boil three quarts of vinegar, adding three-fourths pound mustard wet with cold vinegar. When it thickens pour over the pickle.

641 Sweet Pickle.

Take one peck of good solid green tomatoes, and onions to suit the taste and fancy (five quarts of tomatoes and three of onions), peel the onions as for boiling, wash and dry the tomatoes, cut them in thin lices, cut in small pieces six large green peppers, carefully leaving out the seeds; put the slices in a large pan and sprinkle a pint of fine salt on them; let them stand about twenty-four hours; drain off all the liquor, carefully pressing down the cover; when they are sufficiently drained, put in the preserving kettle and cover well with vinegar, prepared thus: Ten or twelve ounces brown sugar to the quart, a tablespoonful each of ground cinnamon and cloves, and a spoonful of crushed white mustard seed; boil well about fifteen minutes and put in pots or jars.

642 Picked Mangoes.

Young musk or nutmeg melons, English mustard seed, two handfuls mixed with one handful scraped horse-radish, mace and nutmeg pounded, one teaspoonful, two teaspoonfuls chopped garlic, a little ginger, one dozen whole pepper-corns, half a tablespoonful of ground mustard to a pint of the mixture, one tablespoonful sugar to the same quantity, one tablespoonful best salad oil to the same, one teaspoonful celery seed: cut a slender piece out of the melon, save it to replace. Lay the mangoes in strong brine for three days, drain off the brine, and freshen in pure water twenty-four hours, green as you would cucumbers, and lay in cold water until cold and firm, fill with the stuffing; tie up with packthread; pack in a deep stone jar and pour scalding vinegar over them, repeat this process three times more at intervals of two days, then tie up and set away in a cool, dry place; these are very fine; they will keep for months. I use nothing but white wine vinegar. Pepper mangoes can be fixed in the same way.

643 Mustard Pickels.

Two large heads of cauliflower, six heads celery, six white beets. Clean them and boil separately in salt and water until tender. The tender part of the celery is not to be boiled, but cut fine; use just water enough to cover. Mix one-half pound of ground English mustard with vinegar, as for table use, and boil five minutes; then add two bottles of best French mustard (or one pint of German mustard) and boil five minutes longer, adding vinegar enough to cover your pickles, and one tablespoonful of brown sugar. If not salt enough add to your taste. Pour over the pickles boiling hot. As the pickles are used there will be a good deal of the mustard-vinegar left, and small cucumbers can then be put in, or small onions; the latter boiled a few minutes in salt water. This pickle keeps a long time and is very fine. Any vegetables liked can be substituted for cauliflower and white beets.

644 Mustard Chow Chow.

One quart small cucumbers, one quart large cucumbers cut small, two quarts small onions, one quart small green tomatoes, one quart green tomatoes cut up, three good sized heads cauliflower, six green peppers cut in strips, half pound English mustard, one ounce turmeric powder, six cups sugar, two cups flour. Make a paste of these, and stir into one gallon of vinegar, boiling hot. Soak the vegetables separately in a weak salt water brine over night. After draining, put into the scalding vinegar that you have prepared; cook very little, and put into cans.

Mrs. Lapham.

N. B.—This is an admirable receipt, except that as my family disliked the sugar I omitted it.

645 Chow-Chow.

Take fifty small pickles, two quarts of silver onions, two quarts of green string beans, one dozen green tomatoes, three heads of cauliflower; let the onions stand in brine twelve hours, then peel. If the beans are large, break them. Slice the green tomatoes, cut up the cauliflowers; let all stand in brine twenty-four hours. To one gallon of vinegar use one pound of mustard (common is the best), mix it with a little vinegar, and add it to the rest. One or two tablespoonfuls of oil of mustard, one tablespoonful of cayenne pepper—use more spices if preferred. Tie the spices in a white cloth, and boil in the vinegar, before adding the mustard. It can be put in preserve jars in alternate layers; fill three-quarters full; when filling the jars add here and there a little red and green pepper; fill up with the mustard; make air-tight.

646 Filled Peppers.—Very Nice.

Cut the lids off two dozen large green peppers, take out seeds and soak in salt water over night; slice fine a cabbage, mix with it one ounce white mustard seed and one ounce cloves, fill the peppers and tie the lids on; cover with cold boiled cider vinegar.

647 Pickled Cabbage.

Chop a large head of cabbage fine, one teaspoonful of mace, one teaspoonful of cloves; cover with vinegar. Grated horse-radish may be added, if liked.

648 Yellow Pickle.

Two gallons strong cider vinegar, one pint black mustard seed, four ounces ginger, three ounces black pepper, three ounces allspice, one ounce celery seed, one ounce turmeric, four lemons sliced, a few cloves, garlic, say a handful, two pounds sugar, handful horse-radish. Bruise all the spices and put them with the other ingredients in a jar and pour on the vinegar cold. Tie up, but stir every day until the pickles are ready to put in this liquor. Take several small heads of cabbage, wash, quarter and put in strong brine; let them lie in it twenty-four hours well covered, take out, rinse in cold water, put in a preserving kettle with sufficient vinegar to cover and add one ounce turmeric; scald, but by no means suffer to boil, cover with a plate or pan to keep the steam in; let the pickle lie in the same vinegar twenty-four hours, take out and drop in that prepared above. This spiced liquor is good to use with green pickles, leaving out the turmeric, and universally pronounced excellent and a favorite Southern receipe.

649 Peach Pickle.

To seven pounds of fruit take one quart of vinegar, three pounds of sugar, one teaspoonful of ground cloves and one of cinnamon (tied in a muslin bag), rub the peaches clean of their downy coat, prick them with a fork, and put them, a few at a time, into the spiced vinegar. Let them cook till they are tender. Put them into jars, as taken out, and pour the vinegar over them.

This is equally good for plums, quinces, or any other fruit.

650 Sweet Pickled Peaches.

Rub the fur off with a coarse cloth, stick three cloves in each peach, four pounds of sugar to a quart of vinegar, boil and skim, put in the peaches and boil until you can run a stem into them, then take them out, put in a jar, pour the vinegar over hot, cover immediately. These are very fine. The peaches must be hard ones; the yellow are the best.

651 Pickled Apples—Very Nice.

Two pounds of dried apples, one quart of good vinegar, one cup sugar, a little spice and cloves. Soak the apples all night, in the morning put water enough on them to cook until tender. Boil vinegar, sugar and spices, then put in the apples, boil once and you have a good dish for dinner sauce.

652 Chili Sauce.

Take twenty-five large ripe tomatoes, ten large onions, ten red peppers, five tablespoonfuls salt, five white sugar, five cups of vinegar; peel the tomatoes and chop all fine; boil slowly till well cooked; bottle and seal, or put in Mason jars.

653 Spiced Crab Apples.

Take of the large sized apples four pounds fruit, four pounds sugar, one pint vinegar, cinnamon and allspice in a bag, put in the vinegar and boil; stick whole cloves in the apples, steam them until soft, then put them in the syrup and simmer slowly until clear.

654 Watermelon Pickles.

Ten pounds of the rinds, boiled in water till tender; make a syrup of two pounds sugar and one quart of vinegar, half ounce cloves, one ounce cinnamon; this is to be poured over the rinds (boiling hot) three days in succession.

655 Pickled Onions.

Use the small silver skinned onions, remove with a knife all the outer skins, so that the onions look fresh. Pour over them a scalding hot brine made in the proportion of one cup of salt to one quart of water; let stand three days, take up, rinse with cold water and pour on scalding hot vinegar, spiced with stick cinnamon, mace and cayenne pepper, or if the pure onion flavor is preferred, simply boil red or green peppers in the vinegar. If the onions seem hard and raw, scald the vinegar again; let the onions scald in it from five to fifteen minutes; bottle and cork.

656 Red Cabbage.

Choose fine firm heads of red cabbage, remove the outer leaves, cut in quarters and pickle in quarters, or slice very fine with a knife or cabbage cutter; sprinkle thoroughly with fine salt and pack in a large sieve or colander; let it drain for twenty-four hours, then pack in a jar pour over scalding hot vinegar strongly spiced with nutmeg, cloves and pepper.

657 Tomato Relish.

Chop one peck of green tomatoes, sprinkle over them one cup of fine salt, and let them stand over night. Strain off the water. Then chop six green peppers and six onions, add one cup of light brown sugar, one tablespoon ground cinnamon, one of ginger, one-half tablespoon cloves, cover with vinegar. Mix well and cook until tender.

658 To Make French Mustard.

Take one-quarter pound of best yellow mustard, pour over it one-half pint each of water and vinegar; add a pinch of salt and a piece of calamus root the size of a pea. Put it on the fire, and while it boils add a teaspoonful of flour. Let it boil twenty minutes, stirring it constantly. Just before taking it off stir in a teaspoonful of sugar or honey. When cool put it into bottles and cork tightly.

659 Tomato Mustard (Excellent).

One bushel of tomatoes; take out the stalks and boil for an hour with six red peppers; then strain through a sieve and add one-half pound of salt, one ounce of ginger, one-half ounce of cloves, three tablespoonfuls of black pepper, one ounce of allspice, two onions. Boil for six hours to a thick paste; when cold add one-fourth of a pound of mustard and one-half pint of vinegar.

660 Spiced Currants or Grapes (Splendid).

To six pounds of fruit, four pounds of sugar, one pint of vinegar. Boil to a thick jam. Just before taking it up stir in two tablespoonfuls of powdered cloves and the same of cinnamon. Very nice to eat with meats.

661 Currant Catsup.

Boil two pounds of currants in one quart of vinegar, until soft; strain all through a sieve, then add three pounds of sugar, one ounce of nutmeg, one tablespoonful of cloves, two tablespoonfuls of cinnamon, and boil one hour.

662 Spiced Fruit.

For Currants, Damson Plums, Gooseberries, Wild Grapes, Old-fashioned Sour Cherries—five pounds of fruit, four coffee cups of sugar (light brown), one teacup of vinegar, one heaping tablespoonful each of cloves and cinnamon, one even tablespoonful of allspice; mix the vinegar, sugar and spices well together; add the fruit and boil one hour, stirring up constantly.—Cousin Annie Dwight.

663   To Make Good Table Vinegar.

When peeling apples, fill a two gallon jar with the skins, stems and cores; pour boiling water over them and let them stand behind the kitchen stove till cool or lukewarm; then add half a pint (or a pint) of molasses and a teacup of quick yeast, and stir the whole well together; let it stand near the kitchen fire three or four weeks, and when well fermented strain and pour into a jug; it will make fine table vinegar.

PRESERVING AND CANNING FRUIT.

Canning Fruit.—Those who have to buy the fruit they put up, as well as the cans, may perhaps purchase to advantage of the wholesale grocer, but where one has abundance of fruit for the picking, and can give the time and trouble, there is certainly a saving in putting up the family supplies of fruit one's self. The cheapest way of getting cans is to buy them of the manufacturer, and thus save the profits of middlemen. The fruit should be perfectly fresh, and the sooner it is canned after it is taken from the tree or vine the better. If a small quantity, say half a dozen quarts, is cooked at one time the color of the fruit and the uniformity of the cooking will be better than if a larger quantity is attempted. There is no necessity of using an ounce of sugar in a gross of cans. The fruit will keep just as well without it, and be far more grateful to a healthy appetite. Glass cans with glass tops, a rubber band and a screw ring give the best satisfaction, as they can be sealed and unsealed in a moments' time. As for the process, when the fruit is done, pour it screeching hot into the cans; let them remain untouched fifteen or twenty minutes, till the fruit settles, then fill them full again and seal up. If the can is placed on a very wet cloth it will not break when the scalding fruit is put into it. Turn the cans, after screwing them up tightly, bottom side up, and if no syrup leaks out no air can get in. When cold set them away in a dark cool closet.

664 Worth Knowing.

In canning fruit, take a thick cloth (or one folded in several thicknesses), wring it out in hot water and lay it on a table. On this set the bottles for filling, and you may pour in the boiling fruit with impunity, thus avoiding the discomfort of standing over a hot stove during the process, handling heated bottles. If the cloth becomes sticky wring it out again. Some persons think a dry cloth answers the same purpose, but we prefer the wet one.

665 To Prevent Mildew on Preserves.

Take the white of an egg and wet slightly both sides of a piece of letter paper, sufficiently large to cover over the top of the preserves snugly. I have kept them free from mold and spoiling two years.

666 Currant Jelly (Perfect).

This receipt is the only one which we will *warrant* to make good jelly against odds. We have made jelly by it on the 5th of July, and on the 19th, and each time it was a perfect success. While we recommend all persons to make their jelly from fresh fruit *early* in the season, we can still assure those who are behindhand that they need not despair of jelly that will set firm and hard later in the season.

Run the currants through your hand, picking out the leaves, and any stray thing that may adhere to them, but leaving the currants on their stems. Weigh the fruit, being accurate in writing down the number of pounds. Put a pint of water into your preserving kettle, and add a bowl or two of currants, mashing and pressing them till you have sufficient juice to cover the bottom of the kettle, then add the remainder of the currants; let them come to a boil, and boil at least twenty minutes, of course stirring and pressing them from time to time that every berry may be broken up and that they may not burn. Have a three-cornered bag of thin, but strong, unbleached cotton, that has been well scalded and wrung till almost dry; hang it up and pour the boiled currants into it. Let it drip into a stone crock all night, but by no means squeeze it; the currants will drain perfectly dry. In the morning pour the strained juice into the preserving kettle, without measuring; let it come to a boil, and boil thoroughly for three or four minutes, then pour in *half* as many pounds of sugar as you had pounds of currants. For instance, a peck of currants will probably weigh twelve pounds, therefore use six pounds of sugar. The moment the sugar is entirely dissolved and the jelly begins to set on your silver ladle, that is, as you pour it off from the ladle the last few drops will fall in flakes that are no longer liquid, the jelly is nearly, if not quite ready to remove from the stove. From the time you pour the sugar in the boiling juice to the removal of the jelly from the fire does not vary much from twenty-five minutes. Allowance must be made for the quantity of jelly, and the heat of the fire; be the same more or less.

667 Currant Jelly.—A Boston Receipt (Mrs. L.)

Take out leaves, leave stems on; put one peck of currants in a kettle with two quarts of water, or water till you can just see it through the currants; boil till fruit is tender, turn the fruit into a sieve or colander to drip; measure juice and return to kettle, boil ten minutes; while boiling add one pound or pint of sugar to one pound or pint of juice, and follow the instructions given in the foregoing receipt.

668 Crab-Apple Jelly.

Place the fruit whole in water enough to cover it an inch over the top and boil perfectly soft, then pour the contents of the kettle into a coarse cheese-cloth or cotton bag and suspend it on a strip of narrow board laid across the backs of two chairs, with a crock under it, and leave it all night, or until it ceases to drip. Then press it a very little. Allow a pound of sugar to a pint of the juice—if you choose, add the juice of a lemon to every quart of syrup. Boil the juice first and skim it; heat the sugar in a dish in the stove oven and add it as the syrup boils up. Let it scald, but not boil, twenty minutes from the time of putting in the sugar, and pour in tumblers or molds. In the jellying, follow the instructions given in Currant Jelly recipe.

669 Cranberry Jelly.

Cover the cranberries with water, and let boil for twenty or thirty minutes; break the berries and scald once more; then pour into a jelly bag, and let drip over night—do not squeeze; weigh a pound of sugar to every pint of juice. Let the juice come to a boil and boil five minutes; then pour in the sugar and stir till thoroughly dissolved. This jelly will set without coming to a boil. It is also nice to stir the juice through a colander, instead of straining through a bag.

670 Grape Jelly.

Differs only from Currant Jelly recipe by boiling the grapes twenty minutes; bruising them meantime with a ladle or potato masher, until the juice runs freely, then strain through a sieve or thin cloth, and measure one pint for one pound of sugar. Boil the juice fifteen or twenty minutes before putting in the sugar; after adding the sugar let it scald from twenty to twenty-five minutes, but never boil.

All fruit will form more readily in a jelly if not quite ripe.

671 Apple Jelly.

Core and quarter, but *not pare*, tart apples. Cook in a little more water than will cover them till well reduced, as in Crab-Apple Jelly. Strain, add one pound of sugar to one pint of the juice, scald twenty minutes or half an hour, and strain carefully into your molds. Slices of lemon or Jamaica ginger may be added to the apples while boiling,

672 Pieplant Jelly.

Pick the pieplant and wash, but do not peel it, cut in strips, put in the kettle, add enough of water to cook until soft, strain the juice off and weigh, add sugar pound for pound; cook ten minutes, or as thick as you wish, and follow the rule for currant jelly.

673 Orange Marmalade.

Three pounds of oranges, two pounds of lemons, five pounds of sugar.

DIRECTIONS.—Peel the oranges and lemons, put the skins of both in the preserving pan, cover with water and cook till tender; then take them out, and put the pulps into the same water and cook from one to two hours, adding more water if it gets too thick; while the pulp is cooking cut the skins in strips as fine as possible; strain the pulp through a jelly bag, and put the juice back in the pan with the sugar; when it is dissolved put in the skins; boil about fifteen minutes, and it is ready to put in bowls.

674 Raspberry Jam.

One pound sugar to one pound berries. Boil three-quarters of an hour. Seal while hot.

675 Raspberry Vinegar, No. 1.

Red raspberries, any quantity, or sufficient to fill a stone jar nearly full, then pour upon them enough vinegar to cover them, cover the jar closely and set it aside for eight or ten days, then strain through flannel or muslin and add to the clear liquor one and-a-half pounds of sugar to each pint; place over the fire and boil gently for a few minutes, then allow it to cool and bottle for use. This makes, when mixed with ice water, a delightful summer drink, or for sick persons.

676 Raspberry Vinegar, No. 2.

Twelve boxes of raspberries, one coffee-cup of vinegar, one pound of sugar to one pint of juice. After straining the juice add sugar and vinegar. Let it come to a boil. Bottle and seal while hot.

677 Preserved Citron Melon.

Pare, core, and cut the melons into slices; weigh them, and to every six pounds of melon allow six pounds of white sugar, and the juice and yellow rind—pared off thin—of four lemons; also, half a pound of race ginger; put the slices into a preserving kettle, cover with water, and a layer on all of peach leaves; boil about half an hour, or until clear, and a broom-whisk will pierce them; drain them, spread them in a pan of cold water, and let them stand all night; next morning tie the ginger in a thin muslin cloth and boil it in three pints of water until the water is highly flavored; take out the ginger; dissolve the sugar in the ginger-water, put in the lemon peel and boil and skim it till no more scum rises; take out the lemon peel, put in the citron slices and juice of the lemon, and boil in the syrup till the slices are transparent and a straw will go through them; put the slices, while warm, in jars, and pour the syrup on slowly; cover closely with paper which the air cannot penetrate, or air-tight jars.

678 To Preserve Citron for Cake Without its Being too Hard.

Cut a citron and steam it, not too much; then melt your sugar, put the citron into it and cook as you would for preserves; dry it slowly in a warm oven; repeat this process several times. Flavor with lemon, if you choose; brown sugar is the best, if you wish to have it look dark. In order to have it moist and easy to cut care must be taken not to dry it too much. When ready to lay away sprinkle sugar over it and it will keep nicely.

I have just preserved some citron for cake as above directed, and it is just as nice as any you will find on sale at fifty cents per pound.

679 Lemon Marmalade.

Every housekeeper should keep a jar filled with brine, in which she may throw lemon peels after having used the grated rind and juice for creams, jellies, etc. These may remain any length of time. Before preserving, soak in pure water until all the taste of salt is extracted. Boil till soft enough to pierce with a straw. Put in a preserving kettle nine pounds of cut sugar and one quart of water; as soon as it boils add six pounds of lemon peel and three pounds of nice sliced apples (pippins are best); boil till very thick.

680 Lemon Conserves.

Wash and dry ten lemons; pare the yellow rind off clear of the white, and beat it in a mortar, with double its weight of sugar. Pack closely in a jar and cover with part of the sugar.

681 Lemon and Orange Syrup.

Put one and one-half pounds of white sugar to each pint of juice; add some peel and boil ten minutes; then strain and cork. It makes a fine beverage, and is useful for flavoring pies and puddings. The juice of any acid fruit may be used in the same way.

682 Ripe Tomato Preserves.

Seven pounds sound, yellow tomatoes, and six pounds of sugar; the juice of three large lemons. Let them all stand together over night; drain off the syrup and boil it, skimming well; then put in the tomatoes and scald gently for twenty minutes; take out the tomatoes with the skimmer and spread on dishes to cool. Boil down the syrup until it thickens; put the preserves in jars and fill up with hot syrup.

683 Preserved Currants.—Very Nice.

Ten pounds currants, seven pounds sugar; take the stems from seven pounds of the currants, and press the the juice from the other three pounds. When the juice and sugar are made into a hot syrup, put in the currants and boil until thick and rich.

684 Preserved Quinces.

Pare, quarter and core the fruit, saving skins and cores. Put the quinces over the fire with just enough water to cover them, and simmer until perfectly tender, but do not let them break. Take out the fruit and spread on dishes to cool. In another kettle have the paring and cores boiling in water enough to cover them; add this water to that in which the quinces were boiled, and cook on hour; then strain through a jelly bag, and to each pint of this liquor allow a pound of sugar. Boil and skim this, then put in the frnit and boil fifteen minutes. Take it off the fire and let it stand in a deep dish twenty-four hours. Then drain off the syrup, and let it boil again; put in the quinces and cook fifteen minutes. Take out the fruit and spread on dishes to cool; boil down the syrup thick; put the fruit in your jars until two-thirds full, then cover with the syrup.

685 Apples for Tea.

Pare a dozen or more apples, take out the core carefully and fill the center of each apple with sugar and a small lump of butter. Put them in a pan with half a pint of water; baste occasionally with the syrup while baking. When done serve with cream.

686 Grape Jam.

Pick the grapes from the stem and wash them; after they are drained slip the pulp from the skin, keeping them in separate dishes; then boil the pulp until it will easily part from the seeds. Strain through a colander, rinsing the seed with a little water. Boil the skins (adding some water) until they are quite tender, and chop them fine. (The Isabella will not become as tender as other varieties.) Then put all together and weigh one pound of sugar to one pound of fruit. Boil two or three minutes, and put into cups or jars.

687 Ripe Peach Marmalade.

One-half pound of sugar, one pound of peaches, cut up; put the sugar over; cook slowly two hours; put in cups or bowls.

688 Mrs. L.'s Receipt for Preserving Peaches.

One peck of rich yellow peaches, five pounds of crushed sugar, one quart of water. Boil the syrup until clear, and, in the meantime, fill cans or jars with peaches, packed as full as possible, whole or in halves, as you please. Pour the syrup boiling hot over them; then place the jars thus filled in pans of warm water on the stove and let them be heated to the boiling point; then seal. N. B.—There is no danger of breaking the cans if a cloth is folded and laid on the bottom of the boiler.

PICKLING BRINE.

689 To Cure Meat.

For those who raise and cure their own meat, the following will be an excellent recipe: To one gallon of water take one and one-half pounds of salt, one-half pound of sugar, one-half ounce of saltpetre, one-half ounce of potash. In this ratio, the pickle to be increased to any quantity desired. Let these be boiled together until all the dirt from the sugar rises to the top and is skimmed off. Then throw it into a tub to cool, and when cold, pour it over your beef or pork, to remain the usual time, say four or five weeks. The meat must be well covered with pickle, and should not be put down for at least two days after killing, during which time it should be slightly sprinkled with powdered saltpetre, which removes all the surface blood, etc., leaving the meat fresh and clean.

Some omit boiling the pickle, and find it to answer well, though the operation of boiling purifies the pickle by throwing off the dirt always to be found in salt and sugar. If this recipe is properly tried it will never be abandoned. There is none that surpasses it, if so good.

690 Spiced Beef.—Mrs. L. A.

Take a piece of beef from the fore quarter, weighing ten pounds. Those who like fat should select a fatty piece; those who prefer lean may take the shoulder clod, or upper part of the fore leg. Take one pint of salt, one teacup of molasses or brown sugar, one tablespoon of ground cloves, allspice and pepper, and two tablespoons of pulverized saltpetre. Place the beef in a deep pan; rub with this mixture. Turn and rub each side twice a day for a week. Then wash off the spices; put in a pot of boiling water, and, as often as it boils hard, turn in a teacupful of cold water. It must simmer for five hours, on the back part of the stove. Press under a heavy weight till it is cold, and you will never desire to try corned beef of the butcher again. Your pickle will do for another ten pounds of beef, first rubbing into it a handful of salt. It can be renewed and a piece kept in preparation every day. This is good to pickle tongues also.

691 Receipt for Curing Beef and Tongue.

Six gallons of water, nine pounds of salt, three pounds of brown sugar, one quart of molasses, three ounces of saltpetre; boil all together and skim; when cold pour on the beef. This is quantity sufficient for one hundred pounds. Keep closely covered and under the brine.

692 Receipt for Curing Hams.

To eight hams of common size, take eight pounds of brown sugar, one and a half pounds of saltpetre, five pounds of fine salt. Rub the hams with the mixture, and let them remain a week with the skins downward. Then make brine of common salt and water, strong enough to bear up an egg; add two or three quarts of lye made from hickory ashes, refined by boiling and skimming. Cover the hams with this liquid, keeping them down with a weight. Let them remain in it from four to six weeks, according to their size, then take them out and let them drain there for a day before sending them to the smoke house.

WASHING AND CLEANING.

693 The Use of Borax.

The washerwomen of Holland and Belgium, so proverbially clean, and who get their linen so beautifully white, use fine borax for washing powder, instead of soda, in the proportion of a large handful of borax powder to ten gallons of water. They save soap nearly one-half. All the large washing establishments adopt the same mode. For laces, cambrics, etc., an extra quantity of the powder is used; and for crinolines (requiring to be made stiff) a stronger solution is necessary. Borax, being a neutral salt, does not in the slightest degree injure the texture of linen. Its effect is to soften the hardest water, and therefore it should be kept on the toilet table. As a way of cleaning the hair, nothing is better than a weak solution of borax in water; it leaves the scalp in a most cleanly condition, and the hair is just sufficiently stiffened to retain its place. This stiffness, however, can be readily removed, if objectionable, by washing with water.

694 To Wash Flannel Without Shrinking It.

Have plenty of hot soft water, make a suds with good soap, rub the clothes clean and rinse out all the soap. Do not let the clothes cool from the time they are wet till they are ready to put on the line. Put them into the next suds or the rinsing water as fast as wrung out, and the final rinsing be done with water having two tablespoonfuls of amonia to the gallon, and let them cool in the basket before you hang them up. Wash them in the morning, on a sunshiny day if possible, so they will have a good chance to dry.

695 To Wash Colored Flannels.

Make a suds of cold water and ordinary bar soap; wash the garment and rinse in cold water. Press while it is still damp. In this way children's fancy sacques and bright dresses may be kept looking like new, neither shrinking nor changing color. Don't be afraid to try it.

A gallon of strong lye put in a barrel of hard water will make it as soft as rain water.

696 To Remove Grass Stains.

Pour boiling hot water on the stains before washing the garments.

697 Nice Glossy Starch.

To three cups water take three rounded teaspoonfuls of starch, a pinch of salt and one teaspoonful of powdered borax. Dissolve your borax in part of the water, then add starch and salt, dip your collars, cuffs and bosoms into the starch. Your irons must be good; rub them with beeswax, and I promise you a stiff, glossy surface, with never a failure.

698 To Remove Iron Rust Stains.

Salts of lemon is best, but if you do not have it moisten the spot with a solution of epsom salts in a few drops of hot water, and rub in well once or twice; then fill a tin vessel with boiling water and set it on the stain; rinse in cold water. A weak solution of oxalic acid will also remove iron rust and ink stains.

699 To Remove Mildew.

Rub common brown soap on the spot, and scrape white chalk in it. Keep wet and lay in the sun.

700 To Remove Scorches.

Scorches made by overheated flat-irons can be removed from linen by spreading over the scorched cloth a paste made of the juice pressed from two onions, one-half ounce of white soap, two ounces of fuller's earth, and half a pint of vinegar. Mix, boil well and cool before using.

Sometimes when a garment is yellowed by a too hot iron, exposure for a little while to the bright sunlight, if the scorch be not too deep, will cause it to disappear.

701 To Prevent Blue Fabrics from Fading.

Dissolve two teaspoonfuls of sugar of lead in one gallon of water, soak the stockings or cloth in this solution from half to one hour, according to material. Delicate fabrics need to soak only until saturated; rinse before washing and wash quickly.

702 Bluing.

One ounce of best Prussian blue, half ounce of oxalic acid, one quart of soft water. Heat enough of water to dissolve the acid, then stir in the blue, add cold water and bottle for use; keep in the cellar.

703 To Wash Black Prints, Alpacas and Waterproofs.

To a boilerful of strong soap-suds, put two handfuls of logwood chips, and let it boil half an hour; strain. Free the garment from grease spots and wet it thoroughly. Put it into the boiler and let it boil several minutes. Take it out and rinse in clear cold water until the water is colorless. Woolens should be ironed on the wrong side while quite damp.

704 Washing Compound—Mrs. L.'s.

Three tablespoonfuls of ammonia, one tablespoonful of turpentine, five gallons of water, lukewarm; soak the clothes in this three hours.

705 Washing Compound—Our Own.

Cut up one bar of soap in two quarts of water; to this add one-quarter of a pound of commercial borax; in the evening stand a bowl containing this mixture over a kettle of hot water, and in the morning it will be of a wax-like consistency. Put a teacupful of this mixture into every pail of water in your wash-boiler, having previously rubbed some of it on the clothes and soaked them in lukewarm water for two hours, the dirt will shake right out.

706 How Summer Suits should be Washed.

Let the water be tepid, the soap not allowed to touch the fabric, which should be washed and rinsed quickly, turned upon the wrong side, and hung in the shade to dry, and starched (in thin boiled water starch, lukewarm), ironed upon the wrong side as soon as possible. Linen should be washed in water in which a quart bag of bran has been boiled. This last will be found to answer for starch as well, and is excellent for print dresses of all kinds. A handful of salt is very useful also to set the colors of light cambrics and dotted lawns; and a little beef's gall will not only set but heighten yellow and purple tints, and has a good effect upon green.

707 To Clean Silk Dresses.

Equal quantities of alcohol, molasses and soft soap; one pint of each will do two dresses; beat well together, and after spreading a breadth of silk on a clean kitchen table, scour it with an old but clean clothes brush; have three tubs or pails of water, take up the breadth of silk by the top and dip it up and down in first one pail, then the second and then the third. When there is no color left in the water the rinsing is complete. Pin the breadths to the clothes line without wringing. When a little damp press out with a cold iron. Before cleaning, rub the grease spots with pure naphtha or gasoline. We have used this horrid-looking mixture with the best success on even light silks and silks with white stripes.

708   To Restore Old Velvet.

First brush the velvet thoroughly to free it from dust, then sponge the under side with alcohol; have ready a very hot flat iron inverted (this may be kept in place by putting the handle downward between two cold ones), and lay over it a wet cloth. While the steam rises pass the wrong side of the velvet over it to raise the pile.

709   For Removing Grease from Woolen Goods.

Nothing can excel gasoline or deodorized benzine in removing grease, and we sponge bad or old grease spots with gasoline before cleaning the articles with either of the four following receipts:

710   To Clean Woolen Garments and Boys' Clothing.

One ounce of borax, one ounce of spirits of camphor, one quart of boiling water. Lay a thick towel under the spot; then rub the soiled place with a woolen cloth dipped in the mixture.

711 Japanese Cream.

A most admirable detergent; try it and you will keep it always on hand. Four ounces white castile soap, four ounces ammonia, two ounces ether, two ounces alcohol, one ounce glycerine. Cut the soap fine, dissolve in one quart of soft water over the fire. When dissolved, add four quarts more of water, then add the spirits.

712 Paint Spots

When neither turpentine nor benzine will remove paint spots from garments, try chloroform. It will absorb and remove paint which has been on for six months.

713 Stains from Linen, Silk, or Woolen.

Four tablespoonfuls of spirits of ammonia, the same quantity of alcohol, and a tablespoon of salt. Shake the whole well together in a bottle and apply with a sponge or tooth brush. This removes ink, paint, fruit or acid stains from silk, linen or woolen articles, but should be used carefully on colored garments.

714 How to Wash Matting.

Put a mixture of salt and lemon juice on the stains; leave this for some hours without washing off; then wash the whole matting with salt and water.

Ammonia in the water will whiten and brighten old white matting.

715 How to Clean Carpets of Any Kind.

Beat and shake thoroughly clear of dust; then tack smoothly to the floor, and with a scrubbing brush apply the following mixture: Half pound borax, one-quarter pound sal soda, half ounce alum, one and a half pounds of rosin soap; cover with water and boil until dissolved; then pour into two buckets of water (rain water best); let stand until all thickens. When ready to use add half a pint of alcohol and one gill of ammonia. Scrub one place at a time thoroughly, the same as you would scrub a floor. Sponge off with clean, cold water, and leave doors and windows open till dry. This operation requires patience, muscle and elbow grease; but if directions are carefully followed, the "old rag" or any other kind of carpet will smile up at you bright and fresh as new.

716 To Sweep a Carpet.

Peel and wash four large potatoes; put them in a chopping bowl and chop into pieces the size of a pea; sprinkle them over the floor, brush them well over the carpet with your broom, and then sweep thoroughly. After using this you will forever discard salt, tea leaves, corn meal, etc.

ANOTHER METHOD.—Put into a wash basin three quarts of water and one pint of pure naphtha. Sweep the room as above, and then dip your broom in this mixture and sweep again with it.

TO BANISH VERMIN.

Perpetual vigilance is the price of freedom from the world of insects.

717 Bedbugs.

For these there is no sure cure, constant cleaning and watchfulness will keep them down and out of sight, but cease to clean and they will spring up and multiply in a month. Clean very thoroughly in March and April.

Oil of cedar is an excellent and cleanly remedy. Salt and kerosene oil in cracks and under base boards is good.

Carbolic acid is effectual. Sulphurous acid in paperer's paste will prevent them getting under newly papered walls.

Gasoline or a strong solution of ammonia are both good remedies.

A preparation of copperas, one pound to one gallon of boiling water. Sponging or painting the bedstead with this solution will drive them away for months. The only drawback is that it leaves a stain like iron rust, which never can be effaced. In Detroit they thrive on corrosive sublimate.

718 Moths; A Red Pepper Smoke.

This is the surest of all we ever tried: Hang up in a closet or clothes, press all woolen things, such as as dresses, clothes, overcoats, etc., and take a few ounces of cayenne pods (the imported article), or the dried red pepper of our gardens, and putting them upon some live coals in a tin pan, the bottom of which is covered with ashes, shut them close into your closet, and let it remain without opening for twenty-four hours; an attic infested with moths may require this process repeated three or four times. Carpets which are on the floor cannot, of course, be treated in this fashion, but by following the directions for sweeping a carpet with naptha and water, they can be banished. Brush furniture with the same preparation..

719 To Drive Away Red Ants.

Grease a plate with lard and set it where the ants are troublesome; place a few sticks around the plate for the ants to climb up on; they will desert the sugar bowl for the lard; occasionally turn the plate over a fire where there is no smoke and the ants will drop into it; reset the plate, and in a few repetitions you will catch all the ants; they trouble nothing else while lard is accessible.

Red lead and sugar sprinkled around your closet or wherever they come will drive them away.

720 To Get Rid of Water Bugs and Cockroaches.

Powdered borax sprinkled over water pipes, closet shelves, etc., will drive them away. Should this fail, use Paris green or equal quantities of red lead flour and sugar on your water pipes, but to keep them away requires perpetual vigilances—find where they nest and with an insect powder puffer puff in the Paris green.

721 To Drive Away Mice.

Moisten chloride of lime, and stop their holes of ingress with the paste. If the holes are inaccessible, set the chloride around on small plates. Mice do not like it.

722 Rats! Rats!! To Banish Rats!!!

Two parts of well bruised squills, three parts of finely chopped bacon, corn meal as required for consistency. Roll thin and bake in small cakes. Place where the vermin most do congregate. "Sure thing." FROM MR. FRANK B.

723 To Get Rid of Black Ants.

Get five cents worth of tartar emetic, mix in an old saucer with sugar and water, and set in your pantry or cupboard, where the ants trouble you. In twenty-four hours every ant will have left the premises. With me the same dish of tartar emetic answered as well the second year as the first; as the water dries out add more.

DAIRY AND COWS.

724 To Purify Dairy Utensils.

Stand on end, in a convenient place for use, an open-ended vessel of suitable dimensions for the size of the dairy, say from half a barrel to a hogshead. In this slake some good quicklime, enough to make a thin whitewash, then fill full of water, and cover to keep out dust and dirt. The lime will settle, leaving a saturated solution of lime over it, as clear as spring water. After using the milk-pans, etc., wash them as other utensils are washed and rinsed, then dip them in the adjoining cask of lime water, giving them a quick turn, so that every part becomes immersed therein; set them to drain and dry, and the purification is complete, without any scalding process, from the new pan to the worn-out one. The lime in the clear water instantly neutralizes the acidity of the milk yet remaining in the cracks or seams, etc., of the milk vessels, to destroy which the process of scalding has been performed. In the case of a very small dairy, or of one cow. the clear water may, if preferred, be dipped out for the time being and poured gently back again, the lime purifying the water and keeping it good all summer.

725 To Make Cows Give Milk.

A writer who says his cow gives all the milk that is wanted in a family of eight persons, and from which was made two hundred and sixty pounds of butter last year, gives the following as his treatment. He says: "If you desire to get a large yield of rich milk, give your cow, three times a day, water slightly warmed, slightly salted, in which bran has been stirred at the rate of one quart to two gallons of water. You will find, if you have not tried this daily practice, that your cow will give twenty-five per cent more, immediately under the effect of it, and she will become so attached to the diet as to refuse to drink clear water, unless very thirsty; but this mess she will drink almost any time, and 'ask for more.' The amount of this drink necessary is an ordinary water pailful each time, noon and night. Four hundred pounds of butter are often obtained from good stock, and instances are mentioned where the yield is often at a higher figure."

GENERAL INFORMATION.

72 Useful Notes.

To remove paint splashed upon the window panes use a hot solution of soda and rub with soft flannel.

Raw potato will take rust off steel.

A hot shovel held over varnished furniture will take out white spots. So will rubbing with a soft cloth wet in spirits of camphor, followed by another dipped in a mixture of sweet oil and turpentine to restore the polish.

A cement made of gum shellac one part, and aqua ammonia ten parts, will cement rubber.

A good cement for marble may be made by melting and stirring together one part of white wax and eight parts of resin, and then adding four parts of plaster of Paris. It should be used while hot.

The reason lamp chimnys so often crack is because they are not properly annealed. If, before using, the chimney is placed in a kettle of cold water, and the water gradually brought to the boiling point, and the chimney removed after the water has cooled again, it will be far less likely crack. Other articles of glass may be tempered in the same way.

THE COMPLEXION.

It has come to be the custom to put in all receipt books some absurdity as "a face wash." We tested several of these and found them flat failures in every particular. We therefor offer a few hints on the care of the skin. Wash the face thoroughly in warm or very hot water, using a French soap called Suc du Laitu or a paste called Pate d'Amande au Miel, both of these are made by the Parisian perfumers, Violet and Coudray, and are simply designed to give a fine grain and good color to the skin. We also give a receipt for a glycernine lotion that we know to be very nice indeed.

A shrewd and fresh looking woman of fifty with no wrinkles in her face and a skin as soft and fine as a girl's, gives us this advice: "Use tepid water (or pretty warm water if you have an oily skin), the choicest quality of well made soap—the softest towels—then *wash your face with your hands*. No sponge, no wash clothes, but YOUR HANDS, working your fingers into the wrinkles and creases of the face and especially the nose; rinse the face well, dry it carefully and *rub it all over with a flesh-brush*, that is what I do." I know one wise woman who rinses her face with water in which she has stirred a teaspoonful of the finest oat-meal, dries it on a soft towel and rubs it well with a very fine chamois skin.

727 For Removing Sun Burn and Tan.

A famous preparation for removing sun burn and tan is very simple yet excellent, and is composed of equal parts of lemon juice and white of egg beaten together in an earthen pot, set over a slow fire, and stirred with a wooden spoon until it acquires the consistency of soft pomatum. If the face is well washed with rice water before it is applied, it will remove freckles and give brilliancy to the complexion. Cold water and coarse towels will make the skin, in time, harsh and wrinkled; water for the face and hands must be tepid and the towels soft and fine.

728 Another Necessary to the Toilette.

A teaspoonful of oat-meal at a time saturated with water until it assumes the color of milk is deemed by many, indispensable. It washes the skin inexpressibly fine, soft, and smooth, both of face and hands. The soaked oat-meal is so glutinous that it is far superior to soap where the best cannot be had.

729 Care of the Hair.

The Spanish and Cuban women are far-famed for the luxuriant growth and beauty of their hair, and the secret of its culture was told me by a Cuban friend. Every month the head is thoroughly shampooed with the yolk of a well-beaten egg; the cleansing properties are wonderful. Then this rather unpleasant stickiness is removed by the hair and head being carefully washed in a basin of tepid water to which is added half a teaspoonful of ammonia and a pinch of powdered borax

730 Glycerine Lotion for Face and Hands.

Three ounces of glycerine, ten drachms of mucilage of quince, five grains of pulverized cochineal, one and a-half ounces of hot water, two and one-half ounces of deodorized alcohol, eight drops of oil of rose, half a drachm of pulverized gum arabic, eight ounces of water.

Rub the powdered cochineal first, with the hot water gradually added, and then add the alcohol; then triturate the oil of rose well with the powdered gum arabic, and gradually add the water, as in making emulsion. With this mix well the solution first formed, and filter, and to the filtered liquid add the glycerine and mucilage of quince seeds, and shake well.

The mucilage of quince seeds should always be freshly made. If the alcohol is sweet and free from foreign odor, and the glycerine perfectly inodorous, a less quantity of oil of roses may suffice.

If care is taken in its manufacture this will form a beautiful and elegant preparation, with a rich, rosy fragrance.

When applied to the skin it imparts an agreeably soft, smooth and *velvety* feel. It is an excellent application for the face after shaving.

I have tried many similiar combinations, but have never found an article that has been so generally admired and so universally popular as this.

731 Red Lip Salve.

Oil of sweet almonds, two ounces; pure olive oil, six ounces; spermaceti, one and one-half ounces; white wax, one ounce. Color with carmine and perfume with oil of roses.

732 Carrot Salve and Ointment for Chapped Hands.

One-half pound mutton tallow, fresh, one-half pound leaf lard (unsalted), one-half pound scraped and grated orange carrots. Let the lard and tallow render out, strain the grease on the carrots and let boil or rather heat in a basin of boiling water. Add a lump of camphor as large as an English walnut; the same of borax and half as much carbonate of ammonia, let them boil an hour; strain through a fine cloth and when partly cooled whip soft with an egg beater, put into pots, cover with paper and wet with alcohol; good for abrasions and burns.

Daisy Eyebright.

SPECIFICS AND REMEDIES.

733 A Remedy for the Diphtheria.

Dr. Field, of Victoria, used powdered sulphur and a quill. He put a teaspoonful of flour of brimstone into a wine-glass of water and stirred it with his finger instead of a spoon, as the sulphur does not readily amalgamate with water. When the sulphur was well mixed he gave it as a gargle. Brimstone kills every species of fungus in man, beast and plant in a very few minutes. Instead of spitting out gargle, he recommended the swallowing of it. In extreme cases, when the fungus was too nearly closing the throat to allow the gargle, he blew the sulphur through a quill into the throat, and after the fungus had shrunk to allow of it, then the gargling.

If the patient cannot gargle, take a live coal, put it on a shovel and sprinkle a spoonful or two of flour of brimstone at a time upon it; let the sufferer inhale it, holding the head over it, and the fungus will die. If plentifully used, the whole room may be filled almost to suffocation, and the patient can walk about in it, inhaling the fumes, with doors and windows closed.

734 Sulphur in Scarlet Fever.

Thoroughly annoint the patient twice daily with sulphur ointment; give five to ten grains of sulphur in a little jam three times a day. Sufficient sulphur was burned twice daily (on coals on a shovel) to fill the room with the fumes, and of course was thoroughly inhaled by the patient. Under this mode of treatment each case improved immediately, and none were over eight days in making a complete recovery, and I firmly believe in each it was prevented from spreading by the treatment adopted. One case was in a large school. Having had a large experience in scarlet fever last year and this, I feel some confidence in my own judgment, and I am of the opinion that the very mildest cases I ever saw do not do half so well as bad cases do by the sulphur treatment, and as far as I can judge, sulphur is as near a specific for scarlet fever as possible.—*Dr. Henry Pigeon, in London Lancet.*

735 To Cure Croup.

Croup can often be cured by alum and sugar. Take a knife or grater, and shave off, in small particles, about a teaspoonful of alum; then mix with about twice its quantity of sugar to make it palatable, and administer it as quickly as possible. Almost instantaneous relief will follow.

736 A Remedy for Croup.

Let a healthy person fill his lungs with pure air; then slowly breathe upon the patient's throat and chest, commencing at the point of the chin and moving slowly down to the bottom of the windpipe. Repeat for a few minutes and it will give relief in cases where all other means fail.

My boy was always subject to croup; came near dying with the rattling, noisy kind at about eleven months old. I saved him with fomentations of warm water, and ever after prevented a serious attack by watchfulness and water. But when three years old, I let him play in the brook one warm rainy day, and he took a severe cold and had the still kind of croup, the first and last time he ever had it. In spite of all I could do, he grew constantly worse until he could only gasp and breathe with his head thrown back. We thought his last moments had come, when I thought and applied Bronson's remedy for a minute. When I stopped he looked up and said, "Do so again, mother, do," though he could not speak when I began. You may be assured I did so again, and I believe it saved his life.

737 Mothers' Milk.

The bruised leaves of the castor oil plant will cause the mother's milk to return by laying it upon the breast. It is worth trying.

738 To Stop the Bleeding of Wounds.

A piece of an enameled card, used as a court plaster, will almost always stanch bleeding.

739 To Cure Corns.

Apply young peach leaves, bruised and moistened, on the corns every night until relieved. This remedy can only be used from May till November, but it is so excellent that we advise our readers to cure their corns during these months.   Mr. W.

740 Soda Mint.

Bicarb. soda (Eng.), one drachm; pure water, three ounces; spearmint water, four ounces; glycerine, one ounce; ar. spts. ammonia, thirty-two drops. Mix and filter. Dose from twenty drops to a tablespoonful, according to age.

741 Wash for Inflamed Eyes.

Sulph. zinc, two grains; wine of opium, ten drops; distilled water, one ounce; mix. Drop two or three drops in the outer corner of the eye several times a day.

742 For Chilblains (Excellent.)

Burgundy pitch, one ounce; sperm oil, one ounce; beeswax, two ounces; spirits of turpentine, one-half ounce. Simmer first three ingredients well together, and when nearly cool add the turpentine. Spread on a cloth and lay as a plaster on the chilblains, after the feet have been well washed and soaked. Draw a fresh stocking over the plaster and keep on for three days and nights; if not cured repeat the whole process.   Mary Goodrich.

743 An Ugly but Efficacious Remedy for Chilblains.

Take a saucer of kerosene oil and add a handful of salt, mix thoroughly and apply to chilblains; then heat the chilblains at a very hot fire; when the heat becomes unbearable "grit" your teeth and bear a little longer; as soon as the pain subsides a little repeat the operation. Do this three or four times. I tried it six years ago on the worst assortment of chilblains I ever saw.

N. B. This has been of great service to many, but we have to record its failure in at least one instance.

744 Flaxseed Syrup.

This excellent remedy for a cough is made thus: boil one ounce of flaxseed in a quart of water for half an hour; strain and add to the liquid the juice of two lemons, and half a pound of rock candy. If the cough is accompanied with weakness and loss of appetite, add half an ounce of powdered gum arabic. Set this to simmer for half an hour, stirring occasionally. Take a wineglass of it when the cough is troublesome.

745 Lemon for Colds.

Slice the lemon or lemons, add a little water and considerable sugar, and set into the oven until well simmered together.

746 Chronic Diarrhœa.

A teaspoonful of wheat flour mixed into a cup of sweet milk, with a little nutmeg grated into it. Take it cold and raw. Beat it well, so that it foams. To be taken three or four times a day.

747 For Neuralgia and Headache.

Alcohol, one ounce; laudanum, one-eighth ounce, chloroform, five-eights ounce; gum camphor, one-half ounce; oil cloves, one-half drachm; oil lavendar, one drachm; sulphuric ether, three-quarters drachm; rub the part affected and inhale the liniment. It is also a good thing for sick headache, by rubbing the forehead with the liniment, and inhaling the same, the pain is relieved.

748 Senna Figs—For Constipation.

Take four ounces of senna and infuse it two hours in one pint of boiling water. Strain this liquor over one pound of fresh figs or prunes, with a handful of loaf sugar; let the prunes stew till well cooked, soft and pulpy; then put them into a jar for use. Eat one or two at night when retiring or oftener through the day if the bowels are very sluggish.

749 To Take Senna.

Take a pinch of senna leaves, pour a wineglass of cold water upon it and let it stand all day. Drink this at night on retiring. Increase the senna and water if necessary.

750 For Burns.

Procure from a tallow chandler a few ounces of palm oil, which is a brownish yellow substance the consistency of lard; spread it on a cloth and apply to the burn. Should the face or eyes have been burned, paint the oil on with a camel's hair brush every hour. The effect is almost miraculous. By the use of it a terrific gunpowder burn was cured in six days without the sign of a scar.

751 Relief for Scalds Where the Skin is not Broken.

Apply a layer of common salt and saturate it with laudanum; hold it in position a few hours with a simple wrapping. The smarting will disappear almost immediately. This acted like magic on a burn produced by scalding tea.

752 Toothache.

According to the London *Lancet*, can be cured by the following preparation of carbolic acid: To one drachm of collodium add two drachms of Calvert's carbolic acid. A gelatinous mass is precipitated, a small portion of which, inserted in the cavity of an aching tooth, invariably gives immediate relief.

753 Antidote for Poison.

A poison of any conceivable description and degree of potency, which has been swallowed intentionally or by accident, may be rendered almost instantaneously harmless by swallowing two gills of sweet oil. An individual with a very strong constitution should take twice the quantity. The oil will neutralize every form of vegetable or mineral poison with which physicians are acquainted. Follow with emetics of a teaspoonful of mustard, and one of salt; repeat if necessary.

754 For an Overdose of Chloroform.

A curious means of reviving patients who are in danger of death from chloroform is brought out by the recent fatal accident in Boston. It reverses the sentence "to be hung by the neck until you are dead," and declares that a man must be hung by the heels until he isn't dead—to provide the needed supply of blood for the head.

755 For Piles or Sore Nipples.

Take the leaves of sweet clover (the tall garden flower) when they are in milk; pick them and put them into an iron vessel with thick sweet cream; let all simmer or boil gently, without burning, until you can pour off a clear green oil; this, when it cools, hardens into a salve, which can be inserted into the rectum. Mrs. Merrick.

Stramonium prepared in the same way is also recommended.

The sweet clover makes a delightful salve by boiling it in the very best sweet oil, and adding to each cupful of the strained oil half an ounce of beeswax.

756 Nipple Salve ("Sure Cure").

One and-a-half tablespoonfuls of cream from milk that has stood two hours, one tablespoonful of the purest olive oil, piece of white wax the size of a fifty cent piece; put on the stove in a saucer and stir until it boils, then cool a few moments, and put in five cents worth of tannin, and a little camphor gum the size of a small pea. Stir all the time until cold. To be put on fine tissue paper and applied to the nipple. N. B.—There is no "*sure* cure" for any thing, but this salve is most helpful, and has been used with praise by hundreds.

757 To Remove Milk Crust from an Infant's Head.

Moisten well with raw linseed oil. Put on an oil skin cap, fitting close to the head to exclude the air.

758 Remedy for Piles—From Madame R.

Take *inwardly*, for one or more nights, until the bowels act, two teaspoonfuls of sulphur in a little milk, and apply as an ointment one ounce of pulverized nut gall in a tablespoonful of lard.

MISCELLANEOUS.

759 To Hasten Cooking.

All kinds of poultry and meat can be cooked quicker by adding to the water in which they are boiled, a little vinegar or a little piece of lemon. By the use of an acid, there will be considerable saving of fuel as well as shortening of time. Its action is beneficial on old tough meats, rendering them quite tender and easy to be digested.

760 To Keep Meat Fresh.

Here is a Japanese recipe for keeping meat fresh in hot weather: "Place it in a clean porcelain bowl and pour very hot water over it, so as to cover it. Then pour oil on the water. The air is thus quite excluded, and the meat is preserved." This is a very nice way of keeping a calf's liver fresh over night.

761 To Preserve Eggs.

Roll each egg in thin paper; put the small end down into a peach basket or crate, that will admit of ventilation; set in a cool place where they will not freeze, and they will keep all winter. This is a truly good receipt. To rub the egg all over with melted butter or lard is also excellent.

CANDY.

762 Pop Corn Balls.

To six quarts of pop corn boil one pint of molasses, one cup of brown sugar one tablespoonful of vinegar and a piece of butter the size of a small egg for fifteen minutes or more; then put the corn into a large pan, pour the boiled molasses over it, stirring briskly till thoroughly mixed. Then make into balls of the desired size.

763 Mamie's Molasses Candy.

Two cups of brown sugar, one cup of molasses, a piece of butter the size of a nutmeg; boil. When done put in one teaspoonful of soda (dry and fine) and stir well about a minute. Pour into buttered pans, let cool and pull.

764 Molasses Candy.

Two cups of molasses, one and one-half cups of brown sugar, one-half cup of vinegar, one-fourth cup of butter. Made thus there will be no adhering to the fingers in pulling, and sticks as white and delicious as any one could wish for will be the result.

765 Bell's Candy.

Two cups of sugar, one cup of water, juice of two lemons; let the sugar and water boil "to the crack" (or thirty or forty minutes), in a frying-pan or spider; add the lemon and stir ten minutes after removing from the fire.

766 Overton Taffy

One pound of powdered loaf sugar, one teacupful of water, one-quarter pound of butter, six drops of essence of lemon. Put the water and sugar into a brass pan, and beat the butter to a cream; when the sugar is dissolved, add the butter, keep stirring the mixture over the fire until it sets, when a little is poured onto a buttered dish; just before it is done, add the lemon, butter a dish or tin; pour on it the mixture, and when it is cool it will come off.

767 Butter Scotch.

One cup of brown sugar, one-half cup of water, one teaspoonful of vinegar, piece of butter the size of a walnut. Boil about twenty minutes—flavor if desired.

768 Vinegar Candy.

Three teacups white sugar, one of vinegar, boil until it will harden in cold water; just before it is done add a little butter, size of a walnut. Do not stir while boiling; pour in a pan to cool, flour the hands and pull until perfectly white.

Very nice candy is made by using three cups sugar, one cup of water, and one tablespoon cream of tartar, not quite as much butter as for vinegar candy.

769 Caramels.

One cup of Baker's chocolate grated, one cup of milk; one cup molasses, one cup of brown sugar, butter, size of an egg; add one tablespoonful of glycerine. Boil till it will harden in water. Pour upon platters, and when nearly ut into squares.　　　　　　　　Margery Daw.

770 Lemon Drops.

Pour clear lemon juice upon powdered sugar and boil till a thick syrup; then drop upon plates in drops singly and put to dry in a warm place.

Or, pour four ounces of lemon juice upon one pound of loaf sugar with the same amount of rose-water as of lemon juice; boil to a thick syrup, add grated lemon peel and proceed as in the first recipe.

771 Raspberry Drops

Are made by using the juice of either fresh berries, or the preserve syrup, in the place of lemon juice.

772 Cazenovia Caramels—Very Nice.

One half pound grated chocolate, not sweet, one pint of milk or cream, three pounds brown sugar, eight ounces of butter. Mix all together; put over a hot fire and stir constantly until it comes to a boil. Boil hard twenty minutes. Try in cold water, and when hard enough pour out *an inch thick*. When nearly cold mark off in squares.

COOKERY FOR THE SICK.

Beef tea has become an essential in cases of typhoid fever, etc., but as the symptoms and digestion of patients vary, we give three methods: **No. 1** takes long in preparation, and may prove a little heavy for some stomachs. **No. 2** is open to the same objection. **No. 3** is an excellent stand-by. Beef juice can be used when nothing else will be retained upon the stomach.

773 Beef Tea—Dr. Chambers. No. 1.

Take half a pound of fresh beef for every pint of beef tea required, free from all fat, sinew, veins and bone. Cut it into pieces less than half an inch square and soak for twelve hours in half a pint of cold water. Let it then be taken out and simmer for two hours in one pint of water; the quantity lost from evaporation being replaced from time to time; the boiling liquor is then to be placed on the cold liquor in which the meat was soaked; the solid meat is to be dried, pounded in a mortar, freed from all stringy parts and mixed with the rest. Beef tea should not be kept hot but warmed when required.

774 Beef Tea, No. 2, or Essence of Beef.

Is quite different from beef tea, and is made by packing the chopped beef in a Hero or Mason preserve jar or a bottle, and lightly covering or corking the vessel; place it in a pot of cold water and let it come to a boil and continue to cook till the meat which was placed without water in the jar is so dissolved as to produce a teacup or more of liquid; this is much stronger than beef tea, but not nearly as digestible.

775 Beef Tea. No. 3.

Take a pound of fine steak free from skin, fat and sinew. Lay it on a gridiron over hot coals and grill *white* on each side; then put it in your chopping bowl and chop fine; pour over enough cold water to just cover the meat and let stand on the back part of the stove for two hours, then bring to a scald and strain. N. B.—Should the tea be required in great haste, a little can be brought at once to a scald.

776 Chicken and Mutton Tea.

Chicken prepared in same way is good, and mutton thus prepared is especially good for teething children when the bowels are affected. As the patient gets better, rice can be added to the soup, and thyme or parsley, and pepper. This is much less trouble and far nicer than the old way of making beef tea in a bottle and cooking for hours.

777 Beef Juice.

Prepare the beef as in receipt No. 444, and when cut in squares squeeze it dry in a glass lemon squeezer, salt. Give one teaspoonful at a time.

778 Gruel.

The lightest possible gruel is made by taking two heaping tablespoonfuls of yellow corn meal, pour upon it a teacup of cold water and stir thoroughly. While settling pour this water into a teacupful of water at a keen boil and scald for five minutes. Add plenty of salt. Do not put let in the coarse yellow part of the meal that settles at the bottom of the cold water.

779 Milk Porridge.

One pint of milk, reserving two tablespoonfuls, place on the stove and let come to a boil; stir in one heaping teaspoonful of flour that has been smoothly mixed with the two tablespoons of milk. Let boil three minutes. Salt well. Excellent for diarrhœa.

780 Cracker Gruel.

Six tablespoonfuls fine cracker crumbs, one quart of milk, one-half teaspoonful of salt; put crumbs and milk into double boiler: let it come to a boil, add the salt and cook two minutes longer.

781 Oat-Meal Gruel.

Into one quart of boiling water sprinkle two tablespoonfuls of coarse oat-meal; let boil forty minutes; salt and strain. Where the patient can use milk and cream, it can be put into the gruel subtracting an equal quantity of water.

782 Indian Meal Gruel.

One quart of boiling water; stir into this one tablespoonful of flour, two tablespoonfuls of Indian meal. Mix the flour with a little water, add the meal and boil from thirty to sixty minutes; season with plenty of salt.

783 Arrowroot Gruel.

One pint of milk, one teaspoonful arrowroot, salt to taste; let milk come to a boil, reserving a little cold milk with which to mix the arrowroot, stir into the boiling milk and cook ten minutes. If milk is too heavy use water.

784 Ice Cream for the Sick.

One cup of milk, one teaspoonful of arrowroot, one pint of cream, not too rich (scalded). A scant half cupful of sugar; scald the milk and arrowroot together ten minutes and freeze. Nine parts of ice to one part of salt.

785 Scrambled Eggs (for one).

One egg, two tablespoonfuls of milk, a bit of butter as large as a hickory nut, pepper and salt; pour into a hot buttered spider and stir just a minute. Butter a slice of hot toast and pour the egg over it.

786 Cream Toast (for one).

Toast and butter a round of stale bread, pour over it three tablespoonfuls of thick cream and half a saltspoonful of salt, into which has been stirred three tablespoonfuls of boiling water. Serve quickly.

787 The Uses of the Lemon.

The London *Lancet* remarks, few people know the value of lemon juice. A piece of lemon bound upon a corn will cure it in a few days; it should be renewed night and morning. A free use of lemon juice and sugar will always relieve a cough. Most people feel poorly in the spring, but if they would eat a lemon before breakfast every day for a week—with or without sugar, as they like it—they would find it better than any medicine. Lemon juice used according to this recipe will sometimes cure consumption: Put a dozen lemons into cold water, and slowly bring to a boil; boil slowly until the lemons are soft, then squeeze until all the juice is extracted, add sugar to your taste and drink. In this way use one dozen lemons a day. After using six dozen the patient will begin to gain flesh and enjoy food.

788 Milk as a Diet, Its Effect.

Milk, diluted with one-third lime-water, it is said, will not cause any one biliousness, and, if taken regularly, will so strengthen the stomach as to banish these disorders. It may be taken with acid of some kind when it does not easily digest. The idea that milk must not be eaten with pickles is not an intelligent one, as milk curdles in the stomach nearly as soon as it is swallowed. When milk is constipating, as it is frequently found to be by persons who drink freely of it in the country in the summer time, a little salt sprinkled in each glassful will prevent the difficulty. As milk is so essential to the health of our bodies it is well to consider when to take it, and how. It is a mistake to drink milk between meals, or with food at the table. In the former case it will destroy the appetite; and in the latter it is never proper to drink anything. After finishing each meal a goblet of pure milk should be drunk; and if any one wishes to grow fleshy, a pint taken before retiring at night will soon cover the scrawniest bones. In cases of fever and summer complaint, milk is given with excellent results. The idea that milk is "feverish" has long since been exploded, and it is now the physician's great reliance in bringing through typhoid patients, or those in too low a state to be nourished by solid food.

789 To Make Lime-Water.

The way to make lime-water is simply to procure a few lumps of unslacked lime, put the lime in a stone jar, add water until the lime is slacked and about the consistency of thin cream; the lime settles, leaving the pure and clear lime water at the top. Three or four tablespoonfuls of it may be added to a goblet of milk.

790 How to Make a Mustard Poultice.

A mustard poultice should never make a blister at all. If a blister is wanted, there are other plasters far better than mustard for the purpose. When you make a mustard plaster, then, use no water whatever, but mix the mustard with the white of an egg, and the result will be a plaster that will "draw" perfectly, but will not produce a blister, even upon the skin of an infant, no matter how long it is allowed to remain upon the part.

791 Cure for a Felon.

Take the skin of an egg and bind it upon the finger where the pain begins. It will have to be removed from time to time as the contraction is so great that it cannot be borne long.

792 Cure for a Run-Round.

If taken in time a run-round can be greatly benefited by holding it in water as hot as can be endured. Repeat this operation several times.

INDELIBLE INK, PASTE, CEMENT, Etc.

793 To Mend China.

Take a very thick solution of gum arabic in water, and stir into it plaster of Paris until the mixture becomes of the proper consistency. Apply it with a brush to the fractured edges of the china, and stick them together. In three days the article cannot be broken in the same place. The whiteness of the cement renders it doubly valuable.

794 A Cheap Fumigator.

The following will be found to be a cheap and pleasant fumigator for sick rooms, diffusing a healthful, agreeable, and highly penetrating disinfectant odor in close apartments, or wherever the air is deteriorated:

Pour common vinegar on powdered chalk until effervescence ceases, leave the whole to settle, and pour off the liquid. Dry the sediment, and place it in a shallow earthen or glass dish, and pour upon it sulphuric acid until white fumes commence rising. This vapor very quickly spreads, is very agreeable, pungent, and acts as a powerful purifier of vitiated air.

795 To Purify a Sink.

In hot weather it is almost impossible to prevent the sinks becoming foul, unless some chemical preparation is used. One pound of copperas dissolved in four gallons of water, poured over a sink three or four times, will completely destroy the offensive odor. As a disinfecting agent, to scatter around premises affected with any unpleasant odor, nothing is better than a mixture of four parts dry ground plaster of Paris to one part of fine charcoal, by weight. All sorts of glass vessels and other utensils may be effectually purified from offensive smells by rinsing them with charcoal powder, after the grosser impurities have been scoured off with sand and soap.

796 Indelible Ink.

Use a quill pen with this ink, which is first-rate. Half a stick of lunar caustic or nitrate of silver dissolved in a bottle, with one large spoonful of pure strong vinegar. Hang the bottle in the sun, shaking two or three times a day. In two weeks it will be found to be better than any ink that can be bought for marking with a pen, but it is too thin to use with a stencil. It is inexpensive, too, and some of the finest and most artistic specimens of linen marking we ever have seen were done with this ink. It grows black, instead of fading with time.

797 Paste That Will Keep Well.

A perpetual paste can be made by dissolving one ounce of alum in a quart of warm water, in which a dozen cloves have been well boiled; when cold, add flour enough to make it the consistency of cream; then stir into it half a teaspoonful of powdered resin. Boil it to a proper consistency, stirring all the time. Strain it hot through a thin muslin cloth. It will keep for twelve months, and when dry may be softened with water.

798 Mucilage Which Always Keeps Pure.

One pound of gum arabic dissolved in one pint of boiling water; add a piece of borax the size of a walnut; bottle in a large-mouthed bottle; shake up three or four days after it is made. One tablespoonful of alcohol will prevent mold.

799 To Repair Walls.

White walls can be easily repaired without sending for the mason. Equal parts of plaster of Paris and white sand—such as is used in most families for scouring purposes—mixed with water to a paste, applied immediately and smoothed with a knife or flat piece of wood, will make the broken place as good as new. As the mixture hardens very quickly, it is best to prepare but a small quantity at a time.

800 To Extinguish Kerosene Flames.

One of the most ready means is to throw a cloth of some kind over the flames, and thus stifle them; but as the cloth is not always convenient to the kitchen, where such accidents are most likely to occur, some one recommends flour as a substitute, which, it is said, promptly extinguishes the flame. It rapidly absorbs the fluid, deadens the flames, and can be readily gathered up and thrown out of doors when the fire is extinguished. A friend of ours finding her kitchen on fire from an exploded lamp, extinguished the flames by throwing several spadesful of earth upon it.

801 For Indoor Whitewashing.

For every sixteen pounds of Paris white (it is sold at paint stores for three cents a pound), get one-half pound of transparent glue; cover the glue with cold water at night, and in the morning heat it, without scorching, till dissolved. Stir in the Paris white with hot water to give it a milky consistency. Then add and mix well the glue. Apply with a common lime whitewash brush. A single coating will do, except on very dingy walls. It is almost as brilliant as zinc white.

ODDS AND ENDS.

802 Burnt Almonds (for dessert).

Blanch and dry half a pound of almonds, put a bit of butter the size of a nutmeg into a tin dripping-pan, set them in your oven and brown as you would coffee, only a very light brown. As you take them up, give them a light dash of salt; serve cold with figs or raisins.

803 Ice Cream Cake. Very nice.

One cup powdered sugar, one-half cup butter, whites of two eggs, one-half cup of milk, one and-a-half even cups of flour, one teaspoonful baking powder. Frost with the yolks of two eggs. Flavor the cake with vanilla, the frosting with lemon. MRS. TODD.

804 Sweet-Breads Fried.

As they spoil easily, put into cold salted water the moment they come from the market, soaking them one hour; then put into *boiling* salt-water, cook from half to one hour until thoroughly tender. Put aside until *cold*, then remove the little pipes and pieces of skin carefully Cut into slices half an inch thick, sprinkle with salt and pepper, dip in egg and bread crumbs and fry in *boiling* lard. Always test the lard before frying by putting in a small piece of bread, if it turns yellow instantly the lard is hot enough.

805 Sweet-Breads Stewed.

Prepare as above. Cut into small pieces. Make a sauce by heating an ounce of butter and one third of an onion chopped very fine; add a teaspoonful of flour, a little beef stock and milk, salt and pepper. When cooked put in the sweet-breads. Serve for breakfast.

806 Stewed Kidneys.

Soak the kidneys (sheep or lamb kidneys the best) in cold, salt-water for an hour, having previously sliced them into thin pieces. Then put into cold water, and boil steadily until tender as liver, renewing the water frequently. Take them out when done; then take the water in which they have been cooking, add a little cream, butter, salt and pepper, thicken with flour until the consistency of sauce, then put the kidneys back for a moment. Serve on slices of thin toast, adding to the sauce, just before serving, a teaspoonful of Harvey's sauce.

807 Delmonico Croquettes.

Chop the meat very fine. One onion fried in one ounce of butter, add one teaspoonful of flour, stir well; then add the meat and a little beef stock, salt and pepper; stir for two or three minutes then put into a dish until cold. When cold mix well together again. Divide into parts for croquettes, roll into desired shapes, dip in egg and in breadcrumbs, and fry in boiling lard, having previously tested the lard. Serve plain, with fried parsley for a garniture, or with tomato sauce.   F. E.

808 Veal Pasty.

One pound of veal, quarter of a pound of raw ham—lean and fat together—chop both together until quite fine, season with pepper, salt, nutmeg and cinnamon, a bit of butter. Make a good puff paste, spread a spoonful or two in each and fold over as in old-fashioned turn-overs. Wet the edge of the paste and press it together and bake in a slow oven for thirty minutes. This quantity will make five pasties.   Mrs. S—gs.

809 Vanilla Ice Cream.

The foundation given in this rule is suitable for all kinds of ice cream. One generous pint of milk, one cupful of sugar, half a cupful of flour, *scant;* two eggs, one quart of cream, one tablespoonful of vanilla extract, and when the cream is added another cupful of sugar. Let the milk come to a boil. Beat the first cupful of sugar, the flour and eggs together and stir into boiling milk. Cook twenty minutes, stirring often. Set away to cool, and when cool add sugar, seasoning and cream, and freeze.

810 Coffee Ice Cream (Exceedingly Nice).

Make the same as the above vanilla ice cream with the addition of one cupful of strong coffee. This gives a strong flavor. Less can be used. The second cupful of sugar should be large.

A Few Words on the Subject of Lunches and Dinners.

If Americans would graft upon their primitive habits such conservative additions as comport with the genius of their country, it would be well. Half a century ago, five courses for a state dinner were enough and to spare. To-day fifteen are indulged in. After seven, each successive course becomes more and more a weariness of the flesh. A shrewd observer said of a well trained English waiter, "it took a hundred years to produce him." Waiting had been his heritage, as it was his father's before him. Americans are too impatient and intolerant of superficial elegance to be patient with confused or stupid service—*ergo*, never attempt too much. We append some suggestions for courses at dinners.

FIRST COURSE.—Bouillon, Mock Turtle, White Soup, White Almond Soup, Black Bean, Parker House, Tomato, Ockra Soup, Corn Soup, Oyster Soup.

SECOND COURSE.—Boiled Whitefish, Boiled Salmon, Trout, Fried Perch, Turbot, Fried Trout, Baked Pike, Whitefish Mayonnaise, Oyster Croustade, Fricasseed Oysters, Salmon Cutlets, Salmon Mayonnaise, Salmon Pate.

THIRD COURSE.—Roast of Beef, Fillet of Beef, a la Mode Beef, Leg of Veal, Broiled Fore-quarter of Lamb, Hind-quarter of Lamb, Saddle of Mutton.

Fourth Course.—Saddle of Venison, Venison Steaks, Roast Turkey, Boiled Turkey.

Fifth Course.—Partridges, Quails, Canvas-back Ducks, Venison Pasty, Snipe, Teal, etc.

Sixth Course.—Salad, Celery, with Mayonnaise Dressing, Salad, with French Dressing, Water Cress, etc.

Seventh Course.—Deserts, Creams, Ice Creams, Jellies at Discretion, Burnt Almonds.

Eighth Course.—Fruit, Coffee, Confectionery.

811 A Whitefish Mayonnaise.

Boil a fish according to receipt No. 64; carefully take out the bones, leaving the fish in pieces large enough for a helping; pile into shape on an oval platter; make a mayonnaise dressing according to No. 269, only with less onion. Let both fish and dressing get *very* cold, and just before serving pour the latter over the fish, then sprinkle a few capers. This receipt may be followed for pike, bass-lake trout or pickerel, but as these are less delicate fish use a sauce, tartare receipt, No. 93. This makes a fresh and nice fish course.

BILLS OF FARE.

With interest and sympathy for puzzled and perplexed friends, we herewith give a few hints in the shape of "Bills of Fare," nutritious and sufficiently elaborate to suit the wants of a large family or a small one with half a dozen guests added, and which, if not within the reach of all, can be modified to suit the taste and purse.

BREAKFAST, No. 1.

Fruit,
Oat-meal Mush, eaten with Cream and Sugar,
Broiled Spring Chicken,
Potatoes Stewed in Cream,
Rolls, Muffins or Pone.
Tea or Coffee.

BREAKFAST, No. 2.

Fruit,
Oat-meal, Hominy or Cracked Wheat,
Mutton Chops, Baked Potatoes,
Toast, Buckwheat Cakes,
Tea or Coffee,

BREAKFAST, No. 3.

Fruit,
Oat-meal,
Broiled Ham, Omelet, Fried Potatoes,
Rolls, Toast,
Tea or Coffee,

LUNCHES.

LUNCH PARTY, No. 1.

Bouillon, served in small Porcelain Cups,
    Devilled Oysters,
        Stewed Sweet-breads,
            Chicken Salad,
                Minced Ham Sandwiches.
                      Olives, Rolls.
"Tutti Frutti,"
    Chocolate Cream,
        Cake Basket of Mixed Cake,
            Mulled Chocolate, Coffee,
                Fruit and Flowers.

Ice Creams and Charlottes can either be added or substituted. For twenty guests allow one gallon of cream.

LUNCH PARTY, No. 2.—GENTLEMEN.

Bouillon,
Broiled Partridge,   Oyster Pie,   Cold Ham,
Peach or Pear Pickles,   Biscuit and Tongue Sandwiches,
Pound and Fruit Cake,   Pyramids of Jelly,
Quaking Blanc-Mange,   Snow Sponge Cake,
Pine-apple Ice,
Coffee.

LUNCH PARTY, No. 3.

Raw Oysters,
Bouillon,
Sweet-Breads and French Peas,
Lamb Chops, Tomato Sauce,
Potatoes a la Parisienne,
Salad of Lettuce,
Ice Cream, Fancy Cakes,
Coffee.

DINNERS.

DINNER No. 1.

FIRST COURSE.

Mock Turtle Soup.

SECOND COURSE.

Boiled White Fish with Mayonnaise Dressing or Sauce Tartare.

THIRD COURSE.

Roast Saddle of Vension, Sauce, Currant Jelly.

FOURTH COURSE.

Roast Partridges or Ducks,
Oyster Pie,
Macaroni, Celery, Pickles and Vegetables.

DESSERT.

Plum Pudding,
Mince Pie, Squash or Lemon Pie, Peach Meringue,
Cheese, Fruits, Nuts,
Coffee.

DINNER No. 2.

FIRST COURSE.

Raw Oysters.

SECOND COURSE.

Baked Pike, Potatoes, Plain, Boiled.

THIRD COURSE.

Roast Chicken, Mashed Potatoes.
Green Peas, Cranberry Jelly, Celery.

FOURTH COURSE.

Lettuce Salad, Thin Bread and Butter.

FIFTH COURSE.

Black Pudding, Lemon Sherbert, Cake.

SIXTH COURSE.

Coffee, Crackers and Cheese.

DINNER, No. 3.

FIRST COURSE.

Raw Oysters with Lemon Crackers.

SECOND COURSE.

Amber Soup and Croutons.

THIRD COURSE.

Boiled or Baked Fish, Boiled Potatoes.

FOURTH COURSE.

Roast Turkey or Fillet of Beef, Cranberries, Mashed Potatoes, Corn or Macaroni.

FIFTH COURSE.

Venison, or Game, Jelly.

SIXTH COURSE.

Salad, with Thin Bread and Butter.

SEVENTH COURSE.

Plum Pudding.

EIGHTH COURSE.

Ice Cream and Assorted Cakes.

NINTH COURSE.

Crackers and Neufchatelle Cheese, Coffee.

TENTH COURSE.

Fruit.

Allowance of Supplies for a Private Entertainment.

In inviting guests, it is safe to calculate that out of one hundred and fifty guests but two-thirds of that number will be present. If five hundred are invited, not more than three hundred can be reckoned on as accepting, many invitations to so large a company being in a measure perfunctory and declined in the same spirit.

Allow one quart of oysters to every three persons present; five chickens, and fifteen or twenty heads of celery (or what is better, a ten-pound turkey, boiled and cut), are enough for chicken salad for fifty guests; one gallon of ice cream to every twenty guests; one hundred and thirty sandwiches for one hundred guests; six to ten quarts of jelly for a hundred.

Allowance for a Public Entertainment.

The lady managers of the Home of the Friendless and Thompson Home for Old Ladies personally prepare and contribute a supper for the Harvest Home of each institution. These suppers have become quite celebrated because of the dainty cooking and equally dainty service. No money is expected to be made from them, but they are a source of intelligent knowledge of the Homes to hundreds and thousands of our fellow-citizens who only by this means come to an acquaintance with our children and old ladies. We give a list of supplies for each entertainment.

1885. DONATION DAY AT THE HOME FOR THE FRIENDLESS.

Eight gallons ice cream; 8 quarts sweet cream; 10 pounds sugar; 6 pounds coffee; ½ pound tea; 18 cans raw oysters; escaloped oysters: 12 dishes; 3 turkeys; 12 cakes; 300 rolls; 12 chickens.

1885. FOUNDERS' DAY AT THE THOMPSON HOME.

Ten gallons ice cream; 12 quarts of sweet cream; 20 cans raw oysters; 15 dishes escaloped oysters; 5 chickens; 18 chickens for salad; 12 cakes; 200 rolls; 4 pounds Saratoga potatoes; 10 lbs. sugar; 4 lbs. coffee; 12½ lbs. tea.

There were two hundred and seventy-five tickets sold for the Donation Day supper, at 50 cents each, and three hundred and forty tickets for the Founders' Day supper of the Thompson Home, also at fifty cents each.

www.ingramcontent.com/pod-product-compliance
Lightning Source LLC
Chambersburg PA
CBHW022109230426
43672CB00008B/1322